Industrialization and
Developing Countries

Alan Mountjoy graduated from Reading University in 1940 and spent the next six years in the Army. It was during this period, in which he saw service in North Africa, the Middle East and Italy, that he became interested in the problems of the under-developed countries. After the war he was appointed to a junior lectureship in Geography at Bedford College, University of London, where he is now the University Reader. He specializes in the economic and social geography of the developing world. He has published numerous papers and articles, many being concerned with aspects of the demographic and economic geography of the countries of the Nile basin. He is the author of *The Mezzogiorno* (1973), joint author (with C. Embleton) of *Africa: A Geographical Study* (1970), editor of *Developing the Underdeveloped Countries* (1971) and contributing editor of the *The Third World: Problems and Perspectives* (1978) based on 'The Third World' series of articles which appeared in *The Geographical Magazine* (1973–4). He has been a Visitor to the University of Khartoum and in 1975 was invited to lecture on developing countries' problems at the universities of Warsaw and Cracow.

Geography editor
Michael Chisholm
Professor of Geography
University of Cambridge

Industrialization and Developing Countries

Alan B. Mountjoy

Reader in Geography
Bedford College, University of London

Hutchinson

London   Melbourne   Sydney   Auckland   Johannesburg

Hutchinson & Co. (Publishers) Ltd

An imprint of the Hutchinson Publishing Group
17-21 Conway Street, London W1P 5HL

Hutchinson Group (Australia) Pty Ltd
30-32 Cremorne Street, Richmond South, Victoria 3121
PO Box 151, Broadway, New South Wales 2007

Hutchinson Group (NZ) Ltd
32-34 View Road, PO Box 40-086, Glenfield, Auckland 10

Hutchinson Group (SA) (Pty) Ltd
PO Box 337, Bergvlei 2012, South Africa

First published 1963
Reprinted 1964
Second edition 1966
Reprinted 1968, 1969
Third edition 1971
Fourth edition 1975
Reprinted with amendments 1978
Fifth edition 1982

Set in Times by TJB Photosetting, South Witham, Lincolnshire

Printed in Great Britain by The Anchor Press Ltd
and bound by Wm Brendon & Son Ltd
both of Tiptree, Essex

British Library Cataloguing in Publication Data
Mountjoy, Alan B.
    Industrialization and developing countries. – 5th ed. –
    1. Under-developed areas – Industries
    I. Title
    338'.09172'4   HC59.7

ISBN 0 09 146801 9

To my wife

Contents

	List of figures	8
	List of tables	9
	Preface to the fifth edition	11
	Preface to the first edition	13
1	Development and under-development	15
2	The demographic factor: the global setting	30
3	The demographic factor in the under-developed lands	45
4	Industrialization: the panacea?	62
5	Industrialization: theoretical considerations	81
6	Problems of industrialization	94
7	Environmental and human problems	114
8	The form of industrialization	142
9	The progress of industrialization 1: Ghana and Nigeria; Chile; Argentina; Hong Kong	163
10	The progress of industrialization 2: India; Egypt	198
11	Conclusion	232
	Notes and references	237
	Bibliography	243
	Index	247

Figures

1	World *per capita* net incomes, 1978	21
2	World population distribution	36
3	The demographic transition	42
4	Age and sex composition, England and Wales, 1881, 1931 and 1971	49
5	Age and sex composition, Peru 1973, India 1974, Morocco 1973 and Ghana 1970	52
6	Rostow's stages of growth	85
7	Myrdal's process of cumulative causation	86
8	The circle of poverty	97
9	World *per capita* energy consumption, 1977	129
10	World levels of literacy, 1975	137
11	The location of Huachipato	179
12	Economic development in Argentina	189
13	Hong Kong's expansion into the New Territories	194
14	India's iron and steel industry	204
15	Egypt: early industrial structure, 1954	225

Tables

1 Estimates of *per capita* net incomes of selected
  countries in US$, 1977–8   19
2 Estimates of world population by continents,
  1650–1975   39
3 Expectation of life at birth in selected countries,
  1900–78   40
4 Occupational structures of selected countries,
  1978   65
5 Vital statistics for selected countries, 1977–8   78
6 Financial aid to developing countries from DAC
  donor countries, 1961–77   103
7 Estimated years of supply of important minerals
  and metals   128
8 *Per capita* energy consumption for selected
  countries, 1977   131
9 Outlay and investment in India's Five Year Plans,
  1951–83   202
10 India's Five Year Plans (1951–83) by major heads
   of development   203
11 Egypt: industrial and mineral production   223

Preface to the fifth edition

The need for a fifth edition of this book has given the opportunity not merely to revise and update it, but substantially to rewrite a great part of it and to enlarge it with the inclusion of additional material. The original volume was first published eighteen years ago and in Britain was a pioneer study of aspects of economic and social geography of what is now called the 'Third World'. Then the references that could be cited were limited in number and were almost entirely the works of economists, politicians and anthropologists. Today, all this has changed. Third World problems – economic, social and political – command world attention. The volume of relevant published writing is immense and geographers now make a substantial contribution. This book has played a part, and within the context of industrialization it continues to outline a wide range of related aspects of economic development in order to make more understandable the plight and problems of the developing world and the varied paths to betterment that lie before it.

The Brandt Report (1980), which seems to have made a disappointing impact in Third World countries and to have received a mixed reception in the developed world, underlines the growing seriousness of the international economic scene for developing countries. In the Third World, populations continue to increase faster than the means of subsistence; food imports continue to rise; aid in real terms slows down; energy costs continue to climb; GATT with its tariff codes appears to be a rich countries' club; and the multinationals' grip on technology transfer grows tighter. However, there is growing awareness of the 'North–South' dichotomy as probably the greatest challenge facing the world today, and the more thoughtful student also becomes uncomfortably aware of the implications for humanity of the 'limits to growth' suggested by the Club of Rome. The decade we have now entered is critical for us all, for we are one world.

I record my gratitude to David Hilling and Colin Patman, colleagues at Bedford College, for helpful suggestions concerning the updating of material on Ghana and Nigeria and the new chapter on development models. I extend my thanks to Mr Ron Halfhide and Miss Claire Wastie for the drawing of the maps and graphs, and to my wife who wrestled with a recalcitrant golfball and completed the typing under par.

A.B.M.

Preface to the first edition

Since the end of the Second World War, governments and peoples in the richer countries of the world have become increasingly aware of the economic problems of their poorer neighbours. It has become an accepted policy of the advanced countries to assist in furthering the development of the human and material resources of these countries. All too often industrialization is regarded uncritically as the cure for the ills of under-development, with its degree of success held to be related simply to the degree of capital investment. Those who offer this prescription are frequently unaware of the multiplicity of problems such policies must overcome and that industrialization is not a universal panacea.

The volume of relevant research and literature is growing, but emanates mainly from economists, sociologists and political scientists; geographers have been slow to make contributions. One reason may be that geographers have been much concerned with a real differentiation within the geography of production, whereas the new field directs attention to the geography of consumption and a study of economies. This book aims to focus attention on the complex and interrelated problems – social, economic, political and geographical – that attend development, placing particular emphasis on the problems which accompany attempts at industrialization. The field is broad and much compression has been necessary. No apology is offered for the emphasis on the demographic factor, for this is fundamental to the main problem, as this work tries to show.

I welcome this opportunity to record my thanks to my colleague Miss E. M. Timberlake who read the manuscript and made many constructive criticisms, to the staff of Tate Library, Bedford College, for numerous incidental courtesies, to Miss P. Payne for assistance with the illustrations, and to my wife, who coped cheerfully with the arduous task of typing and assisted with the index.

A.B.M.

1 Development and under-development

Soon three out of every four people on this globe will live in the developing world – or 'Third World', as it has come to be called.[1]*
The second half of this twentieth century has opened our eyes to the low living standards, the poverty and ill-health endured by the mass of mankind and to the realization that the great period of decolonization following the Second World War was no more than a preamble to prodigious efforts at economic and social advancement for over two-thirds of the world's population. The granting of political independence to sixty-four former colonies between 1945 and 1970 focused attention upon the established international division of labour as a significant cause of the global poverty engulfing the great majority of humanity. Well over half the populations of these countries are engaged in agriculture, either for subsistence or to produce food and raw materials for export to the industries of the rich and advanced nations. Their economies, responsive to the needs of colonial masters, were restricted to primary production and were little touched by modern science and technology. Much of the poverty of a large part of the world is due to under-development of resources. The United Nations General Assembly recognized this in designating the 1960s as the 'United Nations Development Decade', and the 1970s as the 'Second Development Decade'. In a sense the terms 'under-developed' and 'developing' are euphemisms for 'poor'.

The rich nations of the world are remarkably few in number. Most are found in the temperate zone and are populated mainly by European stock. They include the United States and Canada, the countries of Western and Central Europe, Australia and New Zealand. In recent years they have been joined by Japan and a number of oil-exporting countries such as Kuwait and the United Arab Emirates. These oil-exporting states are rich in monetary terms, but their economies and societies are still under-developed.

*Superior figures refer to the Notes and references section on pages 237–41.

The top twenty richest nations include only one eighth of the world's population; almost three-quarters of mankind live in varying degrees of poverty. The poor countries lie mainly in Asia, Africa and Latin America, and their economies are regarded as under-developed in comparison with the richer countries whose economies reveal a wider diversity of activities embodying the fruits of science and technology and heavy investment of capital.

Developing countries are characterized by a high degree of subsistence production with a very limited application of technology; as a consequence manufacturing industry is relatively unimportant and the agricultural sector is paramount. This book is concerned with the development of the industrial sector of such economies as a part of the process of economic development, but it must be understood that industrialization is not a general panacea for all the poor countries of the world. The problem is not simply that their economies lack a substantial industrial sector, but that in many cases even their agricultural sectors are highly inefficient and generally social and institutional patterns make advance in any field extremely difficult. Economic development is not synonymous with industrialization alone, but applies to all sectors of an economy and implies a relative change in their order of importance with the application of science and technology, raising productivity per worker and releasing labour and resources for yet other productive tasks. All sectors (agriculture, mining, manu-facturing industry, commerce, services) should advance. Industry, therefore is but one part of an economy, albeit a very important one, and there is a close interrelationship between all the parts. It is also implicit in the general argument that there is no ceiling to the degree of development possible and that this applies just as much to under-developed countries as to their richer neighbours. Canada, for all its present wealth and degree of development, has vast resources still under-utilized and in this way resembles Brazil and a host of other under-developed lands. Clearly, then, the epithet of 'developed' or 'under-developed' is not based upon potential but rather upon existing levels of wealth and material welfare, but the term 'developing' has a dynamic implication in that it suggests that there is a margin of resources (human and material) that is being developed.

It is not easy to assess and compare the economic welfare of a diversity of nations, particularly when the poorer ones from their very poverty have not the precise knowledge, let alone statistics, of their own conditions. Moreover, it would be hard to get agreement among different peoples as to the meaning of economic well-being; the cultural wants of a highly developed people might seem incomprehensible to the primitive wants for food, clothing and shelter of the world's poorer peoples. On the other hand, some countries generally accepted as under-developed have cultures and civilizations going far back to the time when temperate Western Europe and North America comprised inhospitable forests and bogs. From this it would seem that 'under-developed' is a broad term encompassing states with a wide diversity of attributes, and that strictly it should be used to reflect only a low standard of technical and economic attainment.

The customary common denominator allowing a measure of comparison between countries is that of *per capita* income, obtained by dividing the estimated total net national income by the total population. The limitations of such a yardstick are apparent if the method of calculation is examined. The net national income is taken to be the sum of all goods and services produced during a year after deduction for fuel, raw materials and all other costs of production including depreciation. Wages, salaries, profits, interest and rent are all included; they are certainly applicable in developed countries but are rather unrealistic for the mass of peasantry in the poorer lands. The difficulty of giving monetary value to peasant production in a subsistence economy is clear, particularly when it is remembered that such peoples perform many services for themselves and neighbours (domestic help, cooking, washing, etc.), which are paid employments in developed countries and appear with some precision in the one reckoning, but scarcely at all (or at best as 'guesstimates') in the other. It is likely that subsistence economies are under-valued; also, not only is it difficult to equate local values with world values, but conditions of living have to be taken into account. Minimum requirements of food and clothing are less in hot countries than in areas nearer the Poles and it usually costs less to live in the village than it does in the town, both of which comparisons serve to underline the approximate character of any estimates of net national income and discount the degree of precision that the use of such figures might imply. To this problem may be coupled the frequent lack of knowledge of the size and composition of the working population.

Incomes per head are not the sole indices available; one other that has received some acceptance is a measure of the available energy per head of population. Historically, development has been characterized by a growing replacement of animate by inanimate energy. A country with plenty of power behind the elbows of its workers is one that lives well; productivity in all sections of the economy is high. This productivity may be evaluated in units of currency but it is also measurable in units of energy, for it is generally accepted that a close relationship exists between levels of energy consumption and levels of economic activity (see Table 8, p. 131). Income per head, being expressed in monetary terms, is the more widely accepted, although, besides the element of unreliability, a number of anomalies are patent. For example, the oil-rich sheikdom of Kuwait records a *per capita* net income nearly three times as high as that of Britain, but it would be ridiculous even to attempt a comparison of the economies of the two countries or the standards of living of the masses of the people in them.

With the help of the table of *per capita* incomes (Table 1), a map (Figure 1) has been constructed to show the world distribution of incomes and therefore, in broad terms, to reveal the rich and poor, the developed and developing nations. An examination of the table and map reveals that the world's wealth is extremely unevenly distributed, that the range between the richest and the poorest nations is surprisingly wide and that, on the whole, the world is still a very much under-developed planet. The inequality of income between various countries is most striking. A United States citizen nominally commands about twice the *per capita* income of each of us in the United Kingdom, while our average income per head is fifteen times that of the world's poorest countries. The correlation between highest incomes and the temperate climatic zones is another striking feature and may well reflect climatic influences upon man's mental and physical productivity, a field of study in which much work remains to be done. The other feature apparent from the map is that the 'poor' world lies mainly to the south of the developed world. During the 1970s, with a polarization of attitudes and positions at international conferences, the terms 'North' and 'South' to describe the advanced and developing worlds became internationally recognized and respectable.[2]

Differences in developing countries

The use of the broad term 'developing' must not blind us to the great differences between the developing countries themselves. Since they comprise the greater part of the world this is hardly surprising, but it is worth drawing attention to these differences to emphazise that there is no omnibus solution to the problems of developing lands, that the final answer for each country is an individual one. Numerous generalizations are frequently made about the developing countries, implying homogeneity rather than heterogeneity. There are some affinities and common characteristics to be sure, but too often generalizations based upon them mask wide diversities.

By definition one characteristic of the developing countries is that they are poor, both in income and capital, but there is a considerable range in degrees of poverty. The average net income per head in Bangladesh is less than £40 per annum, in Burma £60, in Sudan £130, Thailand £200, and so on. At the bottom poverty is utter and absolute, but up the scale it becomes relative and more

Table 1 *Estimates of* per capita *net incomes of selected countries in US$, 1977–8*

Over $9000
Belgium, Canada, Denmark, West Germany, Kuwait, Norway, Sweden, Switzerland, United Arab Emirates, USA

$9000–6000
Australia, Austria, Finland, France, Japan, Netherlands

$5999–4000
Czechoslovakia, East Germany, New Zealand, United Kingdom

$3999–2000
Bulgaria, Gabon, Greece, Hong Kong, Hungary, Israel, Italy, Poland, Singapore, Spain, USSR, Venezuela

$1999–1500
Argentina, Brazil, Costa Rica, Iraq, Iran, Lebanon, Portugal, Romania Uruguay, Yugoslavia

$1499–1000
Algeria, Chile, Fiji, Jamaica,
Jordan, Malaysia, Mexico, Panama,
Korea Republic, Republic of South
Africa, Turkey, Taiwan

$999–800
Colombia, Cuba, Dominican Repub-
lic, Ecuador, Guatemala, Ivory
Coast, Mauritius, Mongolia,
Nicaragua, Paraguay, Syria, Tunisia

$799–600
Albania, Botswana, El Salvador,
Korea Democratic Republic,
Morocco, Peru

$599–400
Bolivia, Cameroon, Congo,
Honduras, Guyana, Liberia, Nigeria,
Papua New Guinea, Philippines,
Swaziland, Thailand, Zambia,
Zimbabwe

$399–300
Angola, Egypt, Ghana, Indonesia,
Kenya, Senegal, Sudan, Togo

$299–200
Afghanistan, Benin, Central African
Republic, China, Gambia, Guinea,
Haiti, Lesotho, Madagascar,
Mauretania, Niger, Pakistan, Sierra
Leone, Tanzania, Uganda, Zaire

$199–100
Burma, Chad, Ethiopia, India,
Malawi, Mali, Mozambique, Nepal,
Somalia, Sri Lanka, Upper Volta,
Vietnam

Less than $100
Bangladesh, Democratic
Kampuchea, Lao People's
Democratic Republic

Source: World Bank, *World Development Report* (New York 1980)

Figure 1 *World per capita net incomes, 1978*

tolerable. Further, when we examine the conditions of individual countries, marked differences are apparent in the distribution of the national income. The *per capita* figures are averages assuming each man as rich as his neighbour, but this is unreal – even in communist countries – and in many under-developed countries (for instance the Middle East oil producers) the bulk of the country's wealth is in the hands of a small minority, the mass of the people existing at a standard far lower than the *per capita* income implies. Developing countries also differ in their rates of economic growth, some have been making advances while others remain static or even recede.

If we now turn to the population factor it is evident that very important differences materially affecting economies and rates of growth lie in the varying degrees of under- or over-population, the structures of the populations and their rates of increase. Some countries, such as India and Egypt, are heavily over-populated, others, such as Brazil and Ghana, are under-populated; both conditions retard economic development. These demographic features are considered in greater detail in Chapters 2 and 3, but here it must be stressed that over-population is but one contributive cause of under-development and national poverty, and that only a few countries in the world so far are seriously affected by it. However, the 'population explosions' of the last two decades are especially marked in many developing countries, particularly of South-East Asia and Latin America, and their present impoverished economies, relying mainly on relatively backward agriculture, are unlikely to expand at a rate comparable with the rapid population increase so that low living standards may fall even more.

A further characteristic of developing countries is the substantial part agriculture plays in their way of life. Again, wide differences exist, ranging from almost complete dependence upon subsistence agriculture to dependence upon agricultural exports and the imports of some foodstuffs. A capitalization of favourable climate and soil linked with organization and experience has led to specialist commercial production, such as tea in Sri Lanka, cocoa in Ghana, coffee in Brazil, sugar in Cuba, rubber in Malaya; much of this agriculture is highly efficient. Land tenure systems also vary considerably, being tribal or communal in some areas and based on individual freeholds in others. In some countries ranked as developing, large-scale irrigation works make natural desert areas habitable and cultivable, in other similarly ranked countries, shifting cultivation still pertains. Some developing countries export minerals, oil being the most outstanding example, but others include copper from Zambia and Chile, tin from Malaya, iron ore and phosphates from Algeria. It is true to say that the majority of developing countries participate to varying degrees in international trade, exporting usually only one or two primary products, and one of their problems is vulnerability to any fall in world prices.

It will be clear from the foregoing exposition that the developing countries are at widely different stages of advancement. Some, judged by their institutional arrangements, the aptitudes and education of the population and their commercial standing, are ripe for the financial, social and economic changes that development brings; others may be less ready. The readiness of investors, both internal and external, to deploy their capital in a country indicates some measure of its potentiality for advance from a traditional economy to a diversified and complex economic structure and to a position where enough capital is engendered for reinvestment to sustain progress and economic growth.

Some reasons for under-development

Many reasons are advanced to account for under-development. By our present-day standards, all countries were once in that condition (although they would not have considered themselves so at the time); what has happened is that over the centuries a few, by energy, invention and determination, have paced further and further ahead of the majority who have moved but slowly, while some have scarcely moved at all. A disturbing feature for the newly awakened world conscience is that the pace of progress of the few leading countries is accelerating rapidly; the progression seems to be geometric – the rich become richer and the poor relatively (and in a few cases, absolutely) poorer. During the years 1952–6 when India had launched her first Five Year Plan, her income per head rose by barely £1, whereas Britain's income per head rose by nearly £40. The large rolling snowball picks up much more snow than the tiny one just beginning to roll. This multiplier element, more and more evident as development gets under way, is an integral factor to be invoked in economic plans for development. Cumulative growth, even at apparently slow rates over the years, can, however, have astonishing results. At the beginning of the twentieth century the United Kingdom and the

United States enjoyed approximately identical levels of real income per head, but since then the American rate of progress has averaged about 2 per cent and the British about 1 per cent per annum. Eighty years' growth at these speeds and allowing for compound interest now gives the United States rather more than double the British average income per head. The differing rates of growth seem small, but the result over a period of time is of great consequence. Geographers are interested in, and can make useful contributions to, problems of development. A particular field the geographer tends to regard as his own and to evaluate highly in importance is that of resource endowment. There is a danger that the role and significance of possession or non-possession of natural resources in economic development may be misunderstood. Development and under-development are often loosely attributed to the maldistribution of natural resources or to particular geographical disadvantages of certain countries, such as their world position, size, character of the relief, soils and climate. These views are somewhat erroneous; certainly, the possession of varied natural resources can be advantageous but in themselves resources are not decisive. It is not difficult for the geographer to name well-endowed countries that are still backward in development and to indicate other countries, highly advanced yet apparently possessing few natural resources. Brazil and Indonesia, Switzerland and Denmark provide two examples of each. Brazil, despite only limited geological survey, is known to have a plenitude of mineral resources; its large size and varied structure offer a diversity of topography, climates, soils and mineral wealth, yet it remains relatively undeveloped and the *per capita* income of about £750 is low. On the other hand, Denmark, despite a lack of minerals and energy resources, a small size, a homogeneity of relief and climate, has developed her economy to such an extent that on a *per capita* income basis she is one of the richest countries in Europe.

These examples also serve to disprove the contention that size of country is a major factor in development. We can see countries of equal size enjoying a very different standard of living and large countries seem to have no advantage over small ones and vice versa. The multitude of factors bearing upon the well-being of different countries make it very difficult to isolate and evaluate the significance of size in this connection. It is true that great areas may connote a rich and diversified endowment of natural resources, but this merely gives a potentiality. Far more depends upon man's numbers, energy, knowledge, and sense of purpose. Capital can substitute for natural resources as we see in the case of Switzerland where, however, among other geographical factors, position plays an important part.

These examples suggest that much more than possession of resources is necessary for the furtherance of economic development; not even the economist's triumvirate, land (that is, resources), labour and capital, are by any means the sole determinants of economic progress. Perhaps the most important factors are human ones: in the last resort everything depends upon the people themselves – their numbers and age structures, their enterprise and initiative, their inventiveness, their level of technical knowledge, and above all their desire for material betterment and their willingness to make necessary sacrifices to attain it. Resources in themselves are quite passive; the understanding of their possibilities, the will to use them, the application of capital and technical know-how are the means by which resources become active elements in economies. We must regard the possession of resources as permissive rather than deterministic.

The value and importance of natural resources are not fixed but vary with the stage of development. Spain, for example, by the middle of the nineteenth century was exporting the high-quality, easily won, low-phosphoric-content iron ores of the Viscayan part of Cantabria. In the last decades of the century exports of these ores had risen to an average of 5 million tons per annum. During the century the ore resources were utilized to earn capital and allowed of capital accumulation. This capital was employed in establishing iron and steel plant on the ore site during the 1880s, and if these development measures had been fully successful, both home and export markets for pig iron and steel might have grown and the ore deposits thus have obtained an enhanced value as an important element in Spain's economic growth. Unfortunately the home market remained remarkably small (there being little comparable development in other branches of the economy) and production costs were too high for successful exports. Moreover, the richer ores rapidly approached exhaustion and probably have only been saved from it by the introduction of the basic steel-making process utilizing phosphoric ores and the open-hearth furnaces utilizing high proportions of scrap, thus reducing the demand for these Spanish ores.

This example of the uncertain beginning of Spain's iron and

steel industry serves to demonstrate a number of points. The initial working of the iron-ore deposits on a commercial scale was due to the shrewdness of certain Spaniards and foreigners in appreciating the locational advantages of the deposits situated near the coast, easily accessible to the growing iron industries of Britain and her continental neighbours, and being of high iron content and chemically suitable for the acid Bessemer process. With energy and enterprise, capital was raised, much of it foreign, and mining and export companies were formed. The entrepreneurial factor is clearly revealed; the conversion of latent resources into positive wealth awaited those who saw opportunities and were prepared to take risks in order to realize them. Next we see the utilizing of these resources providing a means of capital accumulation (one of the major problems of under-developed countries) and the investment of this capital in industrial plant, whereby indirectly the ore resources would act as an accelerator to economic development if other factors of production were favourable. The effect of advances in overseas blast- and steel-furnace technology is also noticeable in a fluctuation of demand and a general decline in ore exports (perennial problems of under-developed lands dependent upon markets for one or two primary products). The diminution of export markets underlined the narrowness of the home market for manufactured iron and steel. Whereas capital had been invested in the iron and steel industry, there had been little complementary growth in the rest of the Spanish economy and the money to buy the iron and steel products was lacking. The interrelationship between all parts of an economy is thus revealed and raises the question of the effectiveness of development investment that does not take full account of this feature – another major problem of developing countries today.

The path to development

It is possible to concentrate on economic growth without commensurate improvement and progress for the mass of the population – but this is scarcely 'development'. Development involves not merely economic changes but also social and institutional ones and, in many developing countries, introduces new sets of values and new concepts of society and government. No path to development is likely to be smooth; the 1848 Chartist disturbances in England and 'year of revolution' in Europe are indicative of the stresses the present developed countries underwent with growing urbanization, the rise of an urban proletariat and the growth in numbers and power of the 'middle class'. In Europe these social, economic and political changes were spread over the greater part of a century, but the process of adjustment must now be speeded up, for newly developing countries today necessarily plan their economic and social metamorphism in terms of a number of Three, Four or Five Year Plans. One of the difficulties in initiating economic development in many developing countries lies in overcoming institutional opposition. Here, social systems, often based upon concepts of inherited value, are far more rigid than those of Western Europe ever were and severely restrain opportunities for individual advancement. This places more responsibility for economic development upon the government than has been usual in most developed countries where governmental influence has tended to be indirect. The West has long turned from the satisfactions of religio-cultural values to acquisitive values, for it has come to view development in economic terms: the maximization of goods and services per head. It does not follow that all developing countries will readily accept these capitalist values, although supported by the views of Karl Marx, that the developed countries present to the less-developed societies a picture of their own future.

A growing body of economic theory supports the view that economic development is not an inevitable process but must be created and energetically advanced. This may be done by a variety of co-ordinated measures designed to interrupt the free play of social and economic forces. The forces of the market are no longer supreme within developed countries, for both state and private organizations so manipulate conditions that opportunity is more widespread, levels of inequality narrowed and demand influenced. By planned measures of investment, innovation, supports and controls, aggressive policies of economic development are deemed capable of overcoming the stagnation characteristic of many under-developed lands. In other words, it is now held that economic development can be induced or even imposed, the goals being determined by governments who become responsible for the co-ordination and planning measures deemed necessary to attain them.[3] These hopeful and stimulating theories are now being proved; in them lies the hope for betterment of four-fifths of the world's population. The next decade will be critical in their application and development.

This broad theory of development is widely held; it is in the precise application that differences emerge, particularly over the degree or priority that developing lands should allow industrialization. Most of the rich countries of the world are highly industrialized, and there might seem a case for rapid industrialization in under-developed lands as a short cut to a better standard of living; this view is favoured by Soviet Russia. The previous example of Spain, however, emphasizes the interdependence of the various sectors within an economy, and most Western economists favour what has come to be called 'balanced growth' whereby, briefly, agriculture is made more efficient, allowing output per worker to rise, freeing some to move into manufacturing, power, transport and other non-agricultural pursuits. The greater productivity and increasing purchasing power allows of imports and expands the home market for newly manufactured goods. In short, there is an all-round expansion and an upward spiral is created. If these views (expressed here in outline only but elaborated in Chapter 6) are accepted it will be seen that concentration on manufacturing industry offers no short cut to prosperity. The simple outline above fails to take into account demographic factors, widely proving to be the most obstructive of the hindrances to economic development in under-developed countries.

The confidence of economists in their growing understanding of economic forces and their manipulation in this field coincides with the growth of world knowledge of under-development, both by the richer countries and by the under-developed lands themselves. Bodies such as the United Nations, the World Health Organization, the Food and Agricultural Organization, have collected and disseminated facts and figures of world under-development and world poverty. These followed the years of the Second World War in which hundreds of thousands of soldiers from the richer countries saw for themselves the poverty and resignation of many alien lands. The blinkers have slipped from the eyes of people in the few rich countries of the world and the gulf between the internationally rich and poor has been revealed. A world conscience has become manifest as economic inequalities between the rich and the poor increase. The poor also have become far more aware of their poverty as increasing knowledge of higher standards of living in the developed countries has become known, and the desire for change and improvement has begun to be expressed. The sympathy of the richer countries is annually growing in expression by means of technical and financial help and advice, and makes possible the application in under-developed countries of the modern economic theories of development. The pre-war term 'backward countries' is no longer current and by our use in turn of 'under-developed countries', 'less-developed countries' and 'developing countries' we imply the feasibility of development; we assume that with help those countries can do better with their human and material resources. The size of the problem is now tacitly recognized by the acceptance of the term 'Third World' to differentiate the mass of under-developed countries from the 'free world' of the Atlantic bloc and the centrally organized European Communist bloc.

The second half of the twentieth century is seeing for the first time in world history an international onslaught on poverty and backwardness; a new form of pioneering and on an unprecedented scale. In the process not only economies but also societies will become remoulded and whole landscapes may change. Each period of earth history has seemed both exciting and critical to its people, but surely none more so than today.

2 The demographic factor: the global setting

The greatest problem our world faces, the more serious in that we have been slow to acknowledge it, is that of the excessive population growth in relation to the development of the earth's resources. The world's population problem is not new, but during this century it has become more widely known and its measurement more refined and more complete, thanks to such agencies as the United Nations' statistical departments. With this greater and more accurate knowledge has come the realization of the growing seriousness of the problems posed by the rapid increase in human numbers. At worst the manifestation of the problem is growing poverty in certain parts of the world where human increase exceeds that of the development of resources (although it must be appreciated that, at the same time in other parts of the world, some peoples also increasing in numbers are growing steadily richer). More serious is where population increase is rapid enough to impede and retard plans for economic development. The prospect of the rapid spread and worsening of this situation is before us. The second half of this century has seen the growth of a social conscience among the better-off nations and greater inter-national co-operation; no longer are eyes closed to the periodic famines that take toll of great populations in South-East Asia and Sahelian Africa; the Malthusian checks are now thwarted.

In any community, population numbers, reproductive rate and composition crucially affect the future in that they have a direct influence upon economic development. Here lies the core of the population problem, and that particularly affecting the under-developed lands: the relation between population growth and economic development. It is therefore surprising to find that little is yet known with precision about the economics of population. Economists have concentrated more upon the mechanics of economic development with the developed lands as their examples and, more recently, upon the creation of a theory of under-development to aid in the analysis of particular situations. We are still uncertain, for example, of the effects of over-population, much less the varying rates of population growth, on development. Theories are advanced but they will be tested only as more precise information and statistics become available.

Population theory

As is well known, population theory hinges on the law of diminishing returns. Briefly, this law states that, so long as techniques used remain the same, additional application of capital and labour to (for example) a given area of land will after a time cause a less than proportionate increase in the output of produce. Similarly industry is subject to diminishing returns, although they can usually be more delayed than in agriculture, since industrial processes are more susceptible of improvements in technique and greater division of labour. In the developed lands the steady increase of population expanding the labour force has led to greater specialization and higher efficiency giving a greater return on each unit of labour. The point of decreasing returns has been avoided by inventions, increases in technical skills and the investment of more and more capital. Unless this happens, from the application of this law, whether in agriculture or manufacturing, after a time we may expect returns to increase by smaller increments until they become constant and then decrease. It follows that there is a point of maximum return, beyond which the application of more capital and labour will not produce proportional returns. It is at this point that a population has reached its optimum or has attained a density which, with given resources and skills, produces the maximum economic welfare or, virtually, the maximum real income per head. It is clear that this concept is highly theoretical if only because it is dealing with a balance between a given people and their resources, where numbers, knowledge and skills are constantly changing. The theory, however, does give a definite meaning to the two states of over-population and under-population. With over-population numbers exceed the optimum and with under-population they fall below it; in each case the individual standard of life is lower than it would be if the optimum prevailed.

To put it another way, we may define these conditions as states of society in which there are too many or too few people for the society to live at the highest standard possible with existing land, capital and technical skills. Over-population is a greater drag on economic expansion than under-population and the most serious problem areas in the world today are those over-populated but under-developed; here further population increases depress living conditions still more. It is salutary to view the world's population problem not as one of numbers but of standards of living. It is true that population expansion was a vital and dynamic factor in the economic development of nineteenth-century Britain, but here, via a technical revolution in agriculture, was burgeoning an industrial economy where decreasing returns were prevented by the invest-ment and ploughing back of more and more capital, by increasing specialization and by steadily developing technical processes and skills. A different state of affairs evolved in South-East Asia, although with fewer records it is less satisfactorily explained. One reason may be the very antiquity of these civilizations in the great fertile river basins, where slow improvements and developments in agriculture took place over a long period, for a time no doubt keeping pace with slow population growth. The West European environment was conducive to movement, intercourse and trade, to the mining and working of metals, and by the end of the six-teenth century it created a class of persons removed from the land, a money economy, such far-reaching institutions as the joint stock company, and it supported an agrarian revolution that opened the way to full industrialization with its harnessing and application of mechanical energy. In South-East Asia the more static agrarian way of life offered less scope for technical advances and division of labour, and the predominantly subsistence economy prevented the generation of much capital. Thus these traditional ways persisted and the onset of decreasing returns was not withstood. Standards of living fell acutely with the heavy population increases of more recent times, which now bleed the economies with their absorption of capital, inflate the problem by their very immensity and impede the belated take-off to a more balanced and productive economy.

The heavy drag of high rates of population increase upon econo-mic development is frequently underestimated. Each new member of society raises the bill for education, health and other public services and the provision of employment for him increases the demand for capital investment. A rate of population increase of 1.5 per cent per annum requires at least a 2 per cent per annum increase in output if the standard of living is to grow at all. This is a substantial task needing capital investment of 8–10 per cent of the national income, whereas most under-developed countries save only about 5 per cent of the national income. In fact, this rate of development would be comparatively modest and would take over 100 years to double the standard of living. Also, rates of population increase in most of the developing lands are in excess of 1.5 per cent per annum; rates of 2.5 and 3 per cent per annum are now being recorded, requiring a capital investment of 10–12 per cent of the national income even to hold the present low living standards. Thus the heavy task of finding the means for the raising of output is made more herculean the greater the rate of population increase. Past experience suggests, however, that once standards of living are raised birth rates tend to fall.

This discussion would be incomplete if opposing views were not cited. The above Malthusian view, widely accepted, is challenged by those who feel that population pressure serves to stimulate innovation, for man exerts himself to the utmost to ward off threats to his living standards. Savings also are mainly accumulated by young people, and therefore a youthful population should have a high rate of capital accumulation and therefore of investment. Some economists also cite economies of scale in this connection, pointing out that densely populated countries need less capital per unit of product than do sparsely peopled countries because utilities and capital equipment (for instance, railways, harbour works, etc.) are used more fully. These views, connected with such names as Adam Smith and Marx, derive mainly from studies of developed rather than under-developed economies.

The growth of world population

There is a great body of literature discussing the varied aspects of the world's population problem and it is not intended here to present more than an outline to serve as a frame for a more detailed consideration of the place, problems and possibilities of industrialization. In these matters the demographic factor carries great weight for the population element underlies and colours the whole economic scene. It would be wrong, however, to ascribe development or under-development simply to the weight of the population force, particularly under- or over-population. Development is the result of the interaction over considerable periods of time of many interdependent factors, mutually cumulative in their effects; there is no simple basic factor. The often quoted 'economic factor' – a compound of capital, land and labour – is only one of the ingredients, and non-economic factors also play quite decisive roles, including for example the physical and mental character of a people in addition to their numbers, sex ratios and rates of increase. Geographical position may even carry more weight than resource endowment and much may depend on the prevailing social and political organization. If this were not the case, national poverty could be said to rest wholly on physical circumstances beyond human control.

A review of the present situation of world population and its recent history serves to underline its dynamic character. Each day changes take place; population is in constant transition. Census coverage and information are constantly improving but still the great majority of peoples in under-developed countries are not adequately enumerated, and the more detailed information, such as age groupings in relation to births and deaths (very necessary in estimating population growth), is rarely available. The margin of error in the United Nations' estimate of world population may be as high as 5 per cent.

The United Nations' *Demographic Yearbook* gives the population of the world in 1978 as 4258 million.[1] The present annual increment to this stupendous figure is of the order of nearly 80 million, or much more than the population of the United Kingdom. The population of the world in 1900 has been estimated at about 1550 million, and this suggests that world population has almost trebled during the following eighty years. The fact that world population increased by about 500 million in the first thirty years of this period (in 1930 a total of 2013 million), by 1000 million during the next thirty years (in 1960 a total of 3000 million) and by a further 1500 million in the remaining twenty years (in 1980 an estimate of 4450 million) makes abundantly clear the multiplying factor that is so alarming in population increase. Not only do the absolute numbers grow steadily, but for most of this century the rate of increase itself increased. However, small reductions in birth rate in some developing countries are now being recorded, and at the beginning of the decade of the 1980s the first small reduction this century in the world's rate of population increase was discerned, the rate dropping from 2.2 per cent of a decade ago to 1.9 per cent. Huxley estimated that the rate of increase in 1650 was 0.5 per cent; it did not reach 1 per cent until well into this century; and twenty-five years ago it was 1.3 per cent. It is the acceleration in the rate of increase that is so serious. 'Population increase proceeds ... by acceleration, and the result has been to convert an early stage of virtual stability into one of slow but appreciable growth, then into rapid expansion, and finally into an explosive process.'[2] At a rate of increase of 0.5 per cent per annum the population will double itself in approximately 140 years; at 1 per cent, in seventy years; at 1.5 per cent, in forty-seven years; and at 2 per cent (which has prevailed in recent years) in thirty-five years. We may expect the staggering total of 6000 million by the year 2000 if the present rate continues. The problem of feeding, clothing and occupying this mass of humanity and of reducing its fertility must be solved urgently. The longer we dawdle, the more intractable the problem becomes. Current changes in rates of population increase will not affect this figure, because for an appreciable time the large numbers of women already born will bear children and will cause an absolute increase in the population numbers. Present reduction in the birth rates, if sustained, will reduce the numbers of potential mothers from the turn of the century and thus it is in the twenty-first century that we may hope for a slowing down, then a levelling off, and eventually even a reduction in world population totals.

The map (Figure 2) displays the very uneven distribution of man on the earth and reveals three principal agglomerations of population, in Europe, in eastern North America and in South-East and Eastern Asia. The character of the earth's surface and the climate help to determine the distribution of man and, to a large extent, to account for the crowding into a small number of favoured but limited areas, although the degree of development and character of the economy play their part, particularly in accounting for local variations within the main areas. Both the European and North American populous areas lie in the zone of cyclonic weather, alleged to favour the greatest mental and physical well-being, whereas the Asian population centres are in the monsoonal zone, where the conjunction of moisture and warmth makes possible the production of abundant food per acre. In these three main areas, 3500 million people crowd into about 4 million square miles – an area slightly greater than that of Canada or a third larger than Australia and under half the size of the USSR. It seems, further, that three-quarters of the world's population lives on no more than a twelfth of the earth's land surface, giving a density of 300 per square kilometre. The wealthier industrial nations are able to draw upon considerable food supplies from more sparsely peopled

POPULATION
One dot represents 100,000 people

Figure 2   *World population distribution*

areas, but the densely peopled agricultural lands lack the wealth to do this and their increasing numbers press directly upon the means of subsistence, usually engendering conditions of extreme poverty. It is notable that more than half the population of the world lives in Asia and that this proportion is steadily increasing.

Rates of increase vary markedly but are generally high among the developing lands and moderate or low in richer countries (Table 5, p. 78). Thus, whereas at the beginning of this century there was one European for every two Asians, by the end of the century this ratio may have become one to four. One of the features of the next few decades will be a continuous decline in the relative importance of Europe, including the USSR. It seems likely that by the year 2000 the present population of Africa (460 million) will have increased to nearly 800 million; that of Asia (2500 million) to nearly 3700 million; and that of Latin America (370 million) to almost 650 million. The rest of the world population will increase by a little less than a fifth of its present level to 1400 million. It will be seen that this growth is proportionately greatest in the regions of low standards of living. It would seem that we have now entered the most explosive period of population growth from which the richer and developed countries can no longer be insulated. The year 2000 is relatively close and since the problems become more acute with each year that passes it would seem that the current decade may be one of the most critical in human history.

The history of population growth

It is probably well realized now that the very great population increases during this century, and particularly since the close of the Second World War, are not the result of an increase in human fertility, but rather of a decline in mortality resulting from advances in, and the wider application of, modern medicine. It is striking to realize that, whereas it took the world 200,000 years to attain a population of 2500 million, it now requires barely twenty years to add a further 2000 million. Of course, our reasonably precise knowledge of the size of the world's population goes back barely two centuries. The further we go back in time, the more we must rely on guesswork and the more flimsy the evidence upon which these guesses can be based. It is clear that for at least 10,000 years there has been a steady increase in world population; temporary decreases or stagnation may have occurred here and there but the trend has been persistently upward. Some 10,000 years ago, during the hunting stage of man's existence, world population is thought to have been between 5 and 10 million; 3000 years later, with the onset of civilization, the figure may have risen to 20 million. A progressive increase of numbers followed with development in agriculture, trade and manufacture, and at the time of Christ, world population may have been about 150 million.[3] By the middle of the seventeenth century, when estimates are more certain, this figure had reached approximately 550 million. Seventeen centuries gave a four-fold world population increase, but the past three centuries have seen that population multiply itself five times. Thus it seems that the modern phase of accelerating population increase began during the seventeenth century and was well under way in the eighteenth century.

The sharp upward turn in the rate of population increase during this period may be related to the striking advances made in the fields of agriculture, industry, medicine and sanitation. In these the countries of Western Europe were in the forefront. Between 1650 and 1900 Europe's population, despite considerable emigration, multiplied itself four times and its share of the world's population increased from 22 to 27 per cent (Table 2). Asia's population grew at a slower rate and by 1900 the increase was about three times. By the end of the first half of this century Europe's population had increased almost six-fold since 1650 and Asia's population had quintupled. Thus the rate of Asia's population increase has gone up appreciably during this century. Admittedly, higher rates of increase since the seventeenth century have been recorded in the comparatively empty lands of the Americas, but the numbers involved have been relatively small. Four-fifths of world population is now in Europe and Asia.

Although there is reason to believe that the population of Japan and China began increasing more rapidly during the latter part of the seventeenth century (that is, before the substantial advance in Europe began), on the whole the rise in the rate of increase of Asia's population came after that of Europe, becoming noticeable during the nineteenth century as a result of European influence. It would seem that in certain respects the great increases of population in Asian countries in the recent decades might be regarded as a repetition of a pattern already passed through in Europe. There are grave differences, however, particularly in the speed of occurrence and the magnitude of the populations undergoing them.

Table 2 Estimates of world population by continents. 1650–1975.

(millions)

	1650	(%)	1750	(%)	1850	(%)	1900	(%)	1950	(%)	1975	(%)
Europe	103	22.0	144	21.0	274	25.2	423	27.0	574	23.0	728	18.3
North America	1	0.2	1	0.1	26	2.5	81	6.0	168	7.0	237	6.0
Latin America	7	1.4	10	1.4	33	3.0	63	4.0	163	6.5	324	8.2
Africa	100	21.3	100	14.3	100	9.1	120	7.7	199	8.0	401	10.1
Asia	257	54.7	437	63.0	656	60.1	857	55.0	1376	55.0	2256	56.9
Oceania	2	0.4	2	0.2	2	0.1	6	0.3	13	0.5	21	0.5
World total	470	100	694	100	1091	100	1550	100	2493	100	3967	100

Sources: W. F. Willcox, *Studies in American Demography* (New York 1940), for 1650–1900; United Nations, *Demographic Yearbook, 1950* (New York 1951); *1975* (New York 1976).

The period of really critical increase in the rate of population growth has been the last four decades. Until 1940 the world's annual increase of population was 1.0–1.2 per cent. Over the next thirty-five years this rate of growth quickened to 2.2 per cent, and only with the 1980s did it ease to 1.9 per cent. This recent excessive acceleration has been due to a series of scientific and medical advances whose application has resulted in what has been termed 'death control'. The vigorous introduction of medical services, new drugs, instruction in hygiene and improved sanitation into the poorer countries has often markedly extended the expectation of life. In Britain the expectation of life at birth is about 70 years, in India at the beginning of the century it was only 24, but by 1960 it had increased to 41 years (Table 3). Postponement of death has been particularly successful in the case of infants, and infant mortality rates in the under-developed countries have started to show astonishing reductions. During the period 1948–67 Sri Lanka's mortality rate fell from 92 to 48 and Chile's from 147 to 92 deaths under the age of 1 year per 1000 live births – examples

Table 3   *Expectation of life at birth in selected countries, 1900–78*

	(Years)					
	1900	*1930*	*1950*	*1960*	*1970*	*1978*
United Kingdom	52	-	67	71	72	73
France	47	-	65	70	73	73
Bulgaria	40	46	-	66	71	72
Japan	44	-	58	70	74	76
Chile	-	38	52	57	63	67
Mexico	-	33	-	57	64	65
Algeria	-	-	43	48	54	56
Paraguay	-	-	52	57	62	63
Botswana	-	-	36	41	46	48
Egypt	-	-	44	53	48	54
Kenya	-	-	-	-	49	53

Note: The average of male and female life expectations is given.
Sources: United Nations, *Demographic Yearbook* (New York annually); World Bank, *World Development Report* (New York 1980), Table 21.

typical of most of the under-developed countries.

The result of all this has been that the death rate has been falling exceptionally fast in many under-developed countries of Latin America and Asia, and is beginning to fall in Africa, whereas no appreciable fall has yet occurred in their birth rates. We find that high death rates of, say, 30 per 1000 have been halved without any corresponding diminution of birth rates of the order of 40 per 1000. It may not be wise to press analogies with Europe too far in these matters, but it is worth noting that there was a considerable time lag in Western Europe (half a century in fact) before a decline in birth rates followed the fall in death rates. The people of Western Europe during the last two and a half centuries have been influenced by four social and economic movements: so-called revolutions in agriculture, industry, medicine and sanitation, and birth control. Analysis of the resultant pattern of population reaction to these movements helped in the formulation of what is conveniently known as the population cycle or the demographic transition.

The demographic transition

As a result of social and economic developments populations usually pass through a number of distinct stages in their growth. In the pre-scientific period both birth and death rates were high; population increase was slow and irregular. This period is known as the 'high fluctuating' stage and in this country was coming to an end early in the eighteenth century. As medical knowledge and sanitation improved, the next phase occurred: the 'early expanding' phase of rapid increase. In this stage, death rates fall markedly but birth rates remain both high and constant and a maximum increase of population occurs. The third or 'late expanding' stage finds death rates continuing their fall but, responsive to rising standards of living, families become smaller and a sharp decline in the birth rate sets in; population still increases, but at a less rapid rate. Finally in the 'low fluctuating' phase, both birth and death rates steady at a low level (in Britain at about 13 and 12 per 1000 respectively), increase still takes place, but very slowly, and the population seems to be reaching a phase of stabilization. These conditions for England and Wales are demonstrated in Figure 3.

It may well be thought that the developing lands currently receiving the benefits of advanced agriculture, industry and medicine

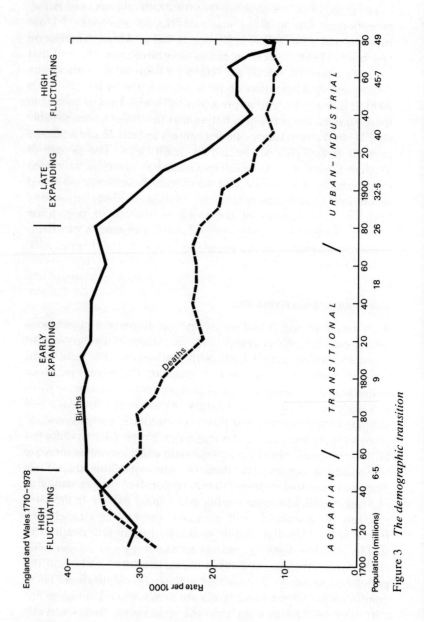

Figure 3   *The demographic transition*

are now passing through the early stages of the population cycle and that a pattern similar to that of Western Europe will ensue. However, the problems of these countries, and indeed the world's population problem as a whole, arise from the very different timing and telescoping of the various phases.

First, it must be realized that in Western Europe, the type area, change was gradual. The knowledge and application of death control arose from a long period of trial and error. The slow but steady accretion of population both stimulated and allowed full advantage to be taken of the new developments in industry and transport; in short, they permitted economic expansion which, throughout the nineteenth century, raised standards of living, making possible, at a price, the choice of comforts and amenities and thus fostering a material desire to limit families. In England and Wales this had started to take effect in the decade 1871–80, when the birth rate, dropping from 35.5 to 34.1, started a downward plunge that was not arrested until during the Second World War. The situation is very different in the developing countries where Europe's hard-won knowledge of two centuries is readily, and relatively instantaneously, available. The reduction of death rates that has taken Western Europe two centuries to accomplish is now occurring in one or two decades in parts of Asia and Latin America. This is graphically illustrated by the much-quoted example of Sri Lanka, where DDT and a well-organized campaign wiped out the malarial mosquito in seven years (1945–52) and the death rate fell from 22 to 10 per 1000. It took about 300 years to clear malaria from England and the comparable fall in the death rate was spread over seventy years. During this time, however, England's birth rate fell from 35 to 15 per 1000, whereas that of Sri Lanka remains above 30, and the population increases at a rate that will double it in thirty years. Here is the explanation of the population explosion now becoming manifest: birth rates are still in stage 2 of the transition, out of phase with falling death rates often already approaching stage 4.

The demographic transition model relating to Western Europe is based upon changing technology and will differ, perhaps substantially, from the transition being experienced in the developing countries. These differences are particularly manifest in the structure of these populations and in the character of the economic development they must necessarily engender. Another differing element is the growing interest by Third World governments in supporting birth control and family planning measures, not taken up by the advanced countries until stage 4 of the model. In Europe reduction of fertility was a 'natural' process, but in developing countries it is becoming 'policy'. In Western Europe, development, particularly industrial development, evolved gradually from within, but in the developing world, this has become, with external contacts, a rapid imposition from without. The scale of development, too, must be very different, since the initial populations are more vast and their standards of living lower than those of Western Europe two centuries ago. The greater these populations, the greater the rate of growth of total output needed to raise the standard of living.

3 The demographic factor in the under-developed lands

Age structures

The dynamic character of population growth and its portents have been outlined; it is now necessary to examine, with particular reference to the developing lands, those aspects of population that leave the greatest impress upon a country's economy. The age structure of a population is a factor of the greatest demographic and economic weight. In the first place age distribution conditions birth and death rates in a community while being itself, of course, an intimate expression of them; or in other words, future population growth is related to past trends because of their expression in the age structure. Crude birth rates are expressed as per 1000 of the total population, but it is an important refinement to consider the ratio of numbers of births to numbers of women in the reproductive cycle (ages 15–45). Variation in the proportions of women in these age groups will alter the birth rate, assuming that the number of children produced by each woman (fertility) remains the same. Actual age distribution within these (the reproductive cycle) age groups is also important. Women approaching the end of their reproductive period are less fertile than younger women, thus a change in the age distribution of women aged 15–45 will also affect the birth rate. If relatively more women appear in the age group 20–24 than before, other things being equal, the birth rate rises.

The proportion of women of child-bearing age to the whole community varies markedly in countries at different stages of the population cycle, implying that some populations are far more fecund than others. Stage 4 populations, for example, are far 'older' than those in earlier stages. In such analyses birth rates related to the specific ages of mothers are valuable but it is very rare for such age-specific birth rates of under-developed lands to be known, consequently one can only examine the patterns in the developed lands, where statistics are available, and in broad terms transpose the resultant trends to assume similar patterns in the developing communities. This relies upon the expectation that future structure of certain populations will resemble the past structure of others.

Death control, that has become so marked a feature in developed lands during the past two or three decades, has the effect of prolonging the lives of some older people. They are less productive but nevertheless need food and shelter; while enlarging the total population they have virtually no effect upon the birth rate and population trend. The main result of death control, however, is a reduction of the crude death rate by a lowering of infant mortality. Children thus saved in infancy are likely to live out an appreciable lifetime, and thus, far more female children will reach child-bearing age and in turn increase the number of babies produced for any given crude birth rate. This is a significant feature that suggests there can be little hope of rapid reduction in population increase in these lands, for even when crude birth rates start to fall, for an appreciable time the large numbers bearing children will cause an absolute increase in numbers born. It is true that the fall in the infant mortality rate is far faster than it was in Western Europe, and there is some hope that when birth rates do fall in the developing lands they will also drop far more rapidly than they did in the developed countries.

Once the numbers of births decline, the age structure of a population will slowly change. The survivors of the former high birth rates become older and pass out of the child-bearing period, to be replaced only partially by the succeeding generations. This was the pattern exhibited by many West European countries immediately prior to the Second World War. In England and Wales the percentage of people over 45 and over in 1881 was just under 20, by 1931 it had risen to 31 per cent, and in 1971 was 37 per cent. Such marked changes in a population's age composition are reflected in a changing rate of increase and affect the degree to which a population is reproducing itself. Differences between crude birth and death rates are inadequate for determining rate of replacement, since a population may still be increasing even when the mothers of a generation are not replacing themselves. The experience of the United Kingdom again demonstrates this. Between 1923 and 1946 our net reproduction rate was below 1.0 (the exact replacement rate), but our population continued to grow because there were large numbers of people born earlier when both the birth rate and number of births per annum were much higher. These people, being both in and after the reproductive age groups but still some way from death, retard the effects of incomplete replacement. However, the use of the measure known as the net reproduction rate clarifies the situation. Here age-specific birth rates of female children are adjusted with similar age-specific death rates and expressed as a proportion of that necessary to maintain a stationary population: in other words it is a measure of how far mothers are reproducing themselves. A rate of 1.0 means that a generation of women of child-bearing age is exactly reproducing itself. During the 1930s the net reproduction rate of England and Wales was barely 0.8, which signified that every ten women of child-bearing age left after them only eight daughters. If such a rate persisted over several generations the total population would level off and then begin to decline.

Other factors affecting birth rates, and related usually to social and economic conditions, are the marriage rate, the age of marriage, and birth control. Here again data are increasingly available for developed countries but as yet scarcely known for the lesser-developed lands. It is sufficient here to notice that subject to certain provisos the greater the marriage rate (that is, the number of persons married per 1000 of the population), the greater the fertility to be expected of a population and, since younger women are more fertile than older women, a lowering of the average age of marriage may well lead to a rise in the crude birth rate. An underlying assumption here is that illegitimate births form but a very small proportion of total births. If the employment of birth control increases and becomes more effective, then a fall in the birth rate is to be expected. This feature, related to under-developed countries, will be discussed in more detail later.

These examples have been mentioned to demonstrate how the vital processes within the framework of the particular stage in the population cycle affect, and in turn are affected by, the age structure of a population. Such structure can reflect the relevant stage in the demographic transition and in broad terms can indicate expanding or contracting populations in the years ahead, always assuming, of course, that existing birth and death rates persist. In turn economic reactions differ in expanding and contracting societies; the long-term requirements of a predominantly young and vigorous population will bear little resemblance to those where half of the population is over 40.

The age and sex pyramid

The examination of the age and sex structure of populations is as necessary a task for the geographer in his interpretation of the human geography as it is for the economist and social scientist concerned with more specific aspects of the economy and its parent society. No examination of the problems of the developing lands can be real or complete without such a study. The most widely used device for illustrating this information is the age and sex pyramid, whereby the information is graphed so that the essential character of the population structure may be clearly seen and the population history readily interpreted. The graph comprises a central vertical scale of age groupings, usually employing five-year groupings with the youngest group, 0–4, at the bottom. The percentage that each of these groups forms of the entire population is plotted on a horizontal scale, males being placed to the left of the vertical scale and females to the right of it. Actual numbers may be plotted horizontally, but this is often less useful than percentages since neither proportions nor comparisons are so easily read off. The graph represents the total population, and its characteristically triangular shape stems from the normally diminishing proportion of males and females in each successively older age group. Such a graph covers nearly a century and reflects the diverse experience of the given society; epidemics, wars, migrations, economic recessions, the advances of medicine are all mirrored in the vital processes and appear on the graph. In turn these features, resembling gashes and scars on an idealized outline, over the years will ascend the scale, contract and vanish, and in this sense the document, in addition to information of the past and the present, can give a partial, but valuable, picture of the future.

A brief examination of the age and sex pyramids for England and Wales in 1881, 1931 and 1971 will demonstrate many of these points (Figure 4). The graph for 1881 is markedly different in shape from the other two and records the age structure at the close of the early expanding stage in Britian's population cycle. A high and steady birth rate related to a steadily diminishing death rate had engendered a rapid increase of population, each succeeding five-year age group has outnumbered its predecessors and a steadily increasing specific mortality rate tapers off the pyramid fairly regularly. This population, in 1881, is basically 'young', some 60 per cent of the population being less than 30 years-old. The

Figure 4   *Age and sex composition, England and Wales, 1881, 1931 and 1971*

period covered by the graph is free from major wars but did see a considerable loss of population by emigration, helping to account for a slight steepening in the adult portion of the graph.

In 1931 a very different picture is presented. This graph records the structure of the population at the end of the late expanding stage in its population cycle. Death rates have continued to fall but birth rates have fallen even more sharply. This results in a pyramid with a narrowed base where succeeding five-year age groups are smaller than their predecessors. A greater expectation of life is indicated by a rather higher proportion in the uppermost age groups, and a thickening in the 15–30-year groups is suggestive of the ageing population that is to come. The effect of the First World War may be seen in the reduction in the proportions of males in 35–50-year age bracket and is a contributive cause of the smaller proportion of children in the 5–10-year-old groups. The shape this pyramid assumes shows that the population is growing older in the sense that the most numerous in it are no longer children but the younger adults.

The tendency for a contraction in the lower age groups was continued through the 1930s. Smaller families had become fashionable, partly as a result of the economic depression and also the desire for increasing amenities – satirized at the time as a preference for the baby Austin rather than the baby. This reduction in fertility from 1881 was brought about mainly by the acceptance and increasing practice of birth control. The result, seen in the third pyramid, was a marked undercutting of the base until the Second World War (this was the period when the net reproduction rate dropped as low as 0.78). There followed the sharp rise in birth that characterized the early post-war years and the emergence of the 'welfare state'. The population has aged further, producing a firm 'middle-aged spread', but the numbers to sustain this burden in the coming years have once more grown. Much more could be gleaned from these three pyramids, but it is irrelevant to the present discussion. An important point that emerges is that the various stages of the population cycle create characteristic pyramids by which they may be recognized.

The difference in outline between populations in the early expanding (stage 2) and the late fluctuating (stage 4) phases of the cycle is striking. The rather squat, broad-based figure contrasts with the taller, more bulbous and pedestalled shape. Pyramids for England and Wales in 1881 and 1971 are good examples. Between them in the late expanding (stage 3) phase the rapidly falling birth rate and still declining death rate is reflected in a narrower base and rather taller structure than for stage 2. The 1921 pyramid for England and Wales (with the effects of the First World War discounted) would serve as an example. Whether, after oscillating through the low fluctuating phase (stage 4), population will settle into a fifth, or stationary, stage we have yet to discover.

A close correlation is discernible between those countries experiencing stages 1 and 2 of the cycle and those countries with the lowest *per capita* income. Little statistical data are yet available for the majority of stage 1 countries (mainly in Africa), but it is reasonable to expect that they in turn will enter, or are already entering, stage 2, as their high death rates become reduced.

Juvenility

Age and sex pyramids for four countries in the early expanding (stage 2) phase (Peru, India, Morocco and Ghana) are plotted in Figure 5 and may be taken as typical. It will be seen that their outlines are remarkably similar. All show the characteristic broad base resulting from high birth rates associated with a low or very low death rate. Each of these countries has a crude birth rate around 35–40 per thousand of the population but only Ghana exhibits typical late (stage 2) death rates (21 per 1000). The other three now have death rates resembling those in stages 3 and 4 in Europe (India and Morocco 15 per 1000, and Peru 12 per 1000), showing the success of death control and the telescoping of a part of the European-type population cycle. The effect of these very low death rates of recent years is to be seen in the exceptionally high proportion of young children, for well over 40 per cent of their populations were under 15 years of age during the early 1970s. It is to be noted that in the 1980s, when the bulk of these children have entered the reproductive period, such populations are of unprecedented fecundity. The fact that youth represents so high a proportion of the total population is also a reflection of the rather low expectation of life in these countries. The pyramids are far more squat that those for West European countries, and it will be seen that the proportion of these populations attaining 65 years and over is very small, averaging 3 to 4 per cent, whereas 11 per cent is more typical of Western Europe. However, expectation of life in these countries is rising quickly (Table 3, page 40), and

Figure 5   Age and sex composition, Peru 1973, India 1974, Morocco 1973 and Ghana 1970

future years will see larger absolute numbers reaching the top of the pyramid, although the proportion of the total population may still be quite small.

These features have economic as well as demographic significance. First, it is clear that juvenility is a prominent characteristic of the majority of the population of developing lands since the proportion of population below 15 years of age is of the order of 40 to 45 per cent. The selection of the fifteenth year is clear cut in the case of the developed lands, for the demands of full-time education up to that age prevent the individual from entering full-time employment. This is far less so in less-developed lands where school-leaving age may well be lower and where school attendance is less obligatory (in fact, if not in law). However, age-group statistics are usually expressed in five-year intervals and there is little doubt that children below 15 years of age should not be regarded as fully productive members of society. Consequently it is felt that a classification into age groups, 0–14, 15–64 and over 65 generally has economic significance in both developed and developing countries. The selection of 0–19 as a first grouping, while revealing that over half the population of under-developed lands is usually children and adolescents, has less economic although much social significance.

The large number of children of low or negligible productivity in these stage 2 countries is a great burden on the economy. They and the smaller proportion of old folk must be supported mainly by the productivity of the remaining adult population. Their numbers, related to the active population (15–64 years), give a 'dependency ratio'. It is not always appreciated that owing to the age structure, the proportion of adults (15–64 years) to the whole population is generally smaller than in developed lands (for example, in 1973 in England and Wales it was 65 per cent, but in Ghana it was 50 per cent). Married couples the world over know that the principal expenditure within a family is on the children, to provide them with food, clothes and housing. Where families are big and incomes low there is little expenditure possible on non-essentials and amenities; standards remain low. With a rapidly increasing population the demand on investment merely to maintain basic living standards will be very great and economic development correspondingly is slowed down.

The degree of return on capital invested may be expressed as the capital:output ratio or capital coefficient. This is a measure of the number of units of net capital investment required to increase the value of output by one unit per annum. Returns on investment vary from one undertaking to another, and the ratio is a guiding figure in the selection of projects for investment and in the most economical deployment of investment capital. The higher the ratio the smaller the increase in national income and vice versa. Our knowledge of rates of capital formation in under-developed lands is, however, very imperfect and here the coefficient can be no more than a general guide.[1] Each individual in a society represents an investment by that society and the able-bodied and skilled man will be capable of giving a greater return (that is, capital producing) than the young and old who are capital absorbing. Expenditure on (or investment in) housing has a high capital:output ratio (that is, a relatively low return), and where capital is scarce and population increase very great the proportion of investment in housing becomes very large. Admittedly the cost of supporting a child is less than supporting an old person, and since the productive years of the child lie ahead it probably represents a better invest-ment, but in this context it is the vast mass of children requiring support and, increasingly, education that keeps standards at subsistence level and absorbs capital so urgently needed for economic development in more remunerative sectors of the economy. In other words heavy increase of population is likely to reduce output per head unless considerable investment is possible. Economists have suggested that a capital:output ratio of up to 4 to 1 may be needed to maintain living standards. This suggests that a population growth of 2 per cent will need a net investment of 8 per cent of the national income to maintain existing standards of living. Few developing lands manage to invest more than 5–6 per cent per annum of their national income and this means that unless other investment (such as foreign aid) becomes available such a population increase will bring about a fall in living standards. Here is the nub of the development problem: that the rate of increase of production needs consistently to surpass the rate of increase of population. To bring this about, countries may, on the one hand, attempt to control and reduce their rate of population growth and, on the other, to increase production by rendering agriculture more efficient and by developing manufacturing industry, where energy supplies and advancing technology make for greater productivity per worker.

An important point of impact upon the economy is when, at the age of about 15 years, masses of work-seeking adolescents annually swamp the labour market. A few years ago the Indian finance minister stated that 4 million new jobs had been created during the initial four years of India's first Five Year Plan, but that the natural increase to the population during this period had thrust 7 million new job seekers on to the labour market. Japan also may be cited; even with industry developing at a higher pace than between the wars it is not expected that employment can be found for more than half the million who join the labour force each year. Such a number of youths competing for not enough jobs might well depress the level of wages and perpetuate the very conditions of poverty it is sought to end. Alternatively, where minimum wage safeguards exist, much purchasing power may go into the pockets of those who have few commitments or responsibilities and little predisposition to save. The legalizing of abortion in 1952 contributed to a sharp reduction in births in Japan during the post-war period. However, well over a million seek to join the labour force each year. These figures give some idea of the magnitude of the scale of development now becoming necessary to keep pace with the current heavy natural increase of population. It is small wonder that all too frequently we read that economic advance in so many developing lands is being cancelled out by the rate at which man is multiplying.

There are further important aspects of juvenility, one being its bearing on fecundity. The unusually large increments at the base of these population pyramids with the passing of years will expand the reproductive age groups; a young population is a highly fecund population. This favours a continuance of high birth rates unless other factors such as later marriage or greater application of birth control reduce fertility. As such factors are usually the outcome of a rising standard of living they are difficult to accomplish with such prolific population. In 1947 about 42 per cent of Japanese women were in the child-bearing age groups (15–45 years), by 1977 this proportion was 46.5 per cent. Such a proportional increase may not seem too serious but, in fact, it represented over 9 million more potential mothers.

Other aspects of juvenility not often comprehended are socio-political. In young populations the enthusiasm, impatience, intolerance and disillusionment of youth do not lack expression. The student demonstrations and riots now becoming characteristic draw much of their vigour from the sheer preponderance of the young in their communities. In Japan more than two-fifths of the population is under 20; in Sri Lanka the proportion is almost a half. It is not only in the West that the teenager has assumed such social and economic importance.

The population explosion of the recent decades and hitherto the low expectation of life in most of the developing lands indicate that their immediate problems concern youth rather than old age. The economic problems associated with ageing populations are now being met in many countries in the low fluctuating population stage and mainly stem from the growing proportion of the pensionable population which constitutes an increasing burden on the body of productive workers. Other and less tangible problems may arise from the changing mental outlook of such populations; less flexibility and go-aheadness may become perceptible. However, these situations are still relatively remote in under-developed lands where an increasing span of life should imply a healthier and more productive working force to sustain both young and old dependents.

Massive emigration is sometimes advanced as a solution to the problems of surplus populations. There is much literature discussing the efficacy and practicability of substantial movements of population, and it is sufficient here to say that history shows that emigration offers little or no relief when high birth rates persist. In theory, however, with a falling birth rate and a rising standard of living the removal of a part of the population might have an upward effect upon the economy. This ignores the general impracticability of such measures; numbers are now too vast, receiving areas inadequate and unwelcoming, the capital costs immense. Further, even with low living standards prodigious capital would be required for the provision of homes, utilities and social services compatible with a reasonable standard of living. To remove from one slum to create another would be no solution.

Urbanization

A further and important manifestation of increasing populations in the lesser-developed lands is in the remarkable increase of the urban portions of the population. Much has yet to be done in recording the distribution of population in these countries, but the increase in the size and number of towns has become characteristic and the rural:urban ratio of these populations is altering. The tendency for urban growth with increasing population, and particularly with growing economic development, is well established. The application of power and the introduction of factory industry saw the beginning of the ascendancy of town over countryside in the developed lands. Towns become workplaces and, as standards rose, service activities grew also; culture wants became added to creature wants. To overcrowded, under-employed, rural populations, towns offer greater opportunity of casual employment, wages are usually better than in the countryside (although living costs are higher too) and they attract by the amenities they offer: electric light, water, health clinics, a chance of a new life. The first signs of development appear in the towns, in the utilities, services and amusement amenities; all act as magnets in attracting further population.

The degree of urbanization is yet unmeasured in many lands and, since there is no universal acceptance of the point at which a village becomes a town, it is unlikely that precise data will ever be available. However, at the upper end of the scale the number, size and growth of cities of over a million people – 'million' cities – is known with tolerable accuracy. Their numbers have increased over six-fold between 1925 and 1970, and from containing 2.9 per cent of world population they had come to hold 10 per cent. This represents a rate of growth of 'million' cities faster than that of world population. Two further significant facts emerge: first, a snowball effect is discernible in that the larger or 'multi-million' cities show a faster rate of growth, and second, that the greatest developments are in the lower latitudes. This is to be expected in that development has lagged in so many of these mainly agricultural countries and rapid urbanization is a reflection of startling population increase and the beginning of economic development. In the early 1950s some 80 'million' cities accommodated 192.5 million people;[2] two decades later in the early 1970s, there were 151 such cities with a total population of 380 million people. Here we have taken the 'million' city as a loose index of urbanization, for each 'million' city is supported by dozens of smaller cities and towns. The rapid growth of towns in the warmer latitudes since the Second World War has been remarkable, and will continue and constitutes the beginning of an 'urban revolution'. Unfortunately acute primacy occurs within the settlement pattern, for usually one city (often the former colonial capital and chief port) alone possesses adequate infrastructure to support industrial growth. It becomes swollen at the expense of the lower order towns, giving a distorted settlement hierarchy but gaining a momentum for expansion that is difficult to check. The tragedy is that migrants from the country passing into such towns greatly exceed the available employment and are gradually changing the character of these metropolitan centres by helping to add shanty towns of squatter settlements.[3]

In addition to the many economic benefits accruing from urbanization which will be discussed in Chapter 4, there are distinct social advantages. Agglomeration of population allows the provision of utilities such as water and power supplies, transport services, education and health provision (hospitals and clinics). In the developing lands, where urban occupations are expanding and agricultural ones are relatively declining, real income per head is generally higher in urban employment and it is in the towns that a rise of living standards first becomes apparent. The spread of education, the desire for comforts and amenities, the raising of the status of women, the growing means of enjoying leisure hours all begin to shape a new mode of life in which children play a less prominent part. Further, with the eventual introduction of compulsory full-time education and establishment of minimum ages of employment, children cease to be an economic asset but instead may represent an encumbrance to social and material advancement. These conditions underlie the well-known fact that urban birth rates are generally lower than rural ones. 'The more urban an area the lower the fertility of the population and the more rural an area the more rapidly its population is reproducing' (T. Lynn Smith).[4] This is precisely a state of affairs urgently to be attained in the world's developing lands. The evolution of a social milieu, where the small family is the rule first in the town and then in the country, is urgently needed but is yet a long way off.

Quality of population

In Chapter 1 reference was made to the importance of population 'quality', a term used here to indicate, in the broadest sense, the physical and mental conditions of a people: their degree of health, education, skill, adaptability, liveliness. These attitudes of a society bear some relation to environmental and demographic conditions and, while less tangible than capital or raw material resources, nevertheless may prove decisive in particular development situations. In this sense the poor 'quality' of their population is probably the greatest handicap to the economic advance of the developing lands. Most of their populations, particularly in the tropical areas, are disease-ridden and undernourished and constitute a great drag on development. A circular pattern can be identified: ill-health = reduced working capacity = lower productivity = poverty = undernourishment = ill-health.

Nutritional diseases such as pellagra, beri-beri and rickets are prevalent. In themselves they are not heavily fatal, but they so debilitate and sap the resistance that endemic and infectious diseases such as cholera, typhus and malaria take immense toll. Not only are diets inadequate in amount (resulting in under-nutrition), but they are usually ill-balanced (resulting in malnutrition), with serious protein and fat deficiences and over-emphasis on starch. In India the average daily intake of calories per person in 1976 was 1949 (this implies that many thousands had less than this amount), whereas dieticians then estimated that the minimum level for well-being in India was 2250 calories. The mass of peasantry in developing countries eats very little meat, fish, milk or eggs but subsists mainly on cereals (principally maize). In the Sudan in 1967 a survey of schoolchildren revealed that 60 per cent of those examined at Atbara and 53 per cent of those at Wad Medani were suffering from protein deficiency. Kwashiorkor or protein malnutrition of young children is another product of these conditions where the period of lactation is reduced and weaning is upon starchy diets such as banana, maize and tapioca. Many of these children die and of those who survive the prevalence of cancer of the liver in later life has been noticed.

These nutritional diseases debilitate and allow a wider incidence of diseases such as malaria, estimated to affect some 300 million people in the world each year. Gourou has pointed out that the most serious fact about malaria is that each death it causes corresponds to at least 2000 days of illness.[5] Much of the apathy of the Egyptian fellahin and tolerance towards their wretched conditions of life has been ascribed to the vicious hold of the intestinal worm diseases bilharzia and ankylostoma – at one time affecting three-quarters of the rural population. These diseases are caught from parasites carried by snails in the irrigation waters. They rarely cause death but sap the vitality, dull the mind, engender feelings of apathy and resignation and reduce the capacity and output of Egyptian labour.

It is difficult for people living in temperate latitudes to appreciate the real significance of disease as a factor retarding the development of a tropical area. The native of West Africa inherits almost all the disorders of temperate climates, and on top of these he may suffer from a multitude of other diseases to which his ignorance of their causes, his poor standards of hygiene and his particular environment make him liable. The inadequacy of the medical facilities and often the reluctance of the sufferers to take advantage of them at least until it is too late aggravates the situation. Trypanosomiasis and onchocerciasis . . . epidemics of cerebrospinal meningitis, the major outbreaks of which have affected the whole of the savana belt of West Africa for at least the past fifty years, occur frequently. Smallpox, malaria, bilharzia, yaws and intestinal disorders are endemic.[6]

Great advances are being made in the eradication of these conditions thanks to the greater use of pesticides and new antibiotic drugs such as DDT and penicillin and improvements in hygiene and sanitation. In one sense the cost has been small in comparison with the immediate benefits. The northern province of Thailand, for example, was cleansed of malaria at a cost of 5p. per head of its population. The benefits are widespread; mortality has decreased and there is greater productivity from both man and beast, freed not merely from malaria but also from fly-borne dysentery, typhoid and ticks. These advances, however, also have a debit side, for unless the resultant death control becomes matched by birth control, or the means of greater productivity are available, then malnourishment and malnutrition may increase. The situation in part of eastern Bangladesh exemplifies this. In the last few years eradication of malaria has led to 15 per cent greater productivity from the rice fields, but fewer of the healthier workers are needed and rural unemployment has increased, for no fresh land is available to put under cultivation. There is no doubt that, in general, productivity per worker in the under-developed lands is low, but with betterment of health it can be considerably improved. This in turn presents further economic and social problems.

Illiteracy is another serious drawback to the advancement of these populations and is the result of the quite inadequate provisions for, and scope of, elementary education in most of these lands. To millions, the world is little more than the village and its contiguous fields, where the methods and sequences of the agrarian life, hallowed by tradition, take their predestined course year after year. It is this illiteracy (used in the sense of general ignorance), coupled with the ingrained resistance to change, that is proving a formidable obstacle in furthering hygiene, in disseminating birth-control information, in introducing new crops or methods of husbandry, in advancing manufacturing industry. Many of these countries have spent much money in the past on university education for the favoured few; the broad bases of the educational pyramids have been neglected. The task of raising the abysmally low level of popular education in the developing lands of the world is gigantic and will take decades to accomplish, but it has begun. Illiteracy in Egypt in the thirty years from 1940 declined from 75 to 55 per cent of the population, but in India the rate has only dropped from 85 to 72 per cent.

To provide and develop successfully a substantial industrial segment in the economies of the developing lands will require a considerable raising of the quality of their populations. The conversion of illiterate, undernourished, apathetic and disease-ridden agricultural workers into alert, healthy and skilled industrial operatives will prove a costly, lengthy and difficult metamorphosis. Even more important will be the emergence of the smaller number of men prepared to take risks in investment and innovation, no longer putting their money into land but bringing in science, new techniques and adventuring into industry. Governmental action may supplement or surpass their efforts, but the need for these entrepreneurs is vital. In short, the whole outlook of such societies must undergo reorientation. Education is the key that must open eyes to possibilities, and society should become permeated with the idea of development, perhaps even dedicated to it as in China, where government and people alike are intent on making up for lost years in the shortest possible time. In all this, one condition would seem to be paramount, namely the reduction of the birth rates of these populations. Without fewer births the work of medicine and science will be jeopardized; numbers increasing at an ever-faster rate may depress levels of nutrition even more, increasing under-employment may spread apathy and misery, while the provision of education for the growing mass of children may become more and more beyond the resources of the countries concerned.

4 Industrialization: the panacea?

Motives for industrialization

In the preceding chapters the value and advantages to be derived
from industrialization have been implied. It is appropriate now to
consider more precisely the reasons why under-developed lands,
many with apparently the most primitive economies, desire so
earnestly to further manufacturing industry. It is clear that a whole
range of reasons may be cited, dependent upon the individual
circumstances of the countries, but broadly we may cite three
conditions that such lands wish to ameliorate, and go on to
consider just why the development of manufacturing industry is
regarded as the best means of such amelioration. The three
customary objects of industrialization policies are to provide work
for growing populations (and in some cases for already under-
employed agricultural populations), to raise the standard of living
by increasing the *per capita* net national income and, often, to
improve balance of payment situations. Various other reasons
have sometimes been cited or imputed in particular cases, one
especially being the desire for national prestige which an industrial
economy could give over fellow primary producers. Another
reason that has appealed to a number of countries is the desire for
economic independence expressed in the attainment of self-
sufficiency in the economy, as with Argentina. Often this has led to
the framing of development programmes that are unbalanced and,
in the event, uneconomic. Industrialization aimed at import-
substitution is pushed at the expense of agriculture, rather than
improving primary production for export where comparative
advantage is held over competition, and then, with foreign exchange
available, developing those industries most likely to have good
economic bases. Often these changes are heralded by political
revolution, by many regarded as an essential precursor of the
desired social and economic transformations.

The most noticeable effect of development which the under-developed lands can see in the wealthy lands is the mass of manu-facturing industry from which the wealth, power and poise of the developed world appears to emanate. Consequently it is not surprising that the introduction of manufacturing industry should be regarded uncritically as a panacea by many members of the 'have-not' nations. Fortunately, major industrial and development schemes nowadays nearly all come under the close scrutiny of international experts, particularly if international capital is sought for them, and this acts as a check on wilder promotions that might have little prospect of success. It should be made clear that the switching of a large mass of humanity to industrial pursuits is in itself no answer to the world's population problem. We have still not reached the stage when we can cheaply mass-produce synthetic food from inanimate matter in our factories, and new industrial populations still need to be fed. It is, of course, in the prospect of greater returns accruing from manufacturing industry making possible the purchase of food from food-surplus countries, as is done in much of north-west Europe, that the hopes of the poorer lands lie. It must be noticed, however, that this state of affairs does not occur overnight, and initially indigenous supplies of food need to be increased, if at all possible, to feed the growing urban-industrial population and thus preserve capital for reinvestment rather than spend it on imported foodstuffs. It follows that developments in agriculture must not be neglected and should continue with industrial development, a situation not followed by most developing countries during the past twenty years and a contributive factor to the lack of success of many development plans.

Occupational structures

As we have seen, it is possible to classify the cycle of population development into stages; in turn it is thought that the cycle of economic development is susceptible to a similar analysis and that stages of economic development may be discovered and classified. Foremost in this field is the work of W. W. Rostow, in whose view an economy moves from a traditional stage through a take-off period to sustained growth, maturity and a stage of high mass-consumption.[1] Development implies changing emphases within an economy, and this is evidenced in the shifting distribution of labour among the major kinds of activity. Colin Clark in his book *The Conditions of Economic Progress* makes a now widely accepted simple division of production into primary, secondary and tertiary groups. The primary activities include farming, fishing and forestry; secondary production includes mining, manufacturing and public utilities such as gas and electricity production; and tertiary production includes all other activities, such as transport, distribution, public administration, entertainment, etc.[2]

From the beginning of time, primary activities have been basic to man's existence, and development signifies a movement whereby primary activities continue but with increasing efficiency so that labour is released for other work involving more application of science, invention and capital. Thus we shall expect the under-developed countries to have an overwhelming proportion of their working population engaged in agriculture with quite small proportions in secondary and tertiary occupations, while fully developed lands might show an opposite pattern. In fact, under-developed lands have around 60–70 per cent of their labour force engaged in primary production, whereas developed countries that have entered the stage of maturity generally have less than 20 per cent thus engaged.

Throughout the world, agricultural incomes per head tend to be less than non-agricultural incomes. Sometimes, as in Australia, the differences are not great but, for example, in Indonesia non-agricultural income per head is five times higher than agricultural income. Such a discrepancy is a measure of under-development and, given the opportunity, spurs labour away to other sectors of the economy. A developed economy gives a high *per capita* income since it is associated with a more varied economic structure whereby science and capital play an increasing part, and agriculture, using a smaller proportion of the labour force, functions with higher efficiency.

These features are demonstrated in Table 4, where it will be seen that in the case of Britain only 2 per cent of our working population is engaged in primary activities, the lowest proportion for any country, whereas nearly half are engaged in secondary activities, among the highest for any country. The special character of our mercantile economy is reflected here, but it should be remembered that the small agricultural labour force produces nearly half the food these crowded islands need. Agricultural efficiency is steadily improving; an increase of capital investment allows each farm-worker to cultivate an increasing number of acres while a greater application of science raises productivity per

Table 4 *Occupational structures of selected countries, 1978*

Country	Labour force as percentage of total population (15–64 years)	Percentage of total active labour force		
		Primary activities	Secondary activities	Tertiary activities
Industrialized				
Sweden	64	5	37	58
USA	65	2	33	65
Canada	66	6	30	64
Australia	64	6	34	60
East Germany	63	10	51	39
United Kingdom	64	2	43	55
Italy	64	13	48	39
USSR	65	17	47	36
Middle income				
Spain	63	18	43	39
Yugoslavia	66	33	32	35
Taiwan	63	37	37	26
Algeria	49	30	25	45
Jamaica	51	28	17	55
Ecuador	52	46	25	29
Morocco	50	53	20	27
Bolivia	53	51	24	25
Egypt	56	51	26	23
Low income				
Kenya	48	79	8	13
Madagascar	53	86	4	10
Pakistan	51	58	19	23
Sri Lanka	58	54	15	31
India	56	74	11	15
Mali	52	88	6	6
Bangladesh	54	74	11	15

Source: World Bank, *World Development Report 1980* (New York 1980), Table 19.

acre. In 1957 one British farm-worker produced enough food for twenty people, the Australian farm-worker produced enough for thirty-two people, and the New Zealander enough for sixty-two people. The development of the United States may be interpreted from her changing occupational structure. The proportions for 1978 are quoted in Table 4, but in 1870 the three groups of activity claimed respectively 53 per cent, 23 per cent, and 24 per cent of the labour force. During the century the numbers of workers in the agricultural sector fell from a maximum of 11.6 million to 4.5 million, but the volume of agricultural production increased two and three-quarter times.

From a comparison of the more advanced and less advanced countries in Table 4 it may be deduced that, as the primary (mainly agricultural) proportions of the working population decline, those engaged in secondary (manufacturing) production increase: a further indicator of economic growth. The demand for foodstuffs is relatively inelastic and as real incomes rise a lesser proportion of the increase is spent on food, thus stimulating the demand for manufactured goods and services. The reasons for the growing proportions engaged in tertiary activities are not always fully understood nor the reasons why, in the eyes of some, the higher the proportion thus engaged, the further the stage of economic development. Tertiary activities include a wide range of occupations, some such as 'pop-singers' and 'beauticians' virtually unproductive in the strict economic sense and others such as dockers and lorry drivers clearly vital to a modern economy. The most numerous members of this group are in shopkeeping, domestic service, sport and entertainment. To claim that the greater proportion of these strange bedfellows in an economy, the more developed it is, may seem odd, but it should be remembered that also in this group are clerks, accountants, directors, bankers, under-writers, teachers, inventors and the professional classes who, by and large, smooth, direct and control the economy.

The disabilities of agriculture

The fact that throughout the world, agriculture is reaching or entering the stage of decreasing returns, whereas industry, in the main, goes on under conditions of increasing returns, raises the question of the differences between the two activities, and in particular the disadvantages of agriculture *vis-à-vis* manufacturing industry. The fundamental disadvantage under which agriculture labours is that the farmer has virtually no control over the natural forces of the physical environment which he utilizes. His crops depend upon sunshine, water, air and mineral salts and, while locally farmers may irrigate or drain, add fertilizer or trace elements to their soils, by and large it is the environment that calls the tune. From this stem a number of other disadvantages, not least being that yields vary from year to year according to the ravages of weather, disease and pests. Consequently farmers cannot foretell accurately the volume of their production each year. Further, production is generally slower than in manufacturing industry, requiring farmers to look ahead and estimate the character of the market at least a year in advance. Crops and animals take months to mature and slow down farmers' reactions to changes in demand, for once crops are in the ground and animals fattening, most farmers prefer to reap their crops, shear their sheep, pick their cocoa beans and so on, despite glut conditions and falling prices. These factors all help to account for the considerable price fluctuations, alternating with gluts and shortages, notable in primary production and of serious consequences to steady economic progress in developing lands. The seasonal character of farming operations in many parts of the world may well impose uneconomic use of labour and certainly of machinery. Farming machinery is costly and generally of a specialized character and may only be in use for a few weeks each year, a great contrast to most factory machinery which may be in almost continual operation.

For the relative inflexibility of agriculture there are a number of reasons, not all of them economic. In many parts of the world the traditional conservatism of the peasantry may present a formidable barrier to progress, especially where the agricultural way of life has become intimately interwoven into the fabric of society, and where changes in agriculture might presage deep repercussions on social groupings and ways of life. This is exemplified in many parts of Africa where the white man's concept of the individual ownership of land has conflicted severely with the natives' concept of tribal ownership and use. Similarly the threat of far-reaching changes in their way of life reinforced peasant opposition to the USSR and East European attempts at collectivization. Agriculture is also at some disadvantage when there is a preponderance of agrarian population, for the onset of decreasing returns comes more swiftly than with industry. Much of the poverty in many developing lands is attributable to this; pressure of population with no alternative employment forcing far too many into agriculture. Labour is applied beyond the point of decreasing returns with consequent inefficiency and low productivity per head.

A further serious drawback lies in the relative inelasticity of demand for agricultural products. The bulk of the products of agriculture are foodstuffs and, being vital to life, are already consumed in great quantities; consequently relatively little extra food is bought if prices fall. Equally, if incomes rise, a less than proportionate extra amount is spent on food; instead, the sale of manufactured goods is stimulated. This suggests that, as the developed lands have become richer, the primary producers selling them their agricultural produce have received a less than proportionate share in the increased wealth. From this it would seem that international trade in primary products does not really produce the equalizing tendencies often claimed for it, but tends to work in favour of the industrialized nations. Even the fruits of greater efficiency of production may not be passed on to the primary producers. Surplus rural populations offering a mass of unskilled labour at the lowest of wages all too often act as a disincentive to greater efficiency and resist innovation. However, where improvements take place and exports are produced more cheaply, the inelasticity of demand prevents the enlargement of the market, which might bring the response of greater productivity and employment; instead the advantages of the cheaper production accrue to the importing country.

A further factor telling against the exporters of primary produce is the greater effect of technical progress upon industry than upon agriculture. This contributes to the fact that industrial countries succeed in increasing their output without a proportionate increase in their imports of raw materials. This comes about in various ways: greater efficiency and reduction of waste; relative decline in textiles which have a high raw material content; the increasing use of synthetic substitutes, such as plastics, man-made fibres, synthetic rubber and dyestuffs. It must be appreciated that the development of synthetics and substitutes is related to price and cost factors. To some extent the general failure of the developing countries to reduce costs and prices of their primary exports relative to those of the developed countries has spurred on invention and technological progress. It has been estimated that in the major industrial countries synthetic materials now account for about 15 per cent of the raw materials used in manufacture whereas the proportion was barely 3 per cent before the Second World War. But for this, imports of natural raw material into these major industrial countries might be 40 per cent higher than they are at present. In all, for every £100 worth of manufactures produced the total import of fuel and raw material declined from £26 in 1938 to £21 in 1955, a decline that still continues. The weight of these disabilities set against the corresponding advantages lying with manufacturing industry help to account for the situation where the primary producers were left behind in the development race. The decade of the 1950s saw the terms of trade swing adversely against the developing countries' primary exports, for whereas export prices of manufactured goods rose by 20 per cent, export prices of primary products rose by only 5 per cent. During the 1960s raw material and fuel export prices declined slightly, but prices of foodstuffs exports rose; however, a 40 per cent increase in the cost of manufactured goods continued the adverse terms of trade pattern. It was not until the early 1970s, when widespread growth in developed economies was unmatched by adequate expansion of primary products and these economies saw shortages and heavy price rises, that terms of trade began to swing in favour of the developing countries. However the quadrupling of oil prices at the end of 1973 had disastrous effects. Large transfers of real income from the rest of the world to the OPEC countries led to balance of payment problems and depression in the industrialized world. Since nearly two-thirds of all developing countries' trade is with the developed states, this had repercussions on the non-oil-developing countries. World prices of many primary products exported fell with reduced demand and again the primary producer suffered. Thus the experience of the last quarter century is that the primary producers' share in the expanding world economy is generally far less than that of the industrialized countries.

The relative advantages of manufacturing industry

On the other side of the coin, the advantages that manufacturing industry holds over primary production might be considered as distinct from the disadvantages of primary production. First it must be recognized that manufacturing industry is far more flexible in methods, competition and output than agriculture. While decreasing returns may be expected in industry as in agriculture, they are, in fact, usually postponed by continual improvements in techniques, by the frequent introduction of new inventions and improved machinery (far less typical in agriculture) and by increasing specialization and division of labour raising the efficiency and productivity of the labour force. The character and scale of operation are also more favourable: it is possible to control production much more closely than with farming, and supply – of a standard quality – can be trimmed more closely to demand, making for greater price stability.

It will be realized that the farmer may have to brief his labour force daily, their tasks depending on the weather, but in a factory it is possible to manage a far larger labour force because their activities are specialized, regular and in general entirely insulated from vagaries of weather. Consequently advantages of scale lie with manufacturing industry which by its organization and specialism aims at mass production through increasing efficiency and the application of power. It is, of course, basically through the application of inanimate energy that manufacturing industry offers greater productivity per worker than agriculture and the amount of power available to each worker is sometimes taken as an indicator of economic stature (Table 8, page 131).

Another advantage to industry but disadvantage to the farmer lies in the proportion of operating costs to fixed costs. A very high proportion of farm costs are in fixed charges and, relatively, the cost of seed, labour, etc., is small. This is a further factor in explaining the sluggish response to adverse conditions, for contraction of a farmer's output in times of difficulty saves relatively less than contraction of a factory's output. In the factory a far higher proportion of costs is in raw materials, labour and services, and these can be more readily cut down. It is the operation and interplay of such factors that help to account for the present state of affairs where so much of world agriculture operates under decreasing returns, whereas manufacturing industry still shows increasing returns.

Effects of agrarian over-population

In most development the two major goals are in the provision of work for growing populations, and the raising of standards of living. The degree to which these aims may be realized seems to depend primarily on the demographic situation in each country. Countries with population problems are faced with the double task; those without such a problem have a much more straightforward path to raising standards of living. It is, of course, possible to envisage populations (for instance in the West Indies) too heavy for their agricultural resources but insufficient to sustain large-scale industrial development. As has been discussed (on pages 30–3), capacity to support population depends upon the character of the economy; an industrial economy can carry a higher population before the onset of diminishing returns than an agricultural one. If population increases over the years and the economy stagnates – possibly as a result of restricted ownership of land or social conditions where equal division of property between the heirs (as in some Moslem countries) leads to a state of chronic and uneconomic fragmentation – then a situation may well be reached when a country's agricultural output will not increase with a further increase of agricultural population. This state of affairs indicates an extreme form of over-population, a stage beyond that occurring with the onset of diminishing returns (where increase of population brings a less than proportionate increase of production).

Over-population, then, should always be thought of as relative to a country's economy. As we have seen, not all under-developed agricultural lands are over-populated although many in Asia are, to which may be added Egypt, and some West Indian islands. In many under-developed lands the poverty of the masses may be related sometimes to land tenure systems, whereby there is an institutional monopoly of land and therefore of capital (as in many states of Latin America), sometimes to poor farming reinforced by social and religious taboos exhausting the soil (as in India), some-times to naturally poor soils, leached or waterlogged, where the application of considerable capital for irrigation or drainage is necessary in order to raise yields. There is, in fact, a wide range of immediate causes of poverty and under-development. It is in the heavily populated under-developed lands that prevailing conditions constitute the greatest spur to development since they build up to increasing unrest, or even anarchy or revolution.

It must not be thought that in over-populated agrarian countries there are necessarily vast masses of unemployed. The onset of over-population is slow and insidious and demonstrates itself rather by growing poverty and increasing under-employment. Excessive numbers are to be found in domestic service, casual employment, and agriculture; one notices a proliferation of news-vendors, bootblacks, porters and petty traders – all doing little business and earning barely enough for subsistence. Similarly in agriculture more and more labour finds employment on the land until the marginal productivity of labour is zero, or even negative. This situation may well lead to a loss of soil fertility by the reduction of manuring and over-cropping. This results in falling output per acre and not merely falling output per head. The term 'disguised unemployment' is sometimes used to describe an element of the working population that can be regarded as surplus in the sense that, if it were removed from the land, the volume of production would not fall. It is in this context that the massive population of South-East Asia, with 70–80 per cent of the workers toiling on the land, should be viewed.

The results of increasing population pressure, slowly grinding poverty, are similar everywhere. The process of descent to such an abject situation may take different forms, generally related to the system of land tenure. These systems are numerous in their variations but may be reduced essentially to three major types:

1 communal ownership, usually tribal as in much of Africa (for example, Lesotho, parts of Zambia and Zaïre) where there is considerable scope for agricultural improvement to raise living standards;
2 peasant proprietorship, demonstrated in other parts of Africa such as Ghana and Uganda, but where the middleman and village usurer may play a significant role, and where holdings become reduced below economic size and owners must offer their labour to larger farmers in order to support their families;
3 large estate farming, of which we may distinguish three types – latifundia, zamindari and plantation. Latifundia are characteristic of southern Europe and Latin America where the larger part of the estate is farmed extensively with hired labour, while the lesser part may be let on a share-cropping basis. In the zamindari system, more prevalent in Asia, the estate is let out in small holdings to tenant farmers on a money rent or share-cropping basis. Plantation estates are usually owned by foreign capital and operated by foreign management, and are efficient large-scale enterprises employing hired labour.

It is instructive to observe the changes, both social and economic, that evolve as pressure of workers on the land increases. The large estates being farmed under the latifundian and plantation systems have a relatively inelastic demand for labour and the more seeking work, the more the level of wages tends to be depressed. Equally, where land is let for rent the increasing numbers desiring land force up rents and land prices to crippling levels. Share-cropping tenancies also become subjected to increasingly unfavourable terms. By 1960 the share of revenue paid to landowners in rents in Oriental countries had come to be out of all proportion to the total productivity of agriculture and to the services the landlord offered. Rent (in various combinations of cash, produce and labour) claimed between one third and one half of the gross output value of agriculture in Middle Eastern and South-East Asian countries. Where conditions of increasing population and limited farmland persist, many of the great landowners are absentees. A combination of absentee landlords, high rents, short leases and impoverished peasantry may eventually lead to ruin of the land for there is neither the incentive nor the wherewithal to improve fertility, but the greatest encouragement to get as much as possible from the soil.

The demographic element has further important effects of both geographical and economic significance. As population pressure mounts so farming character and technique respond. As more and more labour becomes applied, so more labour-intensive methods become adopted (for example, removing spade-excavated earth from new canals in Egypt by baskets on camels and in India by human porterage) and more labour-intensive crops become grown. Quality and variety of crops are sacrificed to quantity; where subsistence farming predominates the most labour-demanding and highest food-yielding plants oust all others and virtual monoculture appears, as in the case of rice in the delta lands of South-East Asia. On large properties where commercial crops are grown, cotton becomes favoured as one of the most labour-intensive of the industrial crops, it is also liked by absentee 'gentlemen farmers' because an impoverished peasantry cannot eat it. In short, it is true to say that farming and tenure systems mould themselves to growing populations, absorbing more and more labour but under increasingly unfavourable conditions as the law of diminishing returns comes into play.

This chain of human misery is incomplete without recognition of the additional and concomitant social consequences. Under such conditions the power and wealth of the landowning classes expand while the mass of the peasantry grows poorer, creating in these agrarian societies a deep gulf between the governing class and the bulk of the population, for a middle or professional and commercial class is too small to span the gap. Money becomes concentrated into the hands of a very few while the mass of the population lives at a level of poverty not readily comprehended in the West. This means that there is virtually no saving and thus a very low rate of capital accumulation and reinvestment. To the wealthy, land is the principal source of wealth and has first claim on further investment, otherwise much tends to be spent on ostentatious living.

We now see that a root cause of the abysmal conditions of the mass of the peasantry in many lands is the excess of hands at work and mouths to be fed – the 'surplus' element in the agrarian population which also provides a disincentive to agricultural improvement. This situation is characteristic of many countries extending from South-Eastern Europe through South-East Asia to China and is also found in the Caribbean area. It is not common in Africa and South America but is probably beginning in parts of Central America. Obviously it is not possible to estimate closely the proportion of the surplus element in these populations. Estimates in the 1930s for some South-East European countries were as high as 25–30 per cent of the agricultural labour force, the proportion in Egypt is probably rather higher, while for India an estimate of at least a quarter has been made (representing 40–50 million people). By their presence these millions drag down the general level of living and, in the sense that, if their labour were removed, the volume of production would not suffer, they contribute nothing to productivity. The magnitude of the problem is becoming greatly increased with the impact of the medical revolution leading to improvements in the health of the peasantry.

As these conditions move from bad to worse, unrest frequently increases. Landowners tend to become more obstinate and reactionary in their resistance to change. Reforms often wait upon crisis and even anarchy (southern Italy, 1950); upon political revolution (Mexico, Egypt); or follow the upheavals of war (Bulgaria, 1880; Yugoslavia, 1918 and 1945). The redistribution of land at the expense of the great landlords is an early reform and under certain conditions can have a number of beneficial effects (see pages 218–19). However, the main problem of too many people on too little land remains, no matter how the ownership is juggled with, and acts as the most powerful incentive to an introduction or expansion of an industrial sector in the economy.

Thus the most weighty factor in the movement for development lies in the abysmal and worsening conditions that can occur under a combination of primary production, population pressure and maldistributed land ownership and tenure. The theory of greater returns and higher living standards from manufacturing industry is easy to grasp and in practice, even where industry is only in its infancy, begins to make itself felt. For example, whereas the annual income of the Egyptian fellah was estimated at £E8 in 1944 the annual income of the Egyptian industrial worker was around £E50, while in Uganda in 1968 the income per head in industry was estimated at over twice the income per head in agriculture. These comparisons may not be pressed too far, for it is not easy to be precise in valuing the self-sufficient element of the farmer, while industrial workers generally live under urban conditions where living costs are much higher.

The social and demographic effects of industrialization

Particularly in its early stage, manufacturing industry is related to the urban centres where market, labour and a range of public utilities are available. Some writers suggest that the ideal industrial development in developing countries should be one of dispersal among rural areas where so much surplus labour is available. This is very much an idealized solution and for many reasons is not practicable, especially in early stages. Furthermore such developments are less likely to capitalize a range of social opportunities and advantages that the development of urban communities makes possible. The agglomeration of people makes it easier and cheaper to provide social, educational, police, sanitary and health facilities, as well as to install such services as piped water, main drainage, gas and electricity. A far higher scale of creature comforts becomes possible and attainable than in the village. Imported goods in the shops give glimpses and knowledge both of a wider world and a high standard of attainment, and desires are raised that become the spur to betterment. Education and training are seen as the keys to better living and these are more readily available in the towns. However, in the long run it is of transcendent importance that with education and increased standards of living the size of family will be reduced by a fall in birth rates, as has happened in the West.

It has already been stressed that the only real and ultimate solution to the world's population problem is a reduction of birth rates broadly commensurate with the fast-dropping death rate.

Development to be completely successful should not only raise living standards and give more employment but should also create conditions that eventually bring birth rates down; industrialization alone will not solve the economic problems of such countries as India, Java, China and Egypt. Despite much study the mechanism by which this has happened in the developed countries of Europe and their overseas offshoots can only be postulated in rather general terms. It is certain that industrialization in itself does not explain the reduction in the size of families, for whereas Britain certainly was industrialized, the overseas dominions were still heavily agricultural when their birth rates began to fall; moreover in their cases the spur of population pressure could not be cited either. Carr-Saunders has pointed out that these countries and Western Europe (and rather later Eastern and Southern Europe) shared a similar mode of life, food, clothes, social fashions and conventions. The practice of family limitation spread among these closely associated countries much as any new habits and novel ideas spread.[3] In other words, attitudes gradually changed as a result of changing social and economic conditions, and not, for example, through any sudden new knowledge of birth-control methods.

Development, embracing urbanization and education, takes a large share in the establishment of the conditions for such changing of social conventions and attitudes. Pure water supplies, improved sanitation and medical facilities in towns reduce the toll on young children and make it unnecessary for eight children to be born in order to rear four. Parents come to realize that the smaller the family the greater the opportunities they can offer their children and the easier their own passage up the social ladder. Much of this social evolution is closely bound up with the position of women. Towns offer women far more opportunities of education and emancipation than the village, and with a lifetime no longer devoted to producing and rearing numerous children, employment outside the home becomes possible. All this takes time: two and possibly three generations in the developed lands. Whether the pattern will be both followed and speeded in the present developing lands are crucial questions. In that it represents social development fructifying from economic development we might regard it as logical and inevitable. Whether a speeding up is possible remains doubtful, for these tendencies evolve, they cannot be imposed. Religious and governmental sanction might do much to clear the path, as also the spread of education and the emergence of a middle class from a newly created or enlarged proletariat; the development of social and cultural standards cannot be accomplished overnight.

It is clear that a wide range of social and economic factors and emotions are involved in accounting for the fall in birth rate that seems to be an early attendant upon a developing urban way of life. One feature deserving of mention is that for a time in developing countries urban birth rates may appear higher than rural rates, but investigation shows that this is usually due to more complete registration. In rural areas the births of a substantial number of babies may never be registered. The more difficult question, to which it would not seem possible to give a definite answer is whether, in fact, economic and social developments in the developing lands will elicit a similar demographic response to that during the past century in the Western world. It would be wrong to assume automatically that the same values will be set upon social position, upon the use of leisure and upon women's emancipation. To our eyes many of the taboos (religious and social) of a number of Asian societies seem odd and anachronistic. In a similar manner it is possible that the response to development by these people may not follow the lines of the Western logic which regards development mainly in economic terms: the move towards an industrial society, to Rostow's phase of mass consumption and to materialism.

So far in only a few of the developing countries are there signs of a commencement of decline in the crude birth rate. Urbanization in the Third World is speeding up, but so far with little effect upon fertility rates. This may be because, while urbanization is occurring at a sharp rate, it is not being matched by growing industrialization. The flood of unskilled peasantry from the countryside far exceeds the establishment of new industries and jobs. Cities expand mainly with the accretion of squatter shacks – 'spontaneous settlements' – but the inhabitants do not easily integrate with urban life-styles and bring village conditions into their shanty towns. Urbanization under these conditions does not bring social and economic betterment, but merely exchanges under-employment in the country for unemployment in the towns.

Fertility decline in the advanced countries occurred spontaneously over a lengthy period; it was not a response to government policies and to government assistance. This aspect of the demographic problem facing the developing world today is urgent and critical to economic progress, although far too many developing countries have been slow to acknowledge it. Now changes are apparent;

Table 5   *Vital statistics for selected countries, 1977–8*

	Crude birth rate (‰ *)	Crude death rate (‰)	Natural increase (%)	Infant mortality rate (‰)	Expectation of life at birth (years)
Industrialized					
Sweden	11.2	10.8	0.04	8	75
USA	15.3	8.8	0.7	14	73
Canada	15.5	7.2	0.8	12	74
Australia	15.7	7.6	0.8	13	73
East Germany	13.9	13.9	0	13	72
United Kingdom	12.3	11.7	0.06	14	73
Italy	13.2	9.6	0.35	18	73
USSR	18.1	8.2	0.09	34	69
Middle income					
Spain	17.2	7.9	0.9	16	73
Yugoslavia	17.4	8.7	0.9	34	69
Algeria	48.8	15.4	3.4	79	56
Jamaica	27.3	5.9	2.2	20	70
Ecuador	36.5	7.8	2.9	66	60
Morocco	46.8	15.7	3.1	–	55
Bolivia	44.2	17.4	2.7	158	52
Egypt	37.6	10.5	2.7	108	54
Low income					
Kenya	20.0	3.6	1.7	54	53
Madagascar	45.1	20.9	2.4	53	46
Pakistan	46.8	16.7	3.0	124	52
Sri Lanka	29.9	7.8	2.2	45	69
India	34.4	15.0	2.0	122	51
Mali	49.0	23.2	2.6	–	42
Bangladesh	47.4	20.5	2.7	139	47

*Per mille.

Source: The World Bank, *World Development Report 1980* (New York 1980), tables 1 and 21.

whereas in 1960 only three of these countries encouraged birth control, by 1971 no less than thirty-three had a population policy and thirty-one others supported family planning. These figures can convey no idea of the degree of support and efficiency of the measures adopted, but they represent a considerable advance over a decade and are contributive to the first ever, albeit small, decrease in world birth rates noticeable in the late 1970s. Computer models have been prepared with a variety of demographic indices and all show the low cost of birth control programmes relative to the gains that follow the prevention of births. A decline in fertility has rapid positive effects: in the short term the working proportion of the population is unaffected, but the number of their young dependants falls. Gradually women with lightened household ties are available for paid work and thus in the longer term, when the labour supply falls they and the body of unemployed and under-employed are available to find a place in the productive economy. As may be seen from Table 5, most developing countries now have rates of population increase of between 2 and 3 per cent per annum. When these rates become below 1 per cent, then the number of future generations will be much reduced and personal betterment in these populations will be occurring.

The case for balanced development

It is not always appreciated that attempts to foster and expand manufacturing industry must be paralleled by development and expansion of the agricultural sector of the economy. There is no simple choice between developing either industry or agriculture, the two sectors are intimately related. Put at its simplest, the farmer should produce more in order to feed the growing population engaged in secondary and tertiary activities and he should be able to do this with a reducing labour force, for successful industrial development necessarily attracts labour from agriculture. This has been the pattern of development in Western countries and it is worth noting that the world's most efficient and productive farming is to be found in those countries, whether the criterion be output per acre or per man employed. However, in that the kind of farming tends to be wasteful of land (considerable emphasis on meat and milk and therefore 'two-stage' agriculture)[4] the supporting power or carrying capacity per acre is exceeded by certain countries such as Japan and Egypt, with their double and treble cropping and emphasis upon 'one-stage' cereal crops.

If agriculture fails to provide food for growing industrial and urban populations then much-needed capital will have to be spent on importing foodstuffs and development will be retarded. Conversely if agriculture can increase its production for export of primary raw materials, then more foreign exchange is available to aid development of the whole economy. It is of course easy to make such suggestions but, for a host of varied reasons (land tenure systems, surplus agricultural population, institutional monopoly of capital), far more difficult for them to be carried out. However, a more prosperous agricultural sector is also needed to provide a market for the products of the new industries. At the moment, the poverty of agriculturists and therefore the smallness of the available market for manufactured goods is probably the greatest hindrance to development. Any enlargement of purchasing power of the peasantry should act as a stimulus to industrial development – one factor cited in favour of land reform.

Hence the successful launching of programmes of industrialization depend upon improvements in agriculture, and the degree to which the improvements can be attained can either provide a curb or act as an incentive to the success of the new ventures. From this it follows that systematic improvement (and therefore investment) in agriculture must be a foremost task of the under-developed lands. The aim should be mutual self-support between these two sectors of the economy whereby agriculture's surplus population may be siphoned off into industry, as agriculture, under the stimulus of greater demand, becomes more efficient and industry in turn raises the market for agricultural produce. Agriculture is one of the major existing sources of wealth in developing lands; from it they must expect to obtain a substantial proportion of the capital needed for development. Thus profits from both the ownership and the working of land need to be made available for productive investment, not only to establish new industries, but particularly to sustain and nourish them during the lengthy period when they are struggling to gather momentum.

5 Industrialization: theoretical considerations

Just as levels of development between nations are unequal, so are levels of development between different parts of a country. The causes of these wide regional disparities in development, and ways of overcoming them so that development and prosperity are spread to all parts of a country, have commanded increasing attention in recent years from economists, geographers and planners. This concern with understanding regional development advanced considerably when a new field of inquiry – regional science – emerged after the Second World War. The old regional geography, consisting mainly of identifying regions and examining regional differentiation, was heavy on description but light on analysis and was becoming discredited. The more rigorous analytical techniques applied by the regional scientists in their study of the interrelationships between economic and ecological systems have gone on to offer explanations of differences in spatial levels of development in newly industrializing countries. The next step has been to indicate ways in which the planners may reduce these interregional variations in prosperity. These studies incidentally have helped to deepen geographers' insight and broadened their methodology and, perceptively used, have given a new life and relevance to regional geography.

It is the spatial differences in levels of development that especially attract the attention of geographers and cause them to study closely development theories that have spatial contexts. The body of economic development theory and models derived from it have proliferated since the Second World War, generally incorporating a greater realism over time and coming to recognize that the path blazed by the present advanced nations is not necessarily the one to be followed identically by the less-developed countries. It has already been shown that there is no close relationship between a country's resources and its wealth or gross national product (GNP), but a close relationship does seem to exist between output and the amount of capital employed. GNP seems to depend directly on two factors: relationship between real capital and output, and the volume of capital utilized.

It is useful for planning purposes to have some idea of the productivity of capital, and the ratio of capital invested to resultant increase of output is frequently quoted and is known as the capital:output ratio. Economists admit that this ratio can be misleading, especially in developing countries where data are scarce, but for planning purposes some such estimates are necessary. It may be applied as a ratio for the entire economy as in summaries of development plans, or it may refer to a particular sector of the economy. In an industrial country an investment of £100 may lead to an increase in the national income of £33 a year – the capital:output ratio thus being 3:1. At such a rate an annual new investment of 12 per cent of national income should result in an annual increase of about 4 per cent in that national income, figures that are generally typical of industrial countries. Estimates of likely coefficients in developing countries vary. India's first Five Year Plan was apparently based on a capital:output ratio of 3:1 and this in fact proved to be an underestimate. Investment in agriculture usually gives good returns, even approaching 1:1, but in heavy industry, where great investment in plant and machinery, power supplies etc. are required, a much less attractive ratio, even as low as 8:1, is experienced. Economists generally agree that in developing countries the marginal capital:output ratio is likely to be more of the order 4:1. Associated with the operation of capital investment is the 'multiplier'. Put simply, money invested provides (*inter alia*) jobs, and the recipients will spend most of their wages on food, clothes, etc. and thus provide work and income for others. These others in turn spend and make employment for yet more, and so on. Thus the initial investment provides direct employment and wages but indirectly provides a multiple of that figure. It is the operation of the multiplier that is one cause of uneven spatial development, discussed on pages 86–8.

Stages of growth: a non-spatial view

There has been no scarcity of economic growth models in recent years. If we examine their characteristics we find non-spatial and spatial groups, and in each some that are mathematical and some conceptual; some apply to regions within countries, some to countries themselves and others to supranational areas.[1] Although geographers have most interest in spatial models, first the non-spatial conceptual model of W. W. Rostow will be outlined; it was made public in 1960 when it attracted remarkable attention and it still commands much allegiance.[2] As an economic historian Rostow was concerned with economic growth over time. He sought to explain why economic growth is not a continuous progression and identified five stages. At first one finds the traditional society characterized by an agrarian way of life, limited technology and knowledge of science, and little social mobility. All this is within a hierarchical feudal-type society. There follows a lengthy transitional phase – creating the preconditions for 'take-off' – where society begins to change. A greater willingness to lend capital is matched by innovation and entrepreneurial enterprise; the growth of infra-structure, such as roads and railways, sees the beginnings of industry; and a new elite emerges to challenge the authority of land ownership and to change society and government. The next and most critical period is the 'take-off' – a relatively short period during which growth becomes self-sustaining, with over 10 per cent of the national income being invested annually. The change from the 5 per cent per annum investment of the precondition stage to over 10 per cent at the 'take-off' period often relates to some sharp stimulus such as the development of certain growth industries (for instance, textiles in Great Britain), the development of major export industries (grain in the USA and Canada, and timber in Sweden) or the availability of investment from agriculture following land reform (in Russia and Japan, where bought-out landowners had capital for alternative investment); occasionally political revolution is involved, suggestive of the social and economic stresses which the society must endure. A most important aspect emerges from the growth-stage theory at this point: it is that for successful take-off, domestic savings and investment must be at least of the order of 10–12 per cent and they must be sustained at this level for two to three decades. This is a tremendous task for countries of weak financial and administrative structures and needs capacity to get savings mobilized and to inculcate a savings propensity over a lengthy period in a population that may increasingly desire to spend in order to enjoy fruits of development as they become apparent. The economic effort has to be severe and needs discipline, adaptability and forbearance – particularly by consumers who may see their level of consumption (living standards) fall even while capital formation and investment is increased to the 10–12 per cent level. The successful take-off leads to a situation where a steady rate of growth can be regularly sustained and momentum maintained by the spontaneous private forces in the economy. This phase constitutes the drive to maturity during which modern technology becomes increasingly applied, new leading sectors emerge, urbanization creates changes in society and service activities expand. Finally the goal is to reach the stage of high mass consumption with its emphasis on durable consumer goods and the welfare state: a phase that only a handful of developed countries have attained.

Rostow's model has been heavily criticized. It is difficult to test the theory for quantitative evidence is lacking, no clear mechanism links the different stages and many economists deny that such distinct phases or stages can be identified in the real world. Nevertheless Rostow's aeronautically worded model has considerable value in development studies. While the links between the stages may be imprecise he does draw attention to phases that economies enter, and in particular his theory involves social and political preconditions and conditions that play composite roles with rates of investment – the 'human aspect' so often ignored in economists' models. His work stimulated new lines of research on the character of economic growth, which has lead to many other models being advanced. The value of comparing, classifying and analysing apparently different economies over time is now recognized and others have advanced models based on Rostow's but related to particular groups of economies. Here the 'degree of fit' appears to be much greater than in Rostow's general model.

Cumulative causation and polarization

Spatial variation in economic growth and development have come to interest economists and geographers in more recent years, although Gunnar Myrdal, whose name is particularly associated with these studies, first put forward his views in the mid 1950s.[3] Traditional views of interregional relationships were based on the concept that differences in levels of income were temporary since, with free mobility of the factors of production, an equalization of income would follow. This static equilibrium concept failed to explain the persistence of variations in levels of development as shown between countries and regions in the real world by *per*

Figure 6 *Rostow's stages of growth (after D.E. Keeble)*

capita income, rates of growth of industrialization, of trade, etc. To account for this, Myrdal advanced his hypothesis of cumulative causation which directly challenged the static equilibrium theory. He pointed out that the widening of differences in levels of development and income negated the theory that disequilibrium situations tend to move towards equilibrium but support the opposite view, that the play of market forces tends to increase rather than decrease inequalities between regions. He cites the situation where a region of a country, by some initial advantage, begins to develop ahead of its neighbours. Now it is well known that labour, capital and entrepreneurship in a free economy move to where the return is highest and where the demand is growing and thus there will accrue to the favoured region more labour, capital, trade and social and economic infrastructure. His proposition is that economic and social forces will create cumulative expansion in the favoured region and widen the differences with other regions; put in another way, a multiplier effect will produce increasing returns in the one region but will have an adverse effect on surrounding regions. This examination of the spatial interactions between such differing regions is a further valuable feature of Myrdal's model. He suggests that the positive flow to the favoured

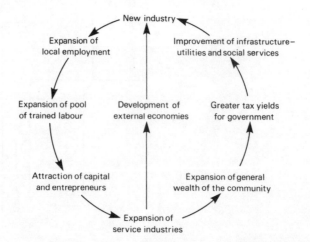

Figure 7   *Myrdal's process of cumulative causation (simplified)*

region will create backwash or negative effects upon other regions, for they will lose skilled and enterprising labour and capital, and will lag even more behind the growth region which will go on increasing its competitive advantage and its real income. Goods and services from the advancing region may swamp local production in the other regions and their reduced economies will give them little strength to attract the range of social services the favoured region receives. This explanation of the interaction between growing and stagnating regions demonstrates polarization effects, but Myrdal also identified what he calls 'spread effects' – eventual momentum from the expanding region which may stimulate growth elsewhere, such as in contiguous areas.

Another model, very similar to that of Myrdal, was published shortly afterwards by Albert Hirschman.[4] He describes similar symptoms as Myrdal: the attraction of labour, capital and other resources to the advancing region; but he envisages a later corrective stage of counterbalances coming into play to restore equilibrium and negate the earlier polarizing forces. These may well be shaped by government economic policy and represent more positive forces than the somewhat uncertain spread effects of Myrdal's model. These spread, or 'trickling down', effects suggested by Myrdal consist of a diffusion of technology and increased demand for the backward region's products (food and raw materials), and a movement of capital to it from the developed regions. This phase is particularly apparent when the developed region can no longer supply its expanding domestic demand and begins to suffer land and labour shortage.

Centre–periphery theories

Some aspects of Myrdal's work were expanded and taken farther by John Friedmann (1963) who, in his centre–periphery model, elaborated some of the relationships outlined by Myrdal.[5] He identifies the major centres of growth and innovation as core regions which dominate dependent peripheral regions ('dominant core and dominated periphery'). The transfer of human, capital and natural resources weakens the peripheral economy but strengthens the core towards more innovation and more linkages; with the success of these movements comes a psychological boost shown by new behavourial patterns which bring growing specialization and economies of scale. The market and supply systems and the administrative control from core to periphery is repeated in hierarchical national systems, and is also applicable on a continental scale and, in a colonial and neo-colonial context, on an international scale. To move from theory to reality one may cite the case of India. Berry describes India's economic system at a regional level as showing an interacting set of economic activities based on major resource complexes and sets of regional economies grouped around major metropolitan centres. 'Both resource complexes and metropolitan nodes (the traditional and colonial elements of India's economy) can be associated with core regions of more intensive activity, surrounded by peripheries in which simple peasant economies remain.'[6]

Friedmann, like Myrdal, postulates eventual spread effects (possibly accelerated by governments) which will reduce the periphery's dependence on the core region and may even lead to new and developing peripheral regions emerging. Some economists fear that the backwash effects may continue indefinitely or that the spread effects will be much delayed because of the strength of cumulative growth at the core. In fact, there is not much evidence to support the assumption that there will be a filtering down of development effects from the core to its periphery. One reason is that the linkages between the rural economy and the urban-industrial and growing core area are usually slight; the economy of the periphery is traditional peasant agriculture with the aim of subsistence and therefore is mainly outside market forces. For diffusion to occur a rural economy needs to be structured in similar ways to its core: to be accessible and to be involved in the market system such as with an agriculture specialized in commercial crop production. Thus one can envisage, as the development process proceeds, a series of transformations in the economy that are related spatially to favoured localities where costs may be minimized or profits maximized and which exhibit rapid economic growth and increase regional inequalities. The astonishing growth of the major cities in the developing world, making for outstanding primacy and sucking in, as they do, the people and resources of the rural areas, is a familiar example of this unequal areal development. If this localized upward spiral is to be checked, then the spread effects must be hastened and reinforced by government intervention, otherwise gross spatial inequalities (with deteriorating agriculture) economically may impair national development programmes and politically may create unrest and strife.

Growth pole strategy

Thus we find that the reduction of regional, economic and social inequalities is now an important part of the planners' tasks in less developed countries and that the stimulation of spread effects to facilitate cumulative growth movements in the peripheral regions receives much attention. What is clear is that economic development never occurs uniformly over a particular region, but is to be found concentrated in favoured areas which benefit from the upward spiral suggested by Myrdal and Friedmann, with growing impetus as industrial linkage and economies of scale grow. The core areas expanding more rapidly than the surrounding regions are 'growth poles', and analysis and understanding of mechanisms and interactions within them is increasingly allowing the creation of 'artificial' growth poles to be a strategy for planners.

The analysis of the expansion mechanism of a growth pole has been the particular work of Perroux and other French economists.[7] The growth pole is fuelled by one or more dynamic industries which attract service and linked industries offering inputs or taking inputs from them, and as this relationship grows, so do economies which serve to attract a wider spectrum of industries. Proximity and ease of communication further technological changes and innovation. Jinja in Uganda and Nairobi in Kenya are the successful outcome of such policies. Another more recent application of growth pole theory has been in southern Italy, the most under-developed region within the European Economic Community. Plans were drawn up for industrial growth in the Bari–Brindisi–Taranto triangle of Apulia, Italy's 'heel'. A comprehensive input–output table of the region was constructed, to show the goods and services consumed and produced in all existing productive activities. These were then analysed and the new industries that might find the region's resources advantageous were listed. Feasibility studies for each such industry were then undertaken, close consideration being given to the needs of these industries within the spectrum of external economies. Upon examination it was found that being surrounded by numerous other industries did not necessarily create adequate external economies, but that specialized auxiliary firms were required. Some of these provide components, others retooling and service activities. With ever-increasing specialization and constant improvements in transport, it is becoming apparent that, for some industries, closeness to auxilaries rather than to raw materials etc. may now be considered vital. The region's peripheral position and lack of a pool of skilled labour were other factors taken into account. Finally, two 'poles of development' were created at Bari and Taranto by the establishment of nine mechanical engineering industries. They in turn require the establishment of thirty auxiliary plants concerned with repairs, tooling, foundry work, gear-cutting, pressing, moulding and galvanizing. These, and the infrastructure established for them, are slowly promoting the growth of allied and service industries and providing non-agricultural jobs so much needed throughout the Italian Mezzogiorno.[8]

Dualism

We may now view the changing social, economic and spatial patterns analysed by Myrdal, Hirschman, Friedmann and Perroux from a different standpoint. The growth centres reflect the coming into play of advanced technologies and capitalist forces, which are demonstrated in the evolution of economies quite distinct from the traditional subsistence way of life of the peripheral areas. In the developing world, what is called dualism has emerged from the introduction in favoured areas of money and cash crop economies and modern manufacturing industry, which have come to parallel the traditional subsistence way of life. Within those countries two differing types of economy with differing technologies are demonstrated. The traditional sector operates usually in small family units, is labour-intensive, with little invested capital; it is concerned mainly with agriculture and principally is aimed at subsistence. The modern sector of the economy operates in large units, uses hired labour, is supported by much capital investment and uses advanced or relatively advanced technologies; it is concerned mainly with plantations, mines, manufacturing industry and utilities.

It will be perceived that not only have we two types of economy, but also that they nurture two very different types of society, the one being an imported social system from the West and the other indigenous and traditional. In these two societies there will be differing values, attitudes and aspirations. Thus there is more to dualism than the mere differences between subsistence and exchange sectors, for dualism is manifested in a money economy and financial services; in economic organization; in technological advances; in new habits and ways of life; it exhibits a marked spatial aspect by bringing about regional inequalities of centre and periphery character. Factors that also need emphasis are the inbuilt features of the modern sector, the lack of which retard change in the traditional sector. These features include access to capital, finance and credit; to economic organization and division of labour; to foreign markets and firms – facilities denied or generally inacessible to the small economic units in the traditional sector. Industrial policies furthering import-substitute industries discriminate heavily in favour of the modern sector at the expense of agriculture and artisanal industry. They even protect the larger scale modern factories from the competition of the village workshop. Consequently such policies further regional inequalities that are already in being and which, from a national point of view, should be reduced. The dual economy is not a passive institutional element, but is dynamic and divisive in its economic, social and spatial effects. It is the quickening dynamism inherent in the fusion of the dual economy elements that carry forward the economic development of Third World economies, and with their social and spatial extensions make the term 'modernization' appropriate. Development – in the widest sense of the term – is proving to be a difficult and uneasy process, mainly because of the evident divisive nature of the growing modern sector of whichever Third World economy one chooses to examine. It is clear that dualism is not a cause of backwardness and under-development but is an inevitable consequence of development and the development process.

The principal interest of the geographer focuses upon the spatial effects of the growth of dualism, for as we have seen the establishment of economic activity at a limited number of localities sets in motion forces leading to regional differentiation and to regional inequalities. Spatial disequilibria of modernization are emphasized principally by imbalance in settlement hierarchy, in income distribution and in mobility of population. The spatial development models already considered have thrown light upon the processes involved and have given a new impetus to the search for a theory of regional development. Although differing in detail, the models emphasize polarizing forces that arise with the initial establishment of industrial activities. Labour and resources tend to be pulled in from the surrounding areas, and increasing infrastructure provision (both physical and social) at the centre reinforces this centripetal effect. In short, logically, growth in one area retards growth somewhere else, and without remedial action a pattern of a lively and developing core area surrounded by a stagnating rural periphery evolves. It is doubtful if regional imbalances will of themselves diminish to a gently undulating economic and social peneplane: the polarizing forces are too great and the diffusing (spread) effects are likely to be weak unless actively strengthened by government planning measures. What is serious is that, if corrective policies are not imposed, the forces of dualism encourage large-scale enterprise and neglect the small-scale operator in his rural setting. Then agriculture is often stigmatized as being backward and primitive without recognition of the fact that it has been denied the resources and privileges – of capital, technology and market organization – amply accruing to the modern and urban sector. Finally, Singer draws attention to a most demoralizing fact of dualism: that a superior and an inferior sector coexist, but relations between the two do not make for equalization, the superior element does little to pull up the inferior but may even push it down.[9]

From the foregoing it would seem that, when development strategies are based on industrialization, a clear need will arise for measures incorporating industrial decentralization, for doles of regional aid to the backward regions and the setting up of social infrastructure makes them even more reliant on the centre: industrialization is a necessary ingredient of regional economic development. Algeria provides us with an example of a country exhibiting acute dualism and where the application of both growth pole strategy and attempts to create spread effects into peripheral backward agricultural areas may be found. The overwhelming core area in the colonial period was Algiers (the capital and chief port) with a lesser industrial core centred on Oran (the second city and port). Ever since independence (1962) the main thrust of Algerian development has been through industrialization, but with attempts to restrict the industrial growth of Algiers and to dissipate new industrial development by the establishment of growth poles at Arzew, Annaba and Skikda. Arzew is a terminal of Saharan oil and gas pipelines and has a gas-liquefaction plant, a refinery and a gas-operated fertilizer unit. Other plants, such as for methanol and synthetic resins, are being added. Annaba has a large iron and steel plant, a phosphatic fertilizer unit, engineering, paint manufacture, food processing, construction industries including a cement plant and a thermal power station. Skikda has a gas-liquefaction plant, a petro-chemical complex (specializing in plastics manufacture) and a new thermal electric power station. It is hoped that as these growth poles develop, they will expand into industrial belts (Oran–Arzew–Mostagnanem and Annaba–Skikda) by the founding of scattered smaller plants concerned with textiles, food-processing and mineral extraction.

The Algerian government is attempting to further spread effects to more peripheral regions by special regional development plans, for relatively small areas, aimed at infrastructural, social and educational provision with industrial proposals related to the region's resource base and potentiality. As an example, we find, in the case of the impoverished mountainous areas of the Grande Kabylie and Aures, that between 1968 and 1975 a textile plant and tannery were completed at Batna, near where quarries have been opened and bricks and tiles manufactured. Clothing, wood and furniture industries now function at Batna, Barika and Kenchela.[10] It is doubtful whether the marked regional disparities dating from the colonial period will be erased, but nevertheless there has been success in these planned attempts to spread industry more widely and thus to reduce the centre–periphery effects and to check the dualism they engender.

6 Problems of industrialization

It is generally accepted that an investment of the order of 12–15 per cent of the net national income is necessary if it is intended to diversify and advance a backward economy by the development of secondary and tertiary opportunities. The rate of return on such a degree of investment exceeds typical rates of population growth and permits of rising standards and cumulative returns. The maintenance of such a rate of investment allows the economy to move into the 'take-off' stage – the small snowball begins to roll. This is an oversimplification in that capital alone does not automatically engineer development, for much depends on the qualities of the people: their ability and desire to learn and apply better methods of production, their enterprise, the removal of institutional obstructions and the provision of incentive to effort and investment. However, capital is a very necessary ingredient and the real nub of the matter lies in overcoming the complex problems standing in the way of attaining or bettering the 12 per cent-plus level. It is this ordering of economic progress by means of formulae, equations and interlocking of planning measures that is typical of the modern attack upon the problem of under-development. One reason for the necessity of the planned approach stems from the wide differences between the present developed lands in their early stages of growth and the present developing lands.

These extensive differences are often overlooked when development plans and theories are propounded, for the planning is generally based upon knowledge derived from the patterns of progress of the already developed lands. That we should draw upon accumulated experience is both natural and proper, but similarities here are only partial, differences must not be ignored. For example, to be told that England at the beginning of the nineteenth century and India today are examples of countries in the 'take-off' stage can be misleading.

Supposing an Englishman of those days met an Indian of these days and discussed their economic problems. The one takes off from London in a stage-coach, the other takes off in a Boeing 707 from New Delhi, and they reach Brighton – roughly speaking – at the same time. What common language of economic development can they talk, when they take off their coats and get down to it?'

Perhaps a fundamental difference to note is that industrial development in the pioneer countries such as Britain did not happen according to plan. The government did not ordain and design the country's industrialization, but rather a series of favourable factors and circumstances converged (expanding overseas trade, the growth of both men and institutions of commerce and credit, the surge of science and inventions becoming increasingly applied to a wide resource base). In short, in a bumbling haphazard way an industrial economy was evolved in Britain and took some eighty years over it. Such continental neighbours as Belgium, France and Germany gradually took the same path, their economic and social revolutions also gathered speed slowly and ran through several generations. In contrast, development in the present under-developed lands must be much more speedy and orderly. Advances are likely to come less from evolution within than as a result of government-sponsored imposition from without.

The earliest industrial countries had virtually no rivals; they were the first in the field and their gains were great and tended to become cumulative. The situation regarding overseas markets for manufactured goods is now very different for the state at present attempting to develop an industrial sector. However, the hard-won technical knowledge and scientific advances of developed countries are rapidly available to backward lands and, at least from the point of view of technology, there need be no long period of trial and error. Whether the human resources of the developing countries can be moulded into the forms and societies of the older industrialized lands and whether such patterns are necessary is more problematical. At any rate, ideas and knowledge flow far more quickly around the world and, incidentally, money and its effects also move and fructify far more swiftly.

There are other very striking differences to be taken into account, such as the very low standards of living and mental attitudes in most of the present developing lands. It is false to think of the masses in these lands as being at the stage and level of people in this country 200 years ago. The present lot of the Indian

ryot, Iraqi fellah and Paraguayan peon suggests a much closer
analogy with the England of Domesday. The leap forward is to be
immense and yet must be relatively sudden; time is no longer with
the developing countries.

Finally, one of the greatest differences lies in the demographic
structure. Populations in so many of the developing lands are
larger and at a lower standard of living than in Western Europe in
the early nineteenth century; also almost all now have a more
rapid rate of population increase and a higher proportion of young
workers. These differences have both advantages and disadvantages.
On the positive side the labour of the dense and growing population
offers a great resource for a developing and expanding industrial
sector. The broad-based population pyramid of Britain in the
nineteenth century provided a dynamic element in economic
development; going hand in hand with increasing 'know-how', it
fostered, and more than supplied, a steadily expanding demand, in
addition to furnishing many millions for the newly developing
lands overseas. Steadily improving agriculture, dispensing with
labour, also contributed its quota to this design. In certain conditions,
therefore, the vast labour resources found in many of the developing
lands are a great economic asset and must be fully utilized.

However, on the negative side it must be remembered that
humanity is capital-absorbing as well as being (by work) capital-
forming. The vast masses inadequately employed in so many
backward lands are a great handicap to capital formation, and the
cost of providing services for large population increments may be
crippling. To train, equip and absorb one individual into non-
agricultural employment in Asia twenty years ago was estimated at
US$1500, and this sum is in close accord with the estimated capital
figure per new worker in India's second Five Year Plan.[2] Such a
figure gives some indication of the enormous cost of programmes
of industrialization to such populous countries as China and India,
where massive populations totalling well over 1700 million are now
expanding at an annual rate of 2 per cent. It has been found that so
far in her planned development India has not provided employment
for the full increment to her population; it may be possible that,
with greater austerity imposed under communist central planning,
China might. India's third Five Year Plan, for example, managed
to provide work for the equivalent of 80 per cent of new members
to the labour force – the great mass of unemployed and under-
employed remaining uncatered for. With the theoretical complementary advance in agriculture and the release of workers to non-

agricultural employment, the problem of the provision of capital assumes immense dimensions. Nothing like this was experienced in Western Europe; Britain's population in 1801 was only 9 million and increasing by about 150,000 per annum (1.6 per cent per annum), but with a far broader-based economy and diversity of economic activity and no condition of agrarian over-population to compare with those of Egypt, India, Java, China and Japan today. The heavy annual increments to the labour force in these countries also serve to depress agricultural wage levels and to keep them low – part of the vicious circle of poverty which in turn impedes saving and the formation of capital.

The place of capital

It is obvious that the developing countries are under-equipped with capital in relation to their populations and natural resources. It has been pointed out that circular forces – the 'vicious circle of poverty' – operate to constrict the formation and accumulation of capital by those countries.[3] In simplified form these forces and their effects are set out in Figure 8, where it may be seen how the

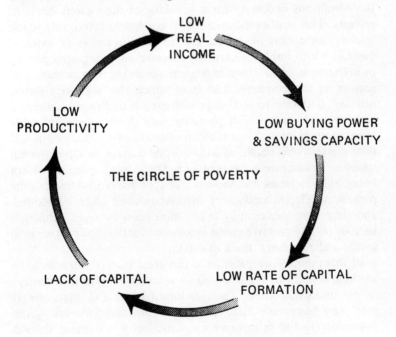

Figure 8   *The circle of poverty*

limitations and deficiences imposed by poverty react upon the size of markets and capacity to save, and thus limit capital attraction and formation. Consequently traditional labour-intensive occupations continue, their low productivity being a cause of the prevailing poverty. To this depressing situation must be added the aggravation of heavily increasing populations laying increasing claims to the very limited supply of capital. The supply of capital has so often been stressed as the key to development and prosperity for under-developed lands, but the supply of unlimited capital will not in itself create development: skilled and willing hands are needed to turn the key to open the door. Professor Kuznets underlines this when he states 'the major capital stock of an industrially advanced country is not in its physical equipment; it is the body of knowledge amassed from tested findings and the capacity and training of the population to use this knowledge effectively'.[4] Capital is but one of a number of economic factors that combine with social, political and cultural forces in bringing about the changes inherent in development. It is an important factor and may be likened to a catalyst in its effects upon other factors.

It is generally accepted that the application of capital is one of the conditions necessary for a breaking of the vicious circle of poverty. This implies the creation of conditions favourable to the internal formation of capital and to the attraction of external capital. It also implies a carefully assessed and integrated pattern of investment, from which maximum advantage may accrue to all sectors of the economy and from which the necessary public utilities conducive to further growth are created or strengthened. The necessity for overall planning, and therefore considerable governmental interest, scrutiny and even active participation, has now come to be regarded as a normal feature of development whereas it was rare a century ago. There is no question of not being able to break the vicious circle of poverty. After all, the present developed lands were themselves once under-developed, and they have successfully taken the necessary steps. Although initially poor, a part of current income was deflected or set aside to create and augment a stock of capital.

In this country we gloss over the great poverty and dreadful working conditions in mills, mines and factories in the first century of our industrialization. The rich industrialists and mine owners may well have built their pseudo-Gothic mansions and given popularity to the term *nouveau riche*, but it was these shrewd, hard-headed men who ploughed back much of their wealth into their enterprises and who saw them expand, proliferate and fructify to an extent never before known. It is on the foundations they laid that Britain fought two great wars and founded her welfare state. Britain pulled herself up by her own bootstraps, for external sources of capital available to her were very limited. To an increasing degree her imitators and successors were helped by foreign investment, and today this is an important potential source of capital for newly developing countries. Even so, the hardships, vicissitudes and sacrifices undergone in the course of industrialization by the present advanced countries are likely to be just as necessary, and must be an accepted part of the process to be undergone by the developing lands. Development will not come without effort, hardship and sacrifices, no matter how much help- may come from outside. Without the right social and political climate investment may be ineffective, but it may not even be attracted, for capital is cautious and will not venture where it may be ill used.

Problems of capital formation

Most developing countries with traditional economies save no more than 5–6 per cent of their net national incomes. To establish themselves in a position for 'take-off' into a fully developed economy requires an annual investment averaging between 10–15 per cent of the net national income, dependent upon the rate of increase of their populations. In broad terms this is the financial target to be arrived at. The low rate of capital formation in underdeveloped countries has barely been sufficient to keep pace with population growth. With a capital:output ratio of 4:1 the investment of 5 per cent of net national income would produce enough to sustain a population increase of about 1.25 per cent at the existing income level. If a higher rate of population increase pertains, and if standards of living are to rise, a far higher rate of investment is clearly necessary.

The general poverty of these countries means that the level of domestic saving is very low, the bulk of the population may have no productive savings, any nest-eggs possessed are usually in the form of gold rings, bracelets, jewellery. To persuade such peoples of the purpose, advantages and safety of such institutions as post office savings banks, thrift societies and insurance is a difficult and lengthy process. It is worth while, but is not likely to result in the saving of much more than 2 per cent of the net national income. An estimate of the value of privately owned gold in India in 1960 was US\$3675 million. 'This is a large amount in absolute terms, being historical accumulation of stocks, but new hoarding is small . . . the role of gold as a savings medium in India is comparatively insignificant.'[5] A point worth noticing here is that a maldistributed national income (such as the United Kingdom's during the nineteenth century, and today in those countries where land ownership still brings in disproportionate wealth) is far more favourable to saving and investment than one which is more evenly distributed. It favours more speedy development, although possibly at the expense of social unrest and dissatisfaction.

No nation should find it impossible to save 12 per cent of its national income given the will and strength of purpose to organize its affairs to that end. All too often under-developed lands are regarded as too poor to do this, yet frequently it will be found that 25–40 per cent of their national income is in the hands of a few thousand landlords who dissipate much of it in ostentatious living and convert a good deal into gold and jewellery. If this money went as taxes to the government for reinvestment, or as profits to industrialists to be ploughed back into business, there would be little difficulty in attaining a high rate of investment. Here, of course, is one of the underlying reasons for land reform measures as an initial step to development in so many poor countries.

It is clear that domestic saving can contribute only a very small part of the investment capital needed; much more should be forthcoming from the ploughing back of profits of existing undertakings. This form of self-capitalization is commonplace in industrial countries, indeed most firms' expansion depends upon reinvestment of undistributed profit although initial investment may have been from external sources. Thus a high level of profits and a population inculcated with the propensity to save, or an austere regime permitting the greatest proportion of reinvestment, would seem to be required. Taxation policies designed to absorb marginal income, whereby money going into circulation returns immediately to the government without creating big price increases, are favoured by those economists who point out that, with such conditions, a controlled inflation favours building up government capital. Developing lands notoriously have very low rates of taxation on marginal incomes and therefore much scope for such measures.

It is illuminating to examine briefly the cases of Japan and Russia to see the principal methods they adopted to obtain the necessary rate of investment for sustained and cumulative economic development. Japanese early development had some unusual facets. During the nineteenth century landowners and nobles were recompensed by the government which took over their duties and administrative functions. This led to many of these erstwhile landowners and feudal lords becoming capitalists, entering banking and interesting themselves in industrial developments, especially after 1880 when the government sold some of the factories it had built for pioneer development. These enterprises were supported by a virtual continuance of the former austere consumption pattern of the people. The semi-isolation of the Japanese at this time, and the discipline of the people, made this possible. It is estimated that before 1914, Japan saved and reinvested annually between 12 per cent and 17 per cent of her national income. Little foreign capital entered Japan before 1920. These policies were fostered and supplemented by the government's taxation and subsidization measures.

Tsarist Russia similarly bought out the feudal landlords and the rents deflected from them became invested in commerce and industry. Banking institutions expanded during the latter part of the nineteenth century and foreign capital became attracted. Undoubtedly the early stages of the 'take-off' were accomplished before the 1917 revolution. Under the subsequent communist regime, isolation from the high and rising consumption standards of developed countries has been a major factor in the economic development of the USSR, where rigid planning and control over personal liberty have become ruthlessly dedicated to economic progress. Where vested interests and institutional obstacles to growth can be swept aside, and where low consumption standards can be maintained, a high rate of capital formation is possible. Other features reinforcing the state capitalist advantage over the private capitalist are the taxation powers and monetary policies it can enforce. The critical 1930s saw tremendous inflation and rising profits which were transferred by taxation to the government. The result of all this has been one of the speediest rates of capital formation in the world, but it should be noticed that such a high rate is only possible where an iron curtain exists preventing free knowledge of the consumption standards elsewhere.

Development of foreign trade in many cases has played a

substantial part in economic developments. National resources permitting export of primary products have helped to finance the import of machinery and equipment, and to pay interest on loans during the 'take-off' period. United States and Canadian grain, Australian wool, Swedish timber, Venezuelan oil provide such examples. However, as has been pointed out, conditions are changing and except for oil the demand for primary products lags behind the expansion of industry partly due to the greater use of synthetics and economies in the use of raw materials.

Problems of capital attraction

Imported capital has played a large part in the economic development of many countries; cases where virtually all capital has been obtained from internal sources are not typical. Foreign investment very often plays a major part in establishing basic utilities necessary for the erection of the industrial superstructure. Enterprises such as railway development are far more costly than establishing individual manufacturing industries and require a long period of gestation before they become really fruitful ventures. Their presence, however, is generally indispensable for further industrial advance.

Foreign capital may be either government or agency controlled (such as loans from the World Bank) or investment by private enterprise. Private investment is now the largest overseas source of capital, but today the enormous demand for capital from the greater part of the world struggling for economic advance is far greater than private investment alone can supply, and the need for aid from public funds of the advanced industrial countries has become accepted. Aid from the rich countries to the poorer ones has gathered impetus from the early 1960s. The United Nations Organization has repeatedly pressed for greater generosity on the part of the donors and an annual aid target of 1 per cent of GNP has been urged, but as yet has rarely been attained. Aid is given in many forms – finance, food, equipment, technicians, scholarships – and can be bilateral (country to country) or multilateral (given through international agencies, such as the World Bank). Financial aid may be in the form of grants (outright gifts) or loans (at hard or soft rates of interest). Generally Britain makes grants to colonies and loans to independent members of the Commonwealth; a pattern possibly reflecting the fact that the poorer countries cannot attract all the private investment they need. Capital, more than ever, has become a scarce resource and needs to be attracted, wooed and cosseted.

The global pattern of aid in recent years is set out in Table 6. Total aid to developing countries in 1961 was $8000 million and increased only moderately over the next few years. The great increases during the 1970s (up to $45000 million in 1977) reflects first a considerable element of inflation and, second a great increase in private commercial capital lending. What is now very serious is the growing indebtedness of the developing countries and their increasing inability to pay the interest on, and repay the capital of, earlier loans now becoming due. The total external debt of non-oil-producing developing countries in 1980 was estimated at $370,000 million, and it is clear that in recent years much of the increase in capital aid has gone straight back to service or repay existing loans. Ways of softening or even cancelling some official loan debts are being examined.

Table 6 *Financial aid to developing countries from DAC donor countries, 1961–77 (US$ millions)*

	1961	1969	1971	1973	1975	1977
Government and agency aid	5647	7,003	8,838	11,648	16,470	17,631
France	948	938	1,131	1,580	2,448	2,424
West Germany	559	433	802	1,115	1,596	1,502
United Kingdom	436	412	550	650	885	924
USA	3069	3,183	3,392	3,300	4,742	4,543
Other countries	635	2,027	2,963	5,003	6,799	8,238
Private long-term capital	2362	6,031	7,478	10,786	20,152	27,023
Total	8009	13,033	16,622	22,434	36,622	44,654

Source: United Nations Statistical Yearbook, 1978 (New York 1979), from Tables 202 and 203.

Foreign capital is rarely popular in overseas countries, especially those which are or have been of colonial status. This arises partly because of feelings of dependence and exploitation and also upon the past pattern of private investment in these countries which concentrated almost entirely upon primary production and extractive industries for export, rather than upon industrial development for a domestic market. This pattern, very typical of the nineteenth century, reflected the poverty of the local domestic market as opposed to the vigorously expanding markets for primary products and raw materials in the industrialized countries. Private investment, after all, is a reflection of market demand, and this explains why so much of it prefers to be reinvested in remunerative enterprises in developed countries. Direct investment from the United States has shown a marked preference for Canada and Western Europe and it should be noted that much of her heavy investment in developing lands, since the Second World War, has been in the oil industry.

It is surprising that so many developing countries, instead of extending inducements to private capital, create deterrents which frighten it away. Restrictions on transfer of profits or of capital, discriminatory taxation, exclusion from particular fields of investment, rules whereby a set (and often very high) proportion of local workers must be employed, immigration and import license restrictions, the fear of arbitrary and ill-recompensed nationalization are all very real difficulties imposed by various countries and deterring the would-be foreign investor. Many developing countries are particularly sensitive to receiving aid with strings, and hypersensitive to anything resembling foreign interference; thus much of the capital supplied may not be used efficiently. Increasingly development projects are carefully vetted before international organizations lend capital, but it is still rare for the actual spending of the money to be overseen or controlled. Direct investment, whereby a foreign firm invests directly in its own subsidiary in a foreign country, is not likely to be misused or wasted, for such investment issues from impartial examinations of commercial possibilities and not from any national or political considerations. A form of aid becoming increasingly fashionable is in tied loans, whereby countries or consortia offer the capital, and often arrange for the construction of distinct large-scale projects – such as a steel mill or a nuclear power station. Such projects are spectacular and can stand as monuments to the foreign power; the more numerous but less spectacular projects lacking glamour are often more difficult to finance and this may become increasingly so as the demand for capital continues to expand.

The total foreign aid needed for India's fifth plan (1975–9) was about £2500 million over the five years. In the next few years, as more countries put development plans into effect, the total foreign capital needed will surpass this great sum many times. Countries and projects will be competing for a scarce resource and inducements rather than deterrents will be necessary, particularly where capital is needed for manufacturing industry. Whereas capital flows moderately well into mining and plantations and to some degree into utilities such as power, and port facilities, it tends initially to shun manufacturing, for here difficulties and risks may be greatest. This situation was noticeable in Egypt after the First World War; much foreign capital was available for financing commerce, land companies and mortgage banks, but early Egyptian industry was less attractive and mainly had to be self-supporting. A big step forward was taken in 1920 with the establishment of the Misr Bank, one of its aims being to float Egyptian companies and to create a body of Egyptian shareholders. The capital and staff of this bank were entirely Egyptian and they promoted eight companies in the following ten years; several, however, having initial capital of only £10,000 or less. The difficulty of forming and attracting sufficient capital was a principal reason for the slow and halting early growth of manufacturing in Egypt, and the conditions then pertaining there are being faced today by other countries which have reached a similar phase of development.

The scarcity of capital, the great demand for it and the risks it must face combine to bring about high rates of interest which have come to be accepted by developing countries, but can be a heavy burden where large investments are involved. The prevalence of high interest rates, however, does help to attract capital from both internal and external sources and also induces the borrower to use available resources wisely. Whereas capital is dear, labour is usually cheap in under-developed lands and an interesting problem lies in the relative uses of the two resources. All too often, advising experts have sought technical efficiency by heavy investment in labour-saving machinery, whereas economic efficiency might suggest a far greater 'homespun' element using a greater amount of labour with a more restrained use of capital. This will be discussed in more detail in Chapter 8, here we may merely underline a further difference between industrialized and developing economies, that, what is both technically and economically efficient in the one, where rates of interest are low and cost of labour high, may not apply in the other where reverse conditions pertain.

The multinational firm

Since the Second World War the large international company
(multinational) has become a predominant form of unit (both in
the primary and secondary sectors) within the world productive
system. Great enterprises of this kind exhibit a concentration and
centralization of capital and expertise on an enormous scale and
through their world-wide operations work towards monopolies
over many key sectors of production. The multinationals' activities
in developing countries account for one third of the world's
foreign investment. It is expected that by 1988 they will control 41
per cent of the world total output. Their overwhelming role in
international trade can be appreciated from the fact that 300
United States' firms with 5200 foreign subsidiaries now account for
28 per cent of world exports.[6] The size and economic power of a
number of multinational firms dwarf those of many small states
with whom they may deal. In such states they may be the major
employers of labour and the bulwark of the economy and are thus
in a powerful position *vis-à-vis* the government. Policies that are
good for the international company are not necessarily best for a
country struggling to develop, and it is over these aspects that
countries of the Third World have been arguing and wrangling at
successive UNCTAD (United Nations Conference on Trade and
Development) conferences, finally coming to some measure of
agreement at the end of 1979 on a voluntary code of conduct
regarding technology transfer and the curbing of the excesses of
Western multinationals.

The establishment of international companies in developing
countries can offer many benefits. The companies facilitate investment of private savings into the developing countries and act as
vehicles for furthering exports into them and for importing raw
material from them. The foreign company, in addition to capital,
brings in management and technical expertise. Factories, plantations,
utilities are run efficiently and help to train local labour, technicians
and management. Some of the companies have educational and
training programmes for this purpose. They contribute taxes to the
government and engender spin-off effects to other local enterprises.
All this is beneficial and desirable. Practice, however, has made
apparent many disadvantages. All too often investment by multinationals is dominant in developing countries' economies, especially
in relation to the modern sector. Thanks to their monopoly
position, their operations may reduce competitive forces in the

market and by their hold of production facilities, may nullify protective policies for local home industries. Many of the industrial plants they introduce are aimed at the home market only, and consequently they may be of small-scale and high-cost producers. Even where prices might be competitive, the parent company can prevent them from entering export markets to compete with their other establishments. Production under licence may also restrict the licencee to the home market. Other practices disliked by developing countries are the remitting of profits to the parent company (a claim on foreign exchange) rather than reinvesting them in the host country, and the forming of cartels by restricting prices. It is also in the transfer of technology that difficulties have arisen.

Technology has been called the 'glue of development', the cardinal means ·of achieving greater industrialization and job creation. Developing countries can afford practically nothing for research into new processes and products; this is left to the advanced countries (which may spend as much as 2.5 per cent of their GNP on it) and means that over 90 per cent of patents are taken out by the West. The multinationals possess the bulk of this vast technological know-how and guard it very jealously. Patents may be registered abroad but they are not used, and recipient countries may not re-export technology because it might result in the international companies competing with their own technology in a third country.

Multinationals are often blamed for introducing technologies that are advanced and capital-intensive, thereby ignoring the local situation in the poor countries where there is a mass of cheap labour. The smaller numbers employed are paid wages above local levels which upsets local social patterns and tends to create a new group of elite workers. These measures and the constant awareness that company policies, dictated from distant countries and with profit-seeking motives, might have serious repercussions on local social and economic conditions, make the problem of the multi-national company particularly severe.

Markets and balanced growth

All discussion, investigation and planning of industrial development necessarily revolves around the potential market. To succeed, industry must sell its wares, either at home or abroad. A feature common to all the under-developed lands is the smallness of the home market. This is the chief obstacle to economic development and reflects a number of factors, but mainly the low purchasing power of the bulk of the population. The national income of the Sudan, for example, has been estimated at about £2000 million per annum or about £120 per head of the population. There is considerable maldistribution of this national income and the mass of the population receives much less than £120 per head per annum. Most of it is spent on basic essentials, particularly food and such items as kerosene, tobacco, cotton cloth (according to the *Yearbook of Labour Statistics*, samples from developing countries suggest that between 60 and 65 per cent of expenditure is on food, compared with 41 per cent in developed countries). Inevitably demands are inelastic at such low real-income levels and there is virtually no effective demand for the products of manufacturing industry. The small market for manufactures is usually supplied by imports and the quantity required is often very marginal to the total output of the overseas suppliers – a few days' production, in fact, being enough to satisfy this small market for the year.

This problem, of course, is a part of the vicious circle already noticed: low buying power and low capacity to save result in both a small formation of capital and small investment. The small market offers no scope for the deployment of capital and economic advances; we are reminded of Adam Smith's thesis that 'the division of labour is limited by the extent of the market'. It is noticeable that even big concerns established in developing countries do not confine their activities to one market; they generally extend their activities into a number of widely different undertakings. An example is the United Africa Company whose undertakings in West Africa prior to redeployment in the 1960s were concerned with oil palm, rubber and banana plantations, with trading in cocoa, cotton, groundnuts, palm oil, hides and skins and with the operation of timber mills, a river fleet and river services.

It follows that a successful expansion of manufacturing for the home market necessarily depends upon raising productivity in a wide range of activities, for the low level of real income is a reflection of low productivity. The downward spiral of poverty embodies a chain reaction, each negative factor being the cause of the suceeding negative factor. Myrdal has pointed out that even as there can be a downward spiral, so theoretically an upward one should be possible (for example, less poverty = more food =

better health = greater productivity), and in fact if developing lands wish to leave the 'traditional' economy of Rostow to attempt the 'take-off' they must make the sacrifices necessary to reverse the direction of their spiral.[7] Opinions as to the methods of reversing the downward spiral vary, but the fact that all sectors of an economy are interlocked and react mutually upon each other leads to the view that investment and incentives to higher production cannot be successful if applied only to one or two industrial (or agricultural) projects, but need to be applied judiciously to a wide range of activities.

If capital is invested in an industrial plant, machinery installed and workers trained, a far greater output per worker may be expected and the greater productivity should bring greater real income to them; but if in the rest of the economy there is no increase in productivity, and therefore buying power, the newly produced goods will lack a market. Much of the enhanced income of the workers will be spent on food, clothing and then a range of other goods; it would be absurd to expect them to spend their greater wealth in buying their own products. Under these conditions such an industrial activity would seem doomed, for the output of any single industry cannot create its own demand. But if simultaneous investment is made in a wide range of carefully selected agricultural projects, utilities and manufactures, the dissipation of the enhanced productivity and real wealth can make an impact, and a wider market is achieved. This theory is often referred to as that of 'balanced growth' and rests upon the well-known fact of the interrelation of activities, whereby the workers in each, now working productively, play their part in consuming goods from the other expanding enterprises.[8] Thus productivity increases and markets can begin to expand and more capital is both formed and attracted.

The two main problems that are appearing as this theory is being put into practice are those of co-ordination (for massive interdependence is the essence of the exercise) and the length of time, perhaps two to three decades, necessary for momentum to be built up for the 'take-off'.[9] An alternative path by 'unbalanced growth' has been propounded by Professor Hirschman. He bases his theory upon the varying degrees of complementarity between particular groups of industries.[10] The balanced growth theory aims at pushing forward on all fronts, in effect assuming that complementarities are equal. Hirschman suggests a concentration upon those industries where interdependence is most marked. He feels that dynamic development may be more rapid if some groups of industries become pace-setters for others.

It must not be thought that these theories apply solely to industrial establishments, but to all sections of the economy including public utilities, upon which many developing industries will depend, and especially upon agriculture. Although this book lays stress upon industrial development, the complementary position of developing agriculture must always be kept in mind. Improvements in agriculture necessarily should go hand in hand with industrial expansion, as has been shown in the history of the more advanced countries. India's first Five Year Plan led to an increase in the national income of 18 per cent, most of this being due to greater investment in and productivity from agriculture. In the decade 1951–61 industrial production in India grew by 120 per cent but her vast agricultural output grew also by 40 per cent, and during this period 20 million acres more land came under irrigation. Thus investment in agriculture – in irrigation, fertilizers, plant breeding, etc., also occasionally associated with land reform (as in Taiwan, Egypt and Syria) – is generally to be expected as development gets under way. There are of course some developing countries where land is plentiful but inadequately used and where agricultural developments should in any case be paramount over the development of an industrial sector.

Planned investment in agriculture and manufacturing industry rests upon two things: first the outlook, adaptability and desire to advance on the part of the people and therefore their acceptance of, and co-operation in, the inevitable changes, and second the presence of the very necessary utilities and services upon which manufacturing industries rely – such facilities as transport, electricity, water, banking and insurance. These features of an economy, both human and material, usually develop slowly and eventually create a springboard from which an economy can take off. Today, when time is limited, the development of utilities and education and training of the people – precondition factors – are built into general development plans and may absorb the bulk of investment in early years and apparently give little return. These conditions differ considerably from those of the advanced countries; they require close and detailed planning and co-ordination and have necessarily become undertaken by governments.

For purposes of simplicity industrial development for the home market has been isolated and considered, but it must be realized that with the majority of present developing countries, even with aims of balanced growth and selected investment injections, the home market although enlarging will be relatively small and cannot be expected to grow very rapidly in the early stages. One reason here is that government will deflect much of the early fruits of development from the people in the interests of reinvestment and the furthering of development, consequently with discipline and austerity their increase in purchasing power will be controlled. Thus it is possible to foresee a sated home market, the growth of manufacturing industry retarded and establishments remaining stunted, denied economies of scale and cheaper production. One answer to this would seem to be a vigorous search for export markets. In finding and developing such a market many difficulties have to be overcome. Much depends upon the nature of resources available and the character of the growing industrial production, for the world market for some goods, such as industrial equipment, electrical goods and vehicles, expands steadily, but for other goods, such as railway equipment, textiles and clothing, it grows much more slowly and these goods are much more difficult to sell by newcomers to the market. One advantage these countries are likely to have is low cost of production stemming principally from low wages. If wages are low enough and the goods otherwise satisfactory, export markets may be obtained as Japan, Taiwan and Hong Kong have shown.

The foregoing may be examined from a different viewpoint if we think in terms of food and population. As was pointed out in Chapter 1, the employment of more and more people in secondary and tertiary activities does not produce more food but may increase the demand relative to the supply. In countries where population is in excess of developed agricultural resources, it is imperative to export manufactures surplus to the home market if full employment is to be both attained and retained, and food and raw materials imported. This is the familiar situation of Britain and Japan but it is also true of Nigeria and Egypt, and is now becoming true of many other developing countries if they do not increase the productivity of their agricultural sectors.

The position of governments: the need for planning

Although it is not true that all the present advanced countries developed mainly as a result of private initiative, certainly the richest countries have done so. Their governments played only indirect roles in the unexpected, unpredictable, pioneer development of their economies. It may well be that in the pioneer period of innovation *laissez faire* was the only sensible policy. These economies developed slowly and almost by trial and error. Japan and Russia provide examples of governmental interest in, and furthering of, economic development, but here the economic wellbeing of their population was secondary to increasing the power of the state. The situation in the post-war world is much changed. Policies of economic growth to combat poverty and ignorance are accepted as prime objectives by many governments of developing countries. With a conscience awake in the advanced countries and a growing awareness of their poverty and lack of opportunity among the developing countries and with the mounting rate of population increase, it has come to be regarded by all that the swiftest way to economic development is necessarily by means of definite economic planning: a duty to be performed by the state.

Not only in the preparation of a plan, but also in its initial carrying out, it has come to be recognized that the government has to take over many of the roles and functions that are within the realm of private business in developed countries. For example, many necessary early investments are unlikely to be profitable for a considerable period – it is in fact necessary to create many facilities to provide external economies for industries yet to be attracted. Had such investments been profitable, private entrepreneurs would already have made them; as it is they are typical and essential measures of the precondition period. Thus we find the state setting out to do, as it were artificially in a short period, what has come to be regarded almost as natural growth over a long period in the advanced countries.

The plans are aimed at increasing a country's productive powers and attracting and forming the necessary capital for increased investment. A central authority is needed to determine total capital needs and to allocate proportions to various projects, to determine the order or priority of undertakings, whereby there is the early creation of facilities for external economies to further and make remunerative succeeding projects, to sustain and develop agriculture, to educate and train the labour force, to inculcate among the population the acceptance of change, of new ideas and methods and to foster the will and determination to make the sacrifices necessary for ultimate success. The new role of governments in under-developed lands and the preparation and publicizing of plans sometimes creates certain misconceptions. Outside the iron curtain, private investment and enterprise still has a large and, as economies move forward, a growing part to play. Nor must rigidity be considered synonymous with planning, for frequently the plan is but a series of guide posts to help departments and sections of the economy to travel the shortest road to the desired destination.

7 Environmental and human problems

Discussion of world development and under-development invariably is in the context of national units, since statistical data are available on a national basis over much of the world. In a sense this is a generalization and a simplification, in that within any country some regions will be developing more rapidly than others, which may even be stagnating (northern and southern Italy come to mind, or even south and mid Wales). Myrdal has pointed out that as a general rule the poorer the country the greater the regional inequalities, for poor countries can spend little on public utilities, school and medical services and most parts of such countries remain backward, contrasting greatly with the few developed areas, such as near the ports where disadvantages to development are less severe. In short, centre–periphery patterns develop. It is probably true to say that economists are more interested at the national level than are geographers, who are much more concerned with analysing and explaining local differentiation and the spatial pattern of development and under-development. It is at, what might be termed, the regional level that the role played by environment in association with economic, social and political factors is most readily discernible, and at this level economic geographers are finding a wide and fruitful field for investigation and analysis. At national level, because of the very diversity of the component parts of most countries, the weight of environmental factors is more difficult to isolate and assess. Such factors include size, position and degree of accessibility to major trade routes, climate, vegetation, topography and natural resources.

Geographical size of a country is not of great significance in itself, but in relation to population size, may have a bearing upon the size of the market. There is, of course, no correlation between size of country and size of population and a wide range of variations may be discerned. It is probable, however, that the larger a country, the greater the amount and diversity of its endowment of natural resources, the greater the range of its climates and variations of topography, land and water and, consequently, the greater the potential for development and the support of a large population. These are, however, only possibilities and we have seen that development depends upon much more than resource endowment. A country of large size, however, has certain economic advantages over smaller countries that stem essentially from economies of scale. Costs of administration, defence, communications and basic utilities do not increase pro- portionately with size and generally bear more heavily upon the small country. On the other hand, small countries having smaller and more closely-knit populations possess greater flexibility and adaptability for social changes concomitant with advancing technology and economic growth.

Climate and man

Climate is one of the most outstanding geographical factors bearing upon economic development. The influence of climate on man is, of course, all-pervasive: it is the predominant factor influencing the growth and distribution of plants; together with vegetation it strongly influences soil characteristics; it plays a part in the moulding of the surface features of the landscape. On man himself climate has both physiological and psychological effects, and influences pests and diseases that prey upon him. From the point of view of large-scale human settlement, the three negative climatic zones are the polar, tropical desert and the high mountain (where terrain, too, plays a major part). Here the rigour and severity of climate demonstrate an omnipotence over the landscape that is unlikely ever to be challenged on any great scale by man. The only economic activities here are local and specialized, such as operating oil wells and mineral concessions; natural circumstances inhibit settlement and economic development. The distribution of man over the globe is remarkably uneven (Figure 2, page 36), but the majority of mankind is to be found in two climatic belts: the temperate cyclonic and the tropical monsoon. The warm humid climates of the tropical monsoon areas are conducive to great fertility of both vegetation and humans, but it is in the more stimulating cooler and variable climate of the temperate cyclonic zone that the greatest economic development has taken place. The bulk of the under-developed countries lie in tropical latitudes and a number of others are in cold climates.

Possible relationships between climate and man, as manifest in his works and the progress of civilization, have interested numerous scientists and evoked a considerable literature. It is possible that the biologists' theory that a combination of certain conditions produce the finest stocks of plant and animal life can also be applied to human beings. Ellsworth Huntington has stressed the importance of climate in this connection. relating the past movement of leadership of the civilized world to past changes in climate.[1] His approach may err in being too enthusiastically deterministic, and a number of his arguments have since been refuted. It seems likely that changing leadership of the civilized world, reflecting successive stages in the upward movement of civilization, has resulted from man's growing means of ameliorating the effects of climate and weather by clothing, housing and firing. This has permitted a gradual shift to cooler, variable and more stimulating areas where the greatest mental and physical vigour is possible. Markham has postulated that the ideal climate, where men can work hardest and with the greatest efficiency, is where the daily temperature is between 15° and 21°C (60° and 70°F) with a moderate humidity (for instance, 40–70 per cent).[2] Dependent upon the amount and nature of clothing worn these constitute ideal indoor (or factory) conditions. Outdoor ideals are harder to assess owing to greater air movement and usually brisker activities, but in general the same band of temperature and humidity seems acceptable.

It follows that annual average temperatures of 21°C or slightly greater were conducive to the rise of early civilizations; the tendency to move northwards came with developments in spinning and the weaving of clothing and the provisions of means of heating by such inventions as the hypocaust, fireplace and chimney. Upper Egypt, Sumeria, India, Babylon and Assyria may be related to the 21°C annual isotherm. Greece and Rome show the first major move from it with the growing knowledge of house heating. After the fifteenth century, improvements in housing materials and heating methods, appliances and fuels brought about a shift of emphasis northwards and to the coal-possessing countries. There, man's energy was no longer expended in surviving the winter cold; the mitigation of winter climate permitted civilization in a stimulating cool winter region, allowed indoor activities and brought coal to prominence. From a source of fuel coal also came to be a source of power and lifted Western civilization far ahead of its predecessors, until Europe and the white man assumed mastery over all the continents. It will be noticed that early civilization did not move to hotter, wetter zones; man has always found it easier to warm and dry air than to cool it, and hotter, wetter climates are far less conducive to mental and physical energy and activity.

The conditions affecting man's efficiency in the tropics stem mainly from the heat and moisture. The human body maintains a constant body temperature of about 37°C (98°F). In health there is little variation from this figure and this is obtained by a physiological mechanism which maintains a balance between heat production and heat loss through the blood circulation, respiration, and secretion by sweat glands. Comfort is obtained at relatively high temperatures by an acceleration in the loss of body heat. Such heat is lost by radiation, conduction and evaporaton; the rate and mode being influenced by temperature, humidity and velocity of the air and by the individual's activity. Dry heat may be resisted at very high temperatures – blast-furnace men work in temperatures approaching boiling point – mainly by surface evaporation via the sweat glands. Moist heat presents a more serious set of problems, for under hot, moist conditions loss of heat by the customary mechanisms is far more difficult. Hot moist air cannot take up much more moisture yet the heat makes the body perspire readily. If body heat is not dissipated, lethargy, weakness, spells of dizziness and a sense of depression characterize the onset of heatstroke, conditions reached when the wet bulb temperature passes 29°C (85°F). On the other hand, warm but very dry air is generally considered less comfortable and less healthy than air of moderate humidity, for dry air irritates the mucous membranes of throat and nose, favours respiratory disorders and leads to sleeplessness and nervous irritability.

It is generally held that the monotony of weather in parts of the tropics is responsible for much ill-health and depression, in that under such conditions the body's adaptability to change is reduced so that changes considered small in a variable climate have serious effects. Colds and chills are common in the tropics and the mortality rate from pneumonia is high. Knowledge of long-term effects of tropical climate is still inadequate and much of the present body of knowledge has been accumulated by studying climatic effects on the white man in the tropics rather than on the indigenous peoples. Yet, broadly it seems that humans, whatever the colour of their skins, are made the same way and react similarly to climatic stimuli. The black man's skin absorbs more solar heat than the white man's, but in compensation he has more sweat glands and he is also better protected against any damaging action of ultra-violet rays. In all humans it is thought that the reactions to warm conditions – a slight lowering of blood pressure from the suffusion of the capillaries and reduction of the blood viscosity ('the tropics thin one's blood') – while allowing of greater sweat volume, generally reduce resistance to infection and pave the way for digestive and gastric disorders.

Although it is possible by means of attention to clothing, diet, exercise and hygiene to keep in good health in warm climates, the physical disadvantages of such climates compared with the 'ideal' cooler and more variable climates remain. There is substantial evidence of the poor productivity of much tropical labour owing to diseases and ill-health, particularly intestinal disorders and worm diseases which debilitate the body and lower output, but additionally tropical climates do not favour muscular activity which generates much body heat and discomfort and induces a disinclination to work. Estate records and observation suggest that agricultural workers in the tropics put in only twenty to thirty hours' work a week, and most of this in the early morning and in the cool of the evening. It has been estimated that, other things being equal, dockers in the Queensland port of Townsville accomplish 5–10 per cent less work than dockers at Brisbane, nine degrees to the south, and they do about 11 per cent more work in the cool season than in the hot. Long periods of sustained physical labour cannot be expected. One is led to the conclusion that labour in the tropics is unlikely to be as efficient as in temperate areas and that it will be more costly to maintain it at any reasonable level of efficiency.

Economic development in lower latitudes, however, demands more than mere physical labour and it is significant that there is a strong body of opinion that the warm wet climates are also inimical to sustained mental work. An investigation in Queensland before the Second World War drew attention to great fatigue and inertia experienced among professional people and clerks. Among psychological disturbances related to tropical climate, a study group of the American Council on Foreign Relations cited in particular loss of mental iniative and the general need for higher concentration to perform a given task.[3] Part of the adaption to warmer and moister climatic conditions is a more leisurely tempo of life and perhaps a greater tinge of fatalism, the *mañana* outlook so exasperating to the Occidental, who has created a civilization in which activity and making provision for the future hold a high place and derive from the demands imposed by cold winters. Tropical climates give less urgency and less value to these habits and the enthusiasm for planning, but procrastination in execution, is well known. Chaudhuri in his *A Passage to England*, underlines this aspect:

The old British official in his sola topee could not escape the heat, and by bringing about a psychological adaptation it endowed him with a sense of the possible which was almost the same as wisdom. But in the artificial cool of the air-conditioned room the Indian and his Occidental friends alike acquire the habit of reckoning without the host.... For the Indian minister or official the mere discussion of his plans with an Occidental in an air-conditioned room is equivalent to execution.... In India the mirages of the mind are produced by coolness.[4]

It is true that the last twenty years have seen great advances in air-conditioning so that, for example, Lancashire air conditions may be simulated in textile mills elsewhere, but these aids are not for the masses; it is a very localized control of climate and ceases on the doorstep. It is an aid to efficiency under warm conditions, especially in factories, but should not be over-rated.

Climate and transport

Accessibility and adequate transport facilities are inherent needs of developing industries. Means of transport in most tropical countries are usually limited in scope and expensive in operation. While it is true that present limited transport nets primarily reflect existing low levels of development, environmental difficulties (and particularly those of climate) exert substantial restraining effects. The range of variation of relief and climate in the tropics is very great and here only general features, but of wide application, will be considered. In many cases, development of roads and railways has either been in response to haphazard demand generated by successful mining ventures or has in itself created conditions where large-scale production for export becomes a worthwhile proposition. Examples are the railway line from Lagos to the tin mines on the Bauchi plateau of Nigeria and the transcontinental line through the copper belt of Central Africa. The development of the beef-cattle industry in Argentina and the growth of cocoa farming in the Gold Coast owe much to the construction of the railway lines, while commercial cotton growing in Uganda and coffee production in Kenya followed the construction of the Mombasa–Kisumu railway in 1902. In that year the line carried 13,000 tons of freight and 73,000 passengers. In 1950 it dealt with 2 million tons of freight and 3 million passengers.

The result, clearly to be seen in tropical Africa, is the lack of a railway net, but instead the presence of a series of disconnected lines striking inland from the ports. A growing road system now feeds and supplements these lines until a rudimentary transport net appears, but the mesh is remarkably coarse when judged by standards of developed countries. In tropical Africa there are 15,500 miles of railway serving an area of over 5 million square miles. In Britain before recent reductions 12,000 miles of railway served 88,000 square miles. Appreciable areas, even with known resources, may remain undeveloped owing to inaccessibility, where the cost of providing transport facilities is in excess of the likely return, as is the case with a number of known mineral deposits in the Brazilian interior. One reason for this lies in the very great size of some of the territories and the great distances involved, often necessitating the crossing of large unproductive areas. The copper belt of Zambia has been described as 'an industrialized oasis in a desert of unproductiveness', for at least 500 miles around there is relatively little settlement or even agriculture.[5] Most of the refined ore has had to travel a single-track line for 1450 miles to Beira in Mozambique (practically the distance from Paris to Moscow). The trade is ill balanced, return freight being far less than outgoing ores and tobacco. The cost of constructing railways over great distances, such as to the African copper belt, is heavy – sometimes even ballast has to be brought great distances – while the frequent use of wood for fuel reduces efficiency and raises operating costs. Consequently today railways are less favoured for opening up new territories. Sixty or seventy years ago there were few roads and new railways had a monopoly of transport stimulation of economic development. Today this is not so and post-war development, such as the southern ('groundnut') lines in Tanzania and the Maiduguri extension in Nigeria, have proved disappointing.[6] Lorry transport is more versatile and rarely more expensive.

Locomotives of the East African railways have to operate in a temperature range of 2°–38°C (35°–100°F), at altitudes ranging from sea-level to over 9000 feet, in tropical rainstorms and dusty semi-desert conditions, nevertheless it is roads that suffer most from tropical weather. The majority of roads in monsoon Asia, Africa and South America are unsurfaced; pot-holes, deep furrows and quagmires come with the rainy season, embankments and bridges on railway tracks may be washed away, while in the dry season corrugations on the surface and choking dust render all movement by road unpleasant and may even render the supply of water for locomotives difficult. The provision of bitumen-surfaced all-weather roads is costly and therefore slow; in Zambia even dirt roads cost £3000 per mile to construct. On the credit side, waterways with which many tropical countries are endowed must be recognized, they persist in many places traditionally as slow but relatively cheap media of movement and transport. However, they too offer obstacles and difficulties such as rapids and falls, seasonal changes of volume affecting both depth and current velocity, and for full development and integration into national transport nets considerable expenditure on dredging, bypasses to rapids, flood control, wharf and handling facilities is to be expected. In short the provision of transport facilities on a considerable scale is recognized as a prerequisite of economic development, and in tropical areas costs and difficulties involved will be far heavier than in developed countries, in large measure due to limitations and obstacles of the environment.

Utilities and services

The provision of infrastructure in the form of public utilities and services in countries aspiring to industry is fundamental and costly. Often in the past these have been painstakingly built up over a long period, but now a swifter pace is becoming essential. Not only are roads, railways, port facilities, telephones and power and water supplies needed, but also law and order, the provision of hospitals and health measures, and education. Investment in these measures for a long period is likely to exceed investment in manufacturing. The capital:output ratio is very high in such an investment, for initially the return is often low; one is putting one's faith and money in future usefulness (as in the case of the Kenya–Uganda railway quoted on p. 120). Industries cannot develop without public utilities and services, and although private capital has been available for these relatively 'safe' investments, often having monopolist attributes, increasingly governments must pay a large share in their finance. This has always been so: in the United States, for example, the Erie Canal was constructed by the New York State legislature, the TVA, a major power producer, was a Federal project, and even the great transcontinental railway nets received Federal subsidy in the guise of land grants. There is no short cut to the creation of these foundations which can absorb vast amounts of development capital. 42 per cent of India's planned expenditure under her first four Five Year Plans was allocated to power, transport and education, while only 20 per cent was allocated to industry and mining.

Development of utilities can never be countrywide and initially in a developing country may well be very limited in spatial distribution. The limitations thus imposed upon location of industrial establishments tend to reinforce a natural gregariousness of many industries. The development of industrial complexes in richer countries is traceable to a number of factors offering locational advantages to the component establishments. Generally the more industries that are located in a given area, the greater the external economies that become possible. Many industries are closely related, using similar raw materials or component parts, others may make the component parts. For example, a furniture-making industrial area is likely to include factories making springs, latex rubber, upholstery fabrics, castors, glue and resins as well as those making furniture. Cardboard container and wrapper factories, and then printing establishments may be attracted to sites near paper mills. Examples in the engineering industry are even greater. Light industries attach themselves where labour and markets are available. In short, natural centripetal tendency may be considerably reinforced if lack of utilities discourages location elsewhere.

In many densely populated developing countries this tendency may conflict with offical ideas. A widespread dissemination of industrial establishments might seem a more direct and healthier method of combating centre–periphery tendencies and of relieving rural under-employment: a physical spread of manufacture rather than a fiscal spread of its rewards. It might be suggested that here lie paths of industrial development differing from those of the developed lands but eminently applicable to meeting the major problems of developing countries. In fact, this overall development within a country is impossible if normal locational forces are allowed free play. Latitude in locational decisions is much restricted, not merely by limitation of utilities and services but in many cases by the character and availability of raw materials. An iron and steel plant within Basilicata (Lucania), south Italy, might bring substantial benefit to the impoverished rural population, but such a situation, remote from the heavy and bulky raw materials, fuel and markets, is doubtful if iron and steel are to be produced at competitive prices. Careful cost studies are essential in deciding the locations of such heavy basic industries; high costs here, emanating from faulty or arbitrary location, can leave an impress on the whole economy. An essential requirement in the developing countries whose populations have limited purchasing power is that production costs and selling price should be low, thus normal locational forces will have to be respected. A conjunction of circumstances suggests that, irrespective of non-economic or social ideals, a pattern of regional specialization will inevitably appear as secondary activities increase. Certain manufactures orientated to market and but loosely tied by raw material needs may show a countrywide distribution. Such establishments are likely to be small, serving only a limited and local market. All in all, a close relationship to existing major urban centres is to be expected (where basic utilities and some manufacturing industry are already likely to be available).

Limited provision of utilities and services will be an important contributive factor to such a growth pattern as conditions in India readily show:

Any city of less than 100,000 population and many cities above this population will have totally inadequate public services. The streets are of mud and become running sewers during the monsoon. Water supply may be inadequate and polluted. Electrical services will be irregular. Delivery of inbound materials from the nearest rail junction may take days or weeks, and the assignment of outbound empties is uncertain. Mail and telegraph services will be regular, if slow, but telephone service will be most difficult. Visiting salesmen and customers may get there only with journeys of many hours on uncomfortable trains .... Their contact with competitors, customers, supplies and the market place in general will be greatly impaired.[7]

It is evident that the largest metropolitan centres in such developing lands have notable advantages that will accelerate their further growth despite policies that may favour more widely disseminated industrial growth. The growing urbanization in the Third World is a social process but is intimately related to the process of industrialization, for where capital is scarce urbanization is necessary as it maximizes the utility of capital and achieves economies of scale. It may well be that the 'megalopolis' tendency in warmer latitudes has scarcely yet begun, despite significant increase in the last decade.

There are undoubted economic and social advantages possible from increasing urbanization, but the views of those attempting to limit it by 'planning' new industry into rural and small town locations should be appreciated. There is a natural reaction against the overcrowded slum conditions and squalor to be found in every city; there is the political fear of a growing urban proletariat: the realization of inevitable social and cultural changes divorced from tradition bred of rural forebears. Above this, there is the realization that there is a limit to economies of scale in relation to economic and urban growth. Cities can become too big for economic efficiency; their arteries can become so congested that they can no longer function, and in the process, maximum discomfort, nervous strain and an artificial way of life are produced. Already the greater city areas of Bombay, Buenos Aires, Cairo, Calcutta, Mexico City, Sao Paulo, Shanghai and Seoul each contain over 10 million people.

Resource problems: raw materials

It was pointed out earlier that the economic prospects of a country cannot be gauged solely by cataloguing its known natural resources (see pages 24–6). This method may suggest potentiality as now in the case of Brazil and China, but resources in themselves are valueless unless they harmonize with a complex network of other economic and social factors. Resources are given value by the application of capital, labour and technical skills. Such application hinges upon the further factor of economic accessibility, itself dependent upon available markets, which in turn involve consideration of cost:price ratios and degrees of competition. It is certainly wrong to dismiss the resource (including energy) base as unimportant, but neither is it paramount. In the modern world, possibilities of industrialization do not hinge upon possession or non-possession of raw material resources; in any case virtually all countries in the world possess some potential or actual agricultural and mineral resources (even the sands of Arabia and the Sahara cloak rich oil deposits). The resource pattern, while not determining whether or not industry shall exist, does exert influence upon the character and intensity of any development that may occur.

In general terms the presence and proximity of iron ore and coal, from the resource point of view, facilitated the growth of great iron (and later steel) industries in Britain, Germany and the eastern United States. Britain's early start and gathering momentum soon led to the import of higher quality foreign ore; the local raw material lost much significance and this was reflected in locational readjustments of the industry. This industry is basic to modern civilization; it ramifies into a great range of constructional, transport and engineering activities and, with its growing links with chemicals and the power industries, makes possible an enormous and diverse industrial superstructure. The case of Britain also demonstrates the decreasing significance of indigenous resources once development is under way and when a growing body of capital, skill, technical knowledge, entrepreneurial experience and wide overseas markets become deployed.

Of a totally different character is the industrial pattern within Switzerland, where two-thirds of the country is mountainous; where there are no mineral resources, no coal, iron or oil, but there are sources of hydraulic energy, scenic beauty and an advantageous position astride international routeways. Switzerland is a small country; her labour force and domestic market are small and, except for a limited range of agricultural products, raw materials have to be imported. These problems are overcome by her concentration on high-quality goods for export markets, and by the application of highly skilled labour and much capital. Switzerland is denied the customary bases of heavy industry and instead concentrates on manufacturing industry. To export, however, she must overcome competition from manufactures of richer countries holding the advantages denied her: they can mass-produce standard articles for their large markets far more cheaply than Switzerland could. Consequently the Swiss find that it pays to concentrate on manufactures where precision and quality predominate, and put emphasis upon the selective rather than the mass market.

Japan has had to overcome different problems. She has a wider endowment of resources than Switzerland, possessing some coal (but unsuitable for coking purposes), limited supplies of oil, some hydraulic energy, iron ore of poor quality, some copper, sulphur and raw silk. Her manner of use of these materials has been greatly influenced by her acute population problem. Like Switzerland she must export, both in order to support her population and pay for the massive imports of raw materials needed to supplement domestic supplies. Her labour costs are far lower than those of Switzerland and other developed countries and, being associated with a high level of efficiency, permit relatively low-cost production. This has facilitated the growth of a wide industrial structure including a base of heavy industry, despite the necessity of importing coking coal, iron ore, non-ferrous metals, crude oil and other raw materials.

Unlike Switzerland, Japan provides exports for the highly competitive mass markets, but in the face of swiftly growing numbers, native skills are being turned increasingly to the 'Swiss type' of product – articles requiring little raw material but much investment of capital and skilled labour, such as in high-quality precision camera and lens manufacture.[8] Japan also combats her shortage of certain raw materials by obtaining concessions and commercial control of supplies in India and crude oil concessions beneath coastal waters in the Persian Gulf – measures which are generally impossible to poorer countries.

Not all natural resources available for transmutation into raw materials offer equal advantages to newly industrializing countries. Deposits of iron ore and coal might be considered superior to an endowment for agricultural raw materials only. The foregoing examples suggest reasons for this. Metallurgical industries being basic to a wide and comprehensive industrial superstructure have a notable advantage, and at the same time it must be recognized that there is a greater world demand for metal manufactures than for, say, textiles or boots and shoes. During the first half of the twentieth century international trade in metal manufactures increased from 31 per cent to 56 per cent of world trade in manufactures, while trade in other commodities increased far more slowly or even declined. Developing countries lacking bases for metallurgical industries must face the problem of competition among themselves for a share of a declining trade in the simple metal goods and in manufactures based on agricultural raw materials.

The future supply of raw materials

The adequacy of the supply of raw materials under conditions of increasing world industrialization presents a further problem, particularly to the poorer nations. A shortage of a range of raw materials, especially minerals (which unlike agricultural products are non-renewable), is much feared. Development and the raising of standards of living create growing demand for capital and consumer goods and thereby increase the world demand for raw materials. So far the rapid increase of raw material consumption reflects the growing wealth of the already developed countries. The United States of America, with barely 6 per cent of the world's population, already consumes about half the non-Communist world's supply of principal minerals and all but a tiny fraction of the remainder is used by other developed countries; the developing lands holding over two-thirds of the world's population use only 6 per cent of these raw materials.

The growing problem of raw material consumption was given publicity in the United States in 1952 by the report of the President's Materials Policy Commission (better known as the Paley Report). This revealed that in the last half-century the tremendous advance in the standard of living in the United States of America saw mineral consumption increase eight times, that of fuel and energy twelve times and the consumption of paper fourteen times, while the population merely doubled. Indeed the United State's appetite has become gargantuan. It is of great significance that, whereas up to forty years ago the United States produced rather more than the materials she required, by 1950 there was a 10 per cent deficit. The report suggested that the demand over the next generation would be double that consumed by the previous generation. The United States purchases more and more of these materials from world markets on an ever-increasing scale, and in addition there is a growing demand from the other developed countries experiencing fast rising standards of living. A more recent study presenting estimates of life of non-renewable resources at various rates of world consumption is given in Table 7. This was calculated by the Club of Rome in the examination of the predicament of mankind – the consequences of the exponential nature of human growth and living standards within a finite world.[9]

Our endowment of minerals is limited to what exists in the earth's crust. There is an abundance of constructional materials (stone, clay, sand and cement) and no immediate shortage of the principal chemical materials is envisaged. The two most important metals, iron and aluminium, form 5 per cent and 8 per cent of the earth's crust respectively and should last man for hundreds of years. Known resources of non-ferrous metals, valuable for alloys, coatings and conductors, however, are much smaller. However, new ore discoveries are constantly increasing known reserves, and the situation is unlikely to be as serious as the figures suggest. Technology advances rapidly and new sources of raw materials and new methods of obtaining them from diverse substances become known, while new metals and synthetic materials increasingly substitute for traditional and more expensive metals.

With the expansion of industrialization and higher living standards in the developing world the demands on the world's non-renewable raw materials and commodities will be critical for industrial growth in developing countries. Sums have been worked out to show the enormous quantities of (for example) metals that a world, developed to the level of the United States in 1970, would need to mine – seventy-five times the current annual extraction of iron ore (which would seem feasible), 100 times that of copper and 250 times that of tin (probably impossible in that they exceed all known reserves and possible discoveries). Thus we must envisage demands upon what in the long run are limited, non-renewable resources. New discoveries in more remote areas may be made,

Table 7   *Estimated years of supply of important minerals and metals*

Mineral/Metal	Years of supply of known reserves		
	at rate of consumption in 1970	at exponential growth rate	with X5 known reserves exponential rate
Aluminium	100	31	55
Chronium	420	95	154
Coal	2300	111	150
Copper	36	21	48
Crude Oil	31	20	50
Iron Ore	240	93	173
Lead	26	21	64
Tin	17	15	61
Tungsten	40	28	72
Zinc	23	18	50

Source: D. H. Meadows *et al.*, *The Limits to Growth* (London 1972). Table 4.

Figure 9   *World per capita energy consumption, 1977*

leaner ores worked, but all will be reflected in an upward spiral of costs. Europe and the United States have built up their industrial civilizations while materials of all kinds have been readily available. The wealth they have accumulated suggests that even in the future their raw material needs can be met, for they have both economic power and purchasing power, but cost to the poorer developing countries will be forced up. Faced with world-wide scarcity of industrial raw materials, a moral problem may be posed: are these resources to be allotted equitably between advanced nations and those seeking to catch up with them? If so, are the advanced nations prepared to accept that there can now be little more growth in standards of living and that, more than likely, there must be a contraction in their economies? The developing countries' requirements are likely to increase perhaps two or three times during the next twenty years, but the succeeding twenty years will see a massive increase with rising momentum, and real scarcities will arise.

Resource problems: energy

The industrial revolution that has affected only a small part of the world, but has transformed world economy, led to the consumption during the last century of half as much energy as was used during the previous eighteen and a half centuries. This suggests that in grasping the fruits of modern technology the developing peoples must increasingly equip themselves with power. We must expect the rapid growth of world energy consumption to continue and although the rate of increase of demand from developed countries may slacken, rising demand from newly industrializing lands may well cause total consumption to double every twenty to twenty-five years. Industrialization depends upon the assured supplies of energy at competitive cost and the provision of this energy in its character and amount helps to decide the nature and scope of industrial undertakings.

Problems arising from the enormously increased demand for energy when a substantial measure of development has been attained by under-developed countries have been eased during the last two decades by the successful introduction of nuclear power for the generation of electricity. That consumption of energy increases markedly as levels of living rise may be appreciated from Table 8, where it will be seen that the majority of under-developed countries use less than 300 kilogrammes (6 cwt) of coal-equivalent per head, whereas Britain uses 5 tons and the United States 11 tons per head. The potential demand for energy during the next twenty years is vast; the developed world is passing into a second industrial revolution involving petro-chemicals, synthetics, nuclear energy and automation, while the developing world is beginning in some ways to undergo the first stages that Britain passed through in the early nineteenth century.

Table 8 Per capita *energy consumption for selected countries, 1977 (kilogrammes, coal-equivalent)*

United States	11,554	Egypt	473
Canada	9,950	India	218
Sweden	6,046	Pakistan	181
United Kingdom	5,268	Ghana	157
Japan	3,679	Senegal	156
Switzerland	3,340	Kenya	152
Venezuela	2,838	Sri Lanka	106
Mexico	1,227	Burma	49
Chile	987	Uganda	48
Brazil	731	Ethiopia	27

Source: United Nations Statistical Yearbook, 1978 (New York 1979), Table 142.

One can foresee problems arising with the enormously increased demand for energy as developing countries attain substantial measures of development. The successful introduction of nuclear power for electricity generation over the last two decades can ease some of these problems but at very considerable cost. Until the OPEC states (Organization of Petroleum Exporting Countries) raised the price of oil six-fold during the 1970s, oil was regarded as a cheap and convenient source of fuel and energy for both the advanced and developing worlds. This is no longer true, and in the hunt for economy and substitution of other fuel and energy sources, the countries of the Third World are hit hard. They have far less scope for energy conservation and development progress will involve the replacement of inefficient firewood, charcoal and dried dung (the chief sources of fuel to nine-tenths of the populations of Third World countries) as living standards rise and industry develops.[10]

Coal, oil and water power

During the last three decades world coal consumption has been expanded faster than ever before, mainly due to industrial development in the USSR, China and India, where coal is available as a major source of energy, and, after 1973, to a recoil from vastly expensive oil by advanced countries. On a global scale coal reserves are plentiful although much is known to be in relatively inaccessible areas remote from population and industry and therefore costly to extract and market. Some two-thirds of world reserves lie in North America; relatively, the eastern hemisphere is poorly endowed. A shortage of certain kinds of coal (for instance, for metallurgical coking) may become apparent, and some industrial countries may find their supplies becoming scarce, for coal in its original bulky form is uneconomic to transport any distance overland. Certainly acceleration in the demand for coal may be expected as new metallurgical and by-product chemical plants increase in number and as coal begins to supplement crude oil as a source of liquid fuels.

Supplies of oil and natural gas, far more convenient and more easily transportable fuels than coal, are expected to be ample until the end of this century but thereafter to become scarcer and possibly to be supplemented by liquid fuel from oil shale and coal. Oil is of importance to the developing countries in that its distribution is more generous to them than that of coal (Latin America and the Middle East hold 75 per cent of current known reserves), it can be transported much more easily, and like coal it has a raw material as well as a fuel and power value. However, many developing countries possess no oil and the cost of oil imports to these states increased more than six-fold between 1973 and 1980 – from US$8000 million to US$51,000 million and acted as a severe brake upon economic and social progress. On the other hand oil-producing and exporting states (and not all are in OPEC) have enjoyed enormously increased revenues, enabling the speeding up of development plans and heavy investment in the industrialized world to ensure substantial returns in the next century when oil revenues become exhausted.

Coal, oil and natural gas are fossil fuels, part of the earth's store of capital and, in our life span, non-renewable. It is because of this fact that hydroelectric developments appear particularly attractive, for here the basic energy appears to be free and perpetual. What is frequently underestimated is the enormous capital cost of creating vast hydroelectrical power stations and the great reservoirs usually necessary to smooth the normal variations of a river's discharge. Further, there is the high cost of transmitting the power to the consumer over any great distance (a much less important factor in thermal-electric costs for those power stations are usually established at the market). Hydroelectricity accounts for only about 6 per cent of the world's total energy consumption, although it represents nearly two-fifths of electrical energy generated. Topography and climate are the principal factors limiting the number and size of stations but there is still a great potential yet to be realized in the world. Unfortunately its distribution is very uneven, much of it being remote from industrial and populated centres and transmission of current over great distances is far too costly. Nevertheless, possession of conditions favouring hydroelectric power development is an important industrial asset, although often acting as a supplement to the other forms and, by its relative cheapness *at the site*, attracting to it, almost irrespective of the location, certain chemical and metallurgical industries requiring vast amounts of power for relatively inexpensive end products, such as nitrogenous fertilizers, aluminium and pulp manufacture.

It is rare for any country to lack a power potential in at least one of the foregoing fields. The real problem in the cases of developing countries has often been one of imperfect geological survey and unsatisfactory location, involving prohibitive cost of extraction and utilization. Since the end of the Second World War many new oil and natural gas discoveries have been made among developing countries, notably in the Algerian Sahara, Ecuador, Libya and Nigeria. Frequently these discoveries are the fruits of many years' exploration and the expenditure of millions of pounds. The Nigerian discoveries came after twenty-one years of effort and exploration expenditure of £27 million by Shell–BP. The wells are very deep (including the deepest oil well in Africa at 14,558 feet) and many of them are situated in mangrove swamps, facts that have helped to make Nigerian oil so expensive to produce.

Nuclear power

The advent of nuclear power offers great promise to many developing countries hampered in their advance by the lack, or high cost, of their energy resources. We are still at the nursery stage in the harnessing of nuclear power and efficiency of utilization is as yet very low, but is improving rapidly as experience is gained. Because of these continual improvements it is impossible to survey performance precisely, but in Britain in the reactors that came into use during the 1960s each ton of uranium fuel did the work of nearly 20,000 tons of coal. In Britain's early nuclear stations only 0.35 per cent of the uranium was burnt; at the 1 per cent rate of utilization which seems attainable, one ton of uranium will equal 30,000 tons of coal. The theoretical limit of utilization is about 30 per cent, when one ton of uranium will do the work of 1 million tons of coal. The uranium fuel in a reactor lasts for several years and, being small in bulk and weight by comparison with coal and oil, can be transported easily about the world. No shortage of the raw materials for nuclear power seems likely for a long time to come.

All this may seem most encouraging for developing countries but a number of limitations must be examined. Nuclear power plants have a far higher capital cost than conventional thermal power stations (in Britain in 1974 about £230 per installed kilowatt against £55 per kilowatt from conventional stations) but a lower fuel cost. It follows that it is important to put the plants to maximum use and so secure the lowest cost per unit of output. Such a plant would work at full stretch to take the base load and might have a load factor, after allowing for maintenance, of about 80 per cent. If the reactor is not put to maximum use, the cost of the power generated rises rapidly. Developing countries examining possibilities of nuclear power must take into account rates of interest which they must pay on the very high capital cost; they must consider the load factor which the station can operate to (whether there will be a market for the continuously high output); and weigh up the costs of coal and/or oil procurement for cheaper conventional power stations. The thermal efficiency of these conventional power stations is also being improved, although less rapidly than rising efficiency in nuclear power stations.

With such a number of variables it is impossible to quote average costs per unit of power, but in Britain electricity from nuclear power stations is no longer dearer than that from conventional stations. However, these estimates apply to developed lands, where established alternative resources compete fiercely. In many developing countries costs of these alternative sources of energy may be higher and their cost advantage over nuclear power much less.

So far nuclear power stations have been constructed in most of the advanced countries, but already it is possible to buy complete nuclear power plants from these countries including the erection and putting into working order, and with a guaranteed supply of uranium fuel. Argentina, Brazil, India, Pakistan and Taiwan are already operating nuclear plants. It is still too early to determine how far the majority of developing countries are likely to benefit by these energy advances; it is worth remembering, however, that in the long run the fact that fossil fuels provide not merely energy but also industrial raw materials may be more decisive to prospects and future industrial status.

Human resources

In this brief survey and appraisal of resources, discussion of human resources, perhaps the most important, has been left to the end. There is now a growing awareness of the paramount place man himself holds in the process of economic development. In the long run, success or failure must depend upon the capacity and adaptability of the people in adopting new techniques and new ways of life, in the will to work and to make sacrifices, in their understanding and discipline as traditional ways are superseded and new social orders and conditions arise. These are enormous demands upon what are all too often communities of illiterate peasants. To train and transform such human resources presents the greatest of problems to newly developing countries and requires much time. The industrial and technological fruits of one or more centuries' growth in developed lands may now be imported and grasped almost immediately by developing countries. Capital may be attracted, skill and 'know-how', in limited quantities, hired or borrowed, but clearly in themselves these things alone do not spell development unless the participation of the mass of the people is included in the forward movement.

Broadly we may discern three kinds of personnel necessary in commercial undertakings; the largest component being the workers and operatives themselves, then the smaller clerical, administrative and executive group, and finally the far smaller body of entrepreneurs – those who are prepared to accept risks and to initiate and translate projects from paper to actuality. Under-developed lands by definition have practically no force of industrially skilled labour available for new development projects. The mass of their peoples are untutored peasants frequently still in loose feudal relationships with the large landowners, conservative in their outlook, their ways moulded by tradition and the rhythm of the agricultural seasons. The absorption of these people into totally different and alien work and ways of life inevitably presents enormous problems and is often attended by unrest and unease at far-reaching social changes. The experiences of African workers in the developing industrial society of the town of Jinja in Uganda have been described as follows:

> The African . . . has to carry out operations which are unfamiliar, on new materials and with new implements, in an unaccustomed environment in which timing and attention to detail have a previously undreamed of importance. He is expected to work for long stretches every day, at a time and place determined by others, to keep working all the time, and to associate during the working day with Europeans, Asians and Africans of other tribes whose behaviour bewilders and often antagonises him. He comes to regard his European and Asian superior as impatient, over-critical and unjust. They are in an incomprehensible hurry to complete every task.[11]

The training and building up of an efficient and reliable industrial labour force will be costly both in time and money. One of the greatest hindrances is the high degree of illiteracy; for example, 79 per cent of the Pakistani and 63 per cent of the Iranian population are illiterate. These populations however, often prove very adaptable and frequently are surprisingly quick at mastering mechanical operations. The lack of experience of industrial occupation is often demonstrated in a resistance to the tempo of factory work, the regular hours and stereotyped regime, by high rates of absenteeism and a large labour turnover. This problem is least in cities where there may be acute competition for work, but is very real in smaller towns and country districts. It is also real in under-populated countries where the urge is rather to earn enough for particular targets – taxes, bride price for example – and then return to the farm. This is both costly and discouraging to the diversity of training and apprenticeship schemes on which industrial development leans. Farming routines and factory routines are very different and an efficient labour force for the one is likely to prove far less efficient in the other. A mixture of the two seems incompatible: the industrial labour force must be divorced from the land, a requirement undoubtedly aided by the concomitant growth of urbanism bringing in its wake social and psychological changes.

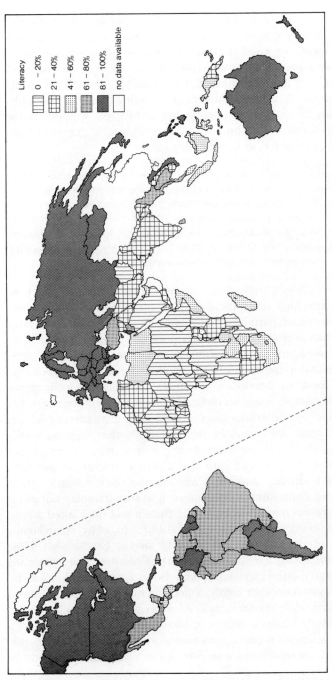

Figure 10   *World levels of literacy, 1975*

It must be recognised that the great populations of so many of the developing countries while in a negative sense a drag upon capital formation also have positive value, for the abundant labour is a major resource provided that it can be trained and used effectively. Much expenditure is necessary to create the varied facilities for training but much of this training of the rank and file, especially in light consumer goods industries, will be in the factories themselves. This suggests a considerable period of high-cost production for, as Lewis points out:

If a factory is opened to weave cotton cloth, the management has to begin by training the workers in this operation. This training takes up to six months, before they are proficient; worse still, they can be trained only by using up yarn in the process of weaving and the material wasted in this way is a heavy item of expense – even more so than their wages. This cost does not arise if a new factory is opened in an already established centre, since the management can hire its workers already trained.[12]

In many newly industrializing countries these costs may be particularly high since there may be no more than one or two factories in each particular trade and with absenteesim and a large labour turnover the creation of a pool of trained labour may be much prolonged. Considerations such as this should bring some qualification to the term 'cheap', applied almost universally to the labour force of developing countries. Wages may well appear cheap in comparison with those paid in developed countries, but the efficiency and productivity of the labour are generally far less for an appreciable time. In the mid 1950s the Egyptian textile industry, then well established, required sixteen operators per 1000 spindles compared with five and four operatives per 1000 spindles in Britain and the United States. Nevertheless simple operations controlling a machine such as that stamping out metal buttons reveal outputs as high as in Britain and the United States. The danger may well be that plentiful and apparently cheap labour may be used wastefully, but the real answer here is that to be competitive and flourish, manufacturing industry must strive for ever greater efficiency. Japan and Hong Kong have shown the capability of Asians for highly skilled and highly efficient industrial production while maintaining low levels of labour costs.

Success in business hinges upon the smooth organization of a host of component parts, both human and material. In developed countries entrepreneurs can rely upon a considerable body of managerial ability, but in under-developed countries opportunities for acquiring such experience are rare and there is a dearth of competent men who possess both the necessary technical and commercial knowledge and the ability to organize labour and maintain efficient production. There are also acute shortages of such very necessary personnel as clerks and accountants, a reflection of the high levels of illiteracy. This lack of managerial talent coupled with administrative and clerical scarcity and shortage of capital has had the effect of furthering small-scale production in which such limitations press less severely. Much depends upon census definitions of 'industrial establishments' which vary considerably, but we find that in 1939 some 74 per cent of Argentina's industrial establishments each employed no more than five workers, and the average number of employees in all establishments in 1944 was only sixteen; in Colombia in 1942 it was only eight and in Egypt in 1964 it was only three. China's recent emphasis upon the value and high place of small-scale enterprises is a notable example of making a virtue out of necessity.

Such small enterprises are of workshop rather than factory character which suggests a lack of modern low-cost methods of production and distribution, for economies of scale are lacking and the operations are labour-intensive rather than capital-intensive. Industrial progress in developing countries is characterized by the growth of such plants; they play an important part in the economy but, as will be discussed on pages 153–4, cannot in themselves constitute the full industrialization that is required.

In developed countries a distinctive feature of growth has been entrepreneurship: the emergence of a relatively small body of persons quick to discern opportunities and willing to promote and advance industrial undertakings despite the attendant risks. Under-developed countries lack such people since they can provide no nursery of the highly organized business society of the developed world. The need for such a body of experienced entrepreneurs is all-important to these countries if a wide front of industry and manufacturing is to be created and a responsible middle class is to develop. The alternative is a passive acceptance of government measures and the lack of flexibility and individuality: an open door to bureaucracy. Knowledge and experience wedded to initiative are the basic deficiences today in developing lands, rather than a dearth of capital which has received undue attention from economists. As we have seen, deficiencies of capital can be much more readily supplied from external sources, but knowledge and experience can be lent only in more limited quantities and indigenous supplies will take years to develop.

The use of foreign knowledge as well as foreign capital is a characteristic of the spread of industrialization; this has applied in the past to the developed countries just as much as nowadays to those newly developing. With the desire for speedy industrial development and because of the increasingly complex make-up of modern industry this need for foreign advisers, technologists, managers, as well as capital, is expanding to huge proportions. Neither foreign capital nor the foreigners themselves are especially welcome in most countries, particularly in many of the newly independent states. Both are costly to borrow and both may constitute sources of friction as time passes. The real measure of help of the foreign expert is not only that he builds and operates industrial establishments, but that at the same time he trains local skill and stimulates local enterprise to take over and continue his tasks. Governments can do a great deal to further or delay development by their attitude to and treatment of foreigners and foreign investment. Foreigners and their money are urgently needed in developing lands; they are likely to become increasingly scarce commodities.

By now it should be quite clear that it takes far more than industry to industrialize. The foregoing discussion has served to outline the extreme complexity of factors concerning development in developing countries. The idea that such development primarily involves only economic and political factors is patently false. Development both demands and produces far-reaching changes in societies and the fabric of social life; it reacts both with and upon demographic factors; the whole operation is affected by, and in turn leaves its impress upon, the physical environment. The period of what might be regarded as spontaneous economic growth and adjustment to environmental conditions is past. The uneven pattern of such development, of rich and poor nations, the potency of demographic factors, the growth of world conscience, all have combined to create an era of economic planning. Time is short and the tasks gigantic, involving the mobilization and harmonizing of both national and international resources. Whether we have yet reached the stage of being able confidently to control and guide economic processes, and in so doing to adjust and mould societies and their vital processes, is uncertain. But immense social and economic experiments are now being made, for in no other way could there be much hope of success within short periods.

8 The form of industrialization

Industrial growth commences in order to supply a growing home demand and begins with simple processing of agricultural and mineral commodities formerly traded in their raw state. Such industries include milling, leather tanning, oilseed pressing, spinning and weaving, brewing and brick-making.

Generally the early processing of agricultural commodities by hand, and later by hand-worked machines, was to remove waste matter, or change the produce into a more edible form, or to one that could be moved or stored more easily. Gradually processing became more complicated and with the development of commerce and communications the handicraft stage began to give way to power-operated machinery. These changes became consolidated with the growth of a money economy and expanding demand which have led to the manufacture of consumer goods both for home and export and finally, in some countries, to industries producing capital equipment.

Factors influencing the selection of industries

The nature and scope of various industries and the possibilities of their adoption in developing countries are influenced by limitations already mentioned: namely, lack of skilled labour, lack of capital, lack of market and scarcity of foreign exchange. These impose restraints upon the kind, size and scope of the industrial development, the methods used, and the order of priorities. The dearth of skilled labour is one very serious handicap, imposing limits not simply on types of industrial activity, but also upon methods of working and the kinds of machinery introduced. Machines requiring individual operations of a comparatively simple level of skill are far more suitable than fewer more complicated machines each capable of a complex series of operations. Not only the operating but also the maintenance of the latter type of machine would be beyond the competence of practically all the local skill. The highly skilled engineer is a product of long training and tradition and plays a vital part in a modern factory; it will be a very long time before developing countries have such personnel in large numbers.

Another limitation is capital: it is both scarce and expensive and must be used to best advantage. The amount of capital investment particular industries require varies enormously. For comparative purposes, it may be expressed in terms of capital required per worker, and in Britain before the heavy inflation of the 1970s this varied from about £620 in the china and earthenware industry to £13,350 in oil refining. In India at this period the initial amounts of capital per worker needed to establish certain industries included £4400 for coal mining machinery manufacture, £7400 for foundry work and £11,900 for iron and steel. These high costs have to be borne in mind in selecting projects, and it does not follow that those projects with highest yield per unit of invested capital are automatically the best. The returns of some projects, notably public utilities, are not to be measured solely in monetary terms, but by the fact that projects such as railways, port facilities and electricity supplies resemble catalysts, reacting upon other industries and making them far more remunerative. Further, some capital-intensive projects produce far greater output than many with a low ratio of capital to labour; thus selection in terms of low capital investment per worker in turn is not necessarily best.

The size of the market limits the division of labour and the inducement to invest and is therefore a further determinant of the character of industrial development. Here we are concerned not merely with numbers but with the size of the subsistence-only element in the economy, of the availability of export markets, and governmental policies regarding competing imports of manufactured goods. It is possible to satisfy the home demand for manufactures of many developing countries with surprisingly few modern industrial establishments and a smaller industrial labour force than is generally supposed. A single modern factory employing about fifty operatives could manufacture enough biscuits to satisfy the complete Ghanaian and Nigerian demand. As we have seen, home demand for manufactures may be expanded if productivity in other sectors of the economy is increased, but where large-scale rural under-employment prevails, industrial development needs to be on a very great scale to absorb surplus population, and is only likely to do this by finding export markets to supplement the limited home demand.

Countries seeking success in export markets must extract the maximum benefit from low industrial wages, the one great advantage they usually possess. To obtain entry into established markets manufactured exports must be highly competitive in price and quality. Low industrial wages do not necessarily imply low labour costs, for this depends upon the productivity of the labour and the degree of skill. It has been estimated that wages in British West Africa are about one tenth of those of the United Kingdom, while the difference in industrial productivity given similar equipment, averages one third to one half. Where wages are moderate and skill and productivity high, as in the Hong Kong textile industry, marked success has attended the penetration of export markets.

Problems of foreign exchange also throw emphasis upon production for export, for even if much foreign capital is available as grants or loans, subsequently interest and capital repayments must be made. Foreign exchange shortage means a favouring of activities requiring a minimum of imported machinery and using indigenous rather than imported raw materials; in other words it favours some emphasis upon labour-intensive technology and small rather than large establishments. Such a pattern of development is also favoured where labour costs (based on low wages) are low, for in this kind of operation labour costs form a major element of total costs.

Theoretically, in examining the character of industrial development in developing lands, the classical doctrine of comparative advantage might seem to have substantial application, but in practice it may not be so, especially in initial phases. According to the theory, a country will gain by specializing in the production of those commodities in which its comparative advantage is greatest, exporting those goods in exchange for ones where its comparative cost advantage is less. The theory underlines optimum use of resources and invokes international levels of cost comparison. However, a substantial body of industry in developing countries cannot be assessed in this way, for its products really do not enter into world trade (for example, much food processing, building, electricity generating, and other utilities). Also we must remember that the pattern of comparative costs is not static; if it were so there might be very little industrial development in under-developed lands and established advantages of the industrial nations would be omnipotent. The reason why governments are so intimately involved is that they alone have the power to interfere with the play of forces in the market and to alter comparative costs in the home market by supporting and sustaining new industries through their birth pangs and early years. A brief discussion of the role of governments in this connection follows on pages 159–61.

Infrastructure needs

Advances in the range of manufactures by means of successful new promotions and the expansion of existing industry from workshop to factory character will depend essentially upon prior or parallel expansion of utilities, education and technical training: the establishment of what is now called the infrastructure. The provision of railways, power stations, harbour installations, schools, hospitals, in themselves large employers of labour, also serves to stimulate local industry, especially the constructional ones such as cement manufacture, manufactures of pre-cast and reinforced concrete, bricks and tiles, metal windows, pipes and tubes.

The considerable capital investment and the lengthy period of fulfilment required in establishing the infrastructure is now an accepted part of planned or systematic development, and reflects changing views during the decade of 1950–60 when economic planning with the enhanced role of government became internationally respectable. A widespread experience in many developing countries was of industries mushrooming during the war and immediate post-war years and failing because their costs were too high and quality too poor or, despite this, surviving at public expense thanks to government support. This has brought home the realization that industrialization cannot afford to develop on a patchy and haphazard trial and error basis with misdirected and misused capital investment, but that first a proper infrastructure, beneficial to all sectors of the economy, is essential. Thus the closing years of the 1950s saw a variety of basic works being put into effect in a considerable number of the world's poorer countries. Afghanistan's first Five Year Plan (1956–61) concentrated on education, the provision of roads, basic irrigation works and power stations. At the end of the period four hydroelectric stations had been built and three others were under construction, while two cement factories were constructed and coal mining began. Pakistan, under its first Five Year Plan (1955–60), devoted 31 per cent of the capital expenditure to agriculture, water and power development; while India in her first five Five Year Plans allotted to communications and power 40 per cent, 38 per cent, 33 per cent, 32 per cent and 36 per cent of total allocations.

Among these basic works are iron and steel plants, not in themselves utilities, but nevertheless the foundation of a large sector of the industrial field. Modern civilization is based on iron and steel, and the establishment of iron and steel works is one of the most desired features of planned development, opening the doors to a great range of other industries, particularly those making heavy capital goods. Not every country possesses raw materials, fuel bases and transport facilities for this industry which, owing to very considerable loss of weight on fabrication, can rarely be operated economically on imported supplies. A number of post-war examples may be cited where these economic factors have been ignored and iron and steel works erected for prestige or strategic reasons. Hungary's iron and steel town of Sztalinvaros, on the Danube forty miles south of Budapest, is such an example. It is a relic of autarkic policies and up to 1960 the works had cost about £200 million and had an annual capacity of 600,000 tonnes of pig iron and 350,000 tonnes of crude steel. Hungary has no iron ore deposits and the plant obtains its ore from Krivoi Rog in the USSR. Four-fifths of the coal is Hungarian, but of indifferent coking quality, and is combined with coking coal imported from Poland. The economic soundness of the project is doubtful, but under a Communist regime this is not made public.[1] A project likely to prove more sound is the iron and steel plant completed in 1969 at Annaba in Algeria. Planned in 1958, it cost £126 million and had a scarcely economic output of 400,000 tonnes of metal per annum. It has now been enlarged to produce nearly 2 million tonnes. Algeria possesses the fuel and raw material supplies necessary for the industry; she is, in fact, a major exporter of high-quality iron ore. A developing country having the resources necessary for an iron and steel industry has much to gain from its establishment. A far wider range of manufactures becomes possible, costs to already established metal-using industries are lowered, foreign exchange will be saved and export possibilities created. It is unlikely that sufficient skill and management ability to run such works will be built up locally for a number of years, but even at very high salaries, the hiring of foreign skill and knowledge (provided that these are passed on) is a good investment here. Great prospects for the future are opened up; as time passes and skills develop, engineering, the manufacture of machinery for factories and of other capital goods becomes possible, and also the development of chemical and fertilizer manufacturing industries based upon the by-products of the coking process, of particular value to agrarian countries.

Oil refineries also offer much scope for associated chemical and plastics industries, but these plants are very expensive and need highly skilled staff. It must be expected that full-scale refineries will not be established easily in developing countries, even if they themselves are crude-oil producers, until substantial home markets for their products arise, but basic refineries without cracking and by-product plants have been built in a number of populous developing countries, including Gabon, Tanzania, Malaya and Costa Rica.

The influence of transport costs

The economic geographer is well aware that the interplay of certain factors, such as value and bulk of raw materials in relation to the character of the end product, cost of assembly of raw materials and of distribution of the finished goods, amounts of fuel, power and labour required, has a bearing upon the location within a country of particular industrial plants. These factors also carry varying weight in determining the character of industry and the nature of the manufacturing that a newly industrializing country may successfully undertake. One of the most decisive among these factors is transport cost. Cost of transport makes local manufacture advantageous where heavy low-value raw materials are required and are available locally; also it is advantageous to set up local industry either on home or imported raw materials where the finished products are bulkier, and therefore more expensive to transport, than the raw materials. In these categories we may include cement, bricks and tiles, furniture and motor-vehicle assembly. Raw materials that vary little in bulk when manufactured are not much affected by transport costs, nor are materials that are of such high value that transport costs form a relatively small proportion of total costs. In these groups we may include cigarettes, clothing, cotton and other textile materials. Transport cost would be similar whether raw materials or finished goods were imported and the high value relative to amount of raw material, bulk and weight makes exports possible.

On the other hand transport costs discourage setting up local industry where raw materials have to be imported and lose weight in processing, for this would incur freight rates being paid on useless waste material (for example, pulp and paper utilizing only two-fifths of the pulp wood, and iron and steel manufacture may be regarded as examples, but it should be remembered in the latter industry, where more than one raw material is involved, that a country may have some of the raw materials at sufficiently low procurement cost to offset freight rates on the import of the others). Also a country lacking good supplies of various fuels is discouraged from establishing those industries where fuel requirements are heavy owing to the high cost of transporting fuel.

This outline, in many respects oversimplified, should help to explain the general pattern of industrial growth in most developing countries, especially those not well endowed with fuel and ore supplies. A range of food-processing industries first becomes established, based upon local agricultural raw materials and proximity to market, and freed from external competition by the perishability of the raw material – milk processing, baking, the canning and preserving of fruit and vegetables, and beverage manufacture such as aerated drinks and beer (where water is an important raw material). Then come industries based upon wood, such as furniture-making, and those concerned with construction and derived from local mineral resources: cement, pre-stressed concrete, bricks and tiles, sanitary ware, glass, pottery, crockery. Assembly industries follow, these being based upon cheaper transport costs of importing component parts assembled locally to make (for example) bicycles and motor vehicles. These are the customary early industrial activities that arise, for their resource bases are either practically ubiquitous or, as we have seen, they are generally sheltered from competition by transport costs and perishability.

With these industries we find others appearing that have less substantial bases and sometimes more hazardous lives. These produce such consumer goods as textiles, clothing, footwear, soap, cigarettes. Unless there is the advantage of local raw materials these industries gain no advantage from the level of freight rates on raw materials against finished goods and are likely to be exposed to competition of mass-produced goods from abroad (often of higher and more reliable quality). The main offsetting advantage they have is low labour costs, but generally this is insufficient and these industries exist (and at times stagnate) beneath a protective tariff.

The industries listed above are the major ones established during the 'pre-take-off' period, generally restricted in character and scale by limited demand, capital, skill and public utilities, etc. However, these articles, which in many cases can be based upon indigenous raw materials, are those that absorb an increasing proportion of spending power as incomes begin to rise above subsistence level, consequently there is a considerable potential home market for them in all under-developed lands. A disadvantage worth remembering, however, is that for these very reasons every developing country is able to make these goods for itself. In such goods there is little scope for export for, as we have seen on page 126, world trade in these commodities is scarcely expanding. For countries that possess resources of fuel and ores the industrial path is likely to be somewhat smoother. Metal manufactures form substantial proportions of the imports of developing countries and command expanding markets in developed lands, consequently world demand for metal goods is increasing and export markets are more readily available. Absence of ores, particularly iron ore, places a curb upon the character and degree of industrial expansion. If fuel is readily available and wages low, some metal manufactures are possibly based upon imported ingots, but generally they are limited to such items as nails, nuts and bolts, pots and pans, and simple agricultural implements.

The need for export markets has been stressed as being a key factor in successful industrial development of over-populated developing countries, but the range of goods likely to be exported successfully is small, particularly so if ores and fuel are not plentiful. Transport costs now act in reverse and only favour goods made from indigenous raw materials that lose weight in manufacture. It is not feasible to use imported raw materials for export industries unless a great deal of labour and skill lavished upon them will materially raise their value (for instance, watches, instruments, high-quality ceramics) or where the ratio of value to weight is sufficiently high for cost of transport to be a minor element in the final cost (for instance, textile raw materials). Success in these activities depends especially upon low labour costs (generally present) allied with considerable skill and technical knowledge (generally absent); it follows that the training and education of the labour force needs to have a high place. Hong Kong provides an example of success here; her millions are supported by widely disseminated exports of textiles, toys, electronic and transistor devices, etc. (see Chapter 9).

However in the real world as opposed to a theoretical world of perfect competition, the forces of the market (and here the effects of transport costs) are frequently influenced and modified by government actions. This is particularly so when industrialization by import-substitution is attempted.

Import-substitute industrialization

The decades of the 1960s and 1970s saw a growing emphasis on industrialization by import-substitution in many countries of the developing world. The rationale here was that, whereas local industry had little prospect of succeeding in export markets, it could be built up to serve the home market if tariffs kept out competing foreign imports. Such a policy might seem to have a great deal to commend it, particularly if it reduced requirements of foreign exchange and stimulated industrial expansion and employment. Another important advantage cited is the fact that the market for these particular products is already in being: the difficult task of creating new markets for new industries against established competition does not apply if government action cuts off the supply of imports, and the policy, by favouring local industries, also serves to attract local investment that otherwise might not have gone into industry. Not all the wide range of imported manufactured goods lend themselves easily to such policies; it has been shown above that transport costs and the nature of the finished product (namely, loss of weight) give solid advantage to certain goods from overseas over home production but many others are no longer disadvantaged if given tariff protection. The industries most favoured for import substitution are those that create the finished consumer goods by the assembly of parts and components, for example, motor cars, radio and television, refrigerators and electrical products.

These import-substitution policies have not been very successful. A principal reason for this being an inevitable *increase* in the economy's dependence on imports. This may seem paradoxical, but new imports are required in the form of finished or semi-finished parts and components and in equipment for the factories that are to assemble them. Further, if the new industries do raise real income per head, the classes who benefit most (the urban sector and high income groups) engender a demand for a wider range of imported consumer goods (this in turn might seem to offer further possibilities of import-substitution and one can envisage a step-by-step expansion of consumer goods industries on this basis). However, with few exceptions (perhaps notably Brazil) results have been disappointing. Considerable protection against foreign imports gives little incentive to improve efficiency; quality remains poor and prices high. Foreign exchange shortages and balance of payments difficulties increase with the growing scale of imports, and stop-go situations leading to under-utilization of manufacturing capacity are common features that contribute to the failure of these policies. Social problems also increase; much of the machinery imported to equip the factories reflects First rather than Third World technology – machinery and methods that require little labour. The discrimination against the agricultural sector inherent in import-substitute policies (see page 185) has led to large numbers leaving the land for the cities, but all too often to unemployment because the new factories can offer only limited employment opportunities.

Import-substitution offers no quick road to greater self-sufficiency, indeed it may render the economy more precarious. When importing finished goods, inability to pay for them makes them unavailable and thus lowers standards of living; but when these goods are produced domestically from imported materials and parts, inability to import will effect the economy more by reducing domestic income through work stoppages and unemployment.[2] Those are the main reasons why import-substitution policies generally have not been successful; remedies are available but they are not easy to achieve. It might be possible to expand foreign exchange earnings from the increased export of primary products, or to set up capital goods industries to make the parts and components otherwise imported or even to find export markets for locally manufactured goods. Reliance on expansion of primary exports may well be hazardous with a generally inelastic demand and fluctuating levels of production and resultant price fluctuations determined by a world market. In the second case higher levels of technology and greater capital inputs are required and these have to be matched by an adequate internal market. As has been shown (page 143), often one reasonably efficient modern factory can satisfy the entire home market and where several factories are established they operate below capacity and invite further government protective measures to sustain them. In short, the economies of many developing countries are too small to nurture capital goods industries (even if the know-how were available), although for a few larger countries (for instance, India and Brazil) it has become feasible. Finally, the problems of finding export markets for the manufactured goods of the developing countries are very great: quality, standardization, packing and price are critical and even more are the trade barriers which established industries in the advanced countries seek to have erected for their own protection. Nevertheless, these hurdles are being passed by a few countries well along the development continuum (notably Brazil, Taiwan, Korea),[3] where early policies of import-substitution become supported by export-oriented measures.

Brazil is worthy of note as being one state that has had a degree of success with its import-substitute strategy, which has been an important part of its development policy since the Second World War. Protection took several forms, including quantitative controls, a multiple exchange rate system and straightforward *ad valorem* duties. Initially there was a reduction in imports and domestic industry expanded, but by the 1960s the growing industrial sector needed increasing quantities of imported raw materials and capital goods, and this led to foreign exchange crises, since exports, particularly from the primary sector, had been neglected. These problems were tackled in the second half of the 1960s. Brazil's rate of inflation was generally higher than that of her trading partners which discouraged exports, so a 'crawling peg' exchange rate system was introduced which, in effect, meant frequent mini-devaluations to make exports profitable. In order to boost exports further and solve the foreign exchange crisis, from 1968 fiscal incentives were provided to exporters of manufactured goods – in reality creating a preferential exchange rate for manufactured exports. There followed a spectacular expansion of exports accompanied by a spread into new markets in the developing countries of Africa, the Middle East and Latin America itself. In the decade 1969–78 exports of manufactured and semi-manufactured goods increased from 20 per cent to over 51 per cent of total exports and in 1978 by value far exceeded that of coffee, Brazil's traditional major export.

Brazil is now practically self-sufficient in manufactured goods, but they are highly priced and the economy is distorted, for agriculture has not benefited by export incentives and suffered under the policy of import-substitute industrialization. Brazil, with its vast resource potential yet scarcely touched, is now one of the first major tropical countries to be far along the development path, and as such is now coming to recognize as an exporter an obligation not to discriminate against exports of other countries, and in particular of other developing countries. Thus phased reductions in the various elements of protection have begun and should be completed by 1983. This move to put greater reliance on market forces in the long term should render Brazilian industry more efficient and improve the allocation of labour and capital resources, although in the short term inflation and related economic pressures may intensify.

The character of industrial development

Labour-intensive policies

Power plants, iron and steel works and oil refineries require immense investments of capital; in themselves they give relatively little employment (that is, the capital investment per worker is very high), but the output per worker is high and particularly beneficial to a very wide sector of the developing industrial economy. It is possible, however, that the return per unit of capital invested in such capital-intensive processes will be less initially than if the money had been invested in a greater number of other, and more labour-intensive, projects. Decisions as to the appropriate capital intensity in the industrialization of a developing country are of fundamental importance, since they will have notable effects upon the character and pattern of the industrial development. They will require early examination of the emphasis to be given to 'heavy' as opposed to 'light' industry and thus the tempo of industrialization itself, for many experts consider there is an implicit correlation between capital per worker and the type of industrial output. In other words, there are not only capital- and labour-intensive *processes* but also capital- and labour-intensive *industries*. Labour-intensive production is assumed to be of small or medium scale of operation and to make 'light' consumer goods, while capital-intensive production is identified with large-scale industrial production of 'heavy' or capital goods. It is sufficient here to remark that these are general concepts; the mutual relationships lack statistical proof, mainly because such data are scarce.

There is a strong body of opinion that where capital is limited it is better to spread it thinly in order to cover a greater labour force, in other words to place emphasis upon labour-intensive industries and methods. Here low labour costs can exert their maximum effects on total costs. By these means there is more development and a wider distribution of purchasing power among those who will quickly spend it, mainly (it is hoped) on consumer goods. Much of the labour used might otherwise be unproductive, and capital saved by the use of this labour can be used for the production of other goods and the employment of yet more labour. As a result total production and income will be greater than if more highly mechanized methods had been used. These views favour small-scale undertakings, between the cottage handicraft unit and the large-scale factory in both size and techniques. Other advantages claimed are that the volume of production from such plants is more likely to accord with the restricted market for the products (a few days' production of a large modern shoe factory would serve to satisfy the present effective annual demand for shoes in a country such as Morocco). Also small-scale industries making use of electric power are less exacting in locational demands and can be widely distributed and thus help to avoid excessive agglomerations of people in large urban areas, necessitating high costs of housing, utilities and sanitation and problems of centre–periphery unbalanced development. There is also the view whereby skill, technique and markets may be developed for subsequent large-scale operations. These views, of course do not rigidly bar large-scale industry, but put most emphasis upon medium- and small-scale ones, believing that they give more employment per unit of invested capital. A real danger is that little of the surplus product is likely to be saved for reinvestment and industrial expansion will be slow.

Capital-intensive policies

The opposite case is also a strong one, and is based on the premise that a cumulative increase in production and national income stems from ever-increasing productivity of labour. This increasing productivity can only come about through the adoption of increasingly efficient techniques and appliances, requiring heavy application of capital. Far higher productivity per worker is possible with capital-intensive processes (although a smaller return per unit of capital than with labour-intensive ones) and, if the profits per worker are continually reinvested, the net product will grow at a faster rate than that of the less intensive ones. This means, in fact, that while employment will be lower in the early years, it accelerates rapidly and soon outstrips the initially higher levels obtaining in labour-intensive industries.

Investment should take as its aim the raising of productive capacity rather than the provision of the greatest number of jobs; with the attainment of one the other will follow. Higher productivity begets higher surpluses, allowing yet more capital for investment; thus an upward spiral may be envisaged. To this end, emphasis on the establishment of capital goods industries rather than consumer goods industries is a further logical step, and some experts favour massive capital-intensive investment in basic industries producing equipment goods which later make possible a more rapid increase of consumer goods. Labour-intensive production lacks this self-accelerating character and with it an economy is likely to stagnate. Early Egyptian industrial development between the wars demonstrates this feature, while modern Indian planned development leans much more upon capital-intensive methods.

It is clear that both policies are vulnerable at some points and also that in any actual country (as opposed to theoretical models for planned purposes) the real decision concerns the proportion of the limited resources to be employed one way and the other. It is here that economic arguments may become subordinated to social and political policies. Thus we find the following industrial activities recommended by a mission to a heavily populated Asian country, their view clearly favouring labour-intensive industrialization: rice milling, coir fibre manufacture, cotton textiles by small-scale production ('The mission recognises that a fairly large and vertically integrated spinning and weaving mill would produce cloth more cheaply ... nevertheless other economic as well as social reasons make it imperative to encourage the development ... of small-scale production'), manufacture of footwear, metal-working industries including hardware, brass and aluminium products, ceramics, agricultural implements, building materials, galvanizing and electro-plating.[4]

Another expert to a different Asian country recommended capital-intensive industrialization with particular emphasis upon large-scale capital goods and heavy machinery industries, and cited the country's economic position as justification. There was a satisfactory foreign trade position and no balance of payments difficulties, a high level of food production and a large reserve of manpower allowing development of basic industries without reducing production in other sectors. He rejected proposals for the expansion of cottage industries on the score that it merely disguised unemployment by means of social relief since differences in the efficiency of production would involve subsidies to the cottage industries and output quotas on competing products of large-scale industries.[5]

Efficiency or output per worker cannot be taken entirely as a reflection of capital investment or size of plant although a general correlation is discernible. Professor Mukerjee, for instance, has shown that from 1946 to 1949 there was an increase in capital intensity in a number of India's manufacturing industries, in most cases accompanied by a rise in output per worker.[6] Studies to discover optimum techniques (capital- or labour-intensive) in various industries are only slowly being carried out, but it is clear that in some there may be room for combinations of methods. Further, it is not always necessary to introduce the latest European or American machinery or equipment, which is often very complicated and designed for very different settings where labour costs are very high. It may be uneconomic to take the newest machines; simple models – even second-hand – may give a better return.

The choice of technologies

The choice of industrial technologies by a developing country is a critical planning decision. Today the advanced countries take for granted the immense technological creations of modern refinery complexes, chemical works, iron and steel plants, etc. that are the end product of generations of intellectual and practical achievement. Of necessity the operators are highly skilled, having been nurtured and educated in technologically dynamic environments where ideas and experience lead to constant innovations that carry the whole process forward.

Given the goodwill of its authors, modern communications now make the transference of much of this technology to developing countries a relatively easy matter. We find that planners and industrial advisers to developing countries, concerned with overcoming the technical and labour problems involved in establishing and raising productivity in industrial plants, show a ready resort to mechanization and advanced technology. To technicians from industrialized countries, faced with the task of improving volume, quality and uniformity of output and in reducing unit costs, this recommendation is in keeping with their experience. They are far less concerned with the social problems surrounding unemployment, or the fact that technologies imported from advanced countries certainly may be more efficient than existing techniques but may economize on the wrong factors. Most advanced technologies represent capital being used to replace expensive labour, but reverse conditions apply in the Third World: capital is dear and labour is cheap. Further, capital-intensive technologies give relatively little employment and need highly trained workers, some of whom may have to be hired from abroad.

Spatially these policies bring about islands of modern and advanced technology amid great areas of a pre-industrial character. Infrastructure requirements restrict the advanced plants and factories to urban areas, and reinforce centre–periphery tendencies and the dual nature of the economy. Migration to the cities – the flight from the countryside – assumes serious and tragic proportions and underlines the fact that this modern sector of Third World economies draws in no more than 20 to 25 per cent of population, the rest are passed by and constitute the disadvantaged traditional sector. It has come to be realized that there is little prospect of these modern sectors expanding to take in entire populations in the near future, and during the decade of the 1970s, the role of science and technology in economic and social development came under closer examination. The necessity of devising indigenous technologies has become recognized, allied with the pressing need for smaller scale, cheaper technologies with lower levels of technical equipment and requirements that can be adopted widely in small town and villages; that is, the workplaces would be where people are living and not only in the large towns.

These policies were supported by the late Dr E. F. Schumacher with his 'intermediate technology' and a charitable trust has been set up in Britain to gather information on low-cost technologies and on self-help techniques. Intermediate technology (now generally referred to as 'appropriate technology') comes between primitive traditional methods and the costly sophisticated technologies of the advanced world; it seeks to devise technologies where the capital cost of a workplace may be no more than about £100 and where simple techniques and local raw materials are employed.[7]

Recent development plans in a number of countries reflect these views (see Nigeria and India in Chapters 9 and 10), which may help to arrest the flood of rural unemployed to the towns and to increase rural purchasing power. By no means can all types of manufacture be fitted into this smaller frame; for the most part heavy industries must be accepted with little change. Iron and steel works, chemical industries producing sulphuric acid, caustic soda and nitrogenous fertilizer need much capital and cannot be operated economically on a small scale.

Planning strategy

As a preliminary to planning for industrialization, the adoption of a broad strategic framework is a necessary first step. Those favouring balanced development, and with Rostow's economic history as guide, point out the dependence of industry upon agriculture: the pace of development in the one depends upon the pace of advance in the other. In less-developed countries agriculture is the principal source of employment, capital and foreign exchange. It provides the internal purchasing power that creates the home market for manufactures, and its food surpluses determine the number of workers that can be sustained outside agriculture. Thus, logically but paradoxically, in the early stages of an industrialization programme resources should be concentrated upon the development of agriculture.

This 'agriculture first' model is stoutly opposed by an 'industry first' school. Their view is that agriculture will not become more productive unless it can be stimulated by expanding markets and better prices. Many farmers produce no more than what is needful for subsistence, but if tempted by cheap manufactured goods they would produce more to earn enough to buy them. The early establishment of industry would create these conditions, spurring on the expansion of food and raw material production and siphoning off labour from the land. Output per head would be raised and foreign exchange would be saved.

That these are deceptively simple arguments becomes clear if real-life conditions are examined. Rostow's examples relate mainly to the nineteenth century, when industry was less sophisticated and cost per work place was moderate; also populations are far heavier today and pressure upon the land limits its response as a source of investment capital, which would be far below the huge sums needed. Further progress would depend upon the efficient development of capital-intensive industry with export markets, for with prevailing heavy rates of population increase, the expansion of the home market would be limited and the whole project hazardous. Clearly choices between alternatives, or a judicious blending of them, provide the development planners with their most difficult task.

The role of governments

This discussion has been designed to demonstrate the variety of conflicting interests involved in determining development targets, and the choice of means to achieve them. Social, economic, technical and strategic factors must be evaluated and governments must decide upon the tempo of development by means of their power of controls and emphasis upon long-term or short-term measures. To mobilize and employ all the forces available in the struggle for development requires that each government of developing countries prepares and puts into effect a general economic plan. The heart of such a plan is to procure the necessary capital in order to raise the amount of investment and so increase productivity, utilizing both internal and external sources. Given the capital, the plan should allocate proportions of it to the various sectors of the economy: transport, communications, power production, manufacturing industry, both 'heavy' and 'light', agriculture, health and education. In turn, detailed proposals for these should be made.

Problems affecting the formation of capital have been discussed in Chapter 6. No developing country can hope to raise anything like the total capital it needs entirely from external sources; increasing quantities must come from investments and savings of its own population, and governmental policies become shaped to encourage and often to enforce this. The discipline of a developing population becomes most tried after the first fruits of development gradually appear. Expanding incomes lead to an increasing demand for consumer goods, and government measures designed to encourage saving and reinvestment attempt to damp down this demand in order to keep control over the development process. There is the further advantage that keeping demand for consumer goods in check allows for more investment and for the growth of the more expensive capital goods industries. Some of the enhanced demand will be for imported goods, and this has the added disadvantage of affecting the foreign exchange position. Consequently developing countries invariably impose import restrictions in one form or another, and these have the further effect of working to protect home manufactures.

Policies of protection are frequently criticized, yet if a developing country is ruthlessly determined to dedicate its powers to development, such a policy becomes attractive particularly, as we have seen, if import-substitute industries are to be nurtured. While the aim that new industries should pay their way is laudable, it should also be clear that these standards have less immediate application in under-developed lands where investments are being made which for a long period may be unprofitable, yet are necessary to create external economies for subsequent industries. Much early investment in manufacturing industry is on a similar basis; it would not take place if some protection or inducement were not afforded, for the disincentives to manufacturing at that stage are too great, which is the reason why the investments were not made earlier.

New industries in developing countries take some time to become going concerns; they must train their labour, which will affect both quality and quantity of production; they may have to pay high rates for services and power; with few other industries operating there will be few external economies, they may find difficulty in breaking into the market, probably supplied by imported goods, and may work below capacity for a considerable period. Not surprisingly, costs of production are likely to be high during this initial period and these industries are in a competitively weak position. All these difficulties should lessen as development proceeds and, provided there is a reasonable chance that the industry will duly pay its way, there is a good case for protection or some form of government help.

The main justification, however, is that the very existence of these young industries is giving a substantial return to the developing state beyond the mere value of their production. It is generally true that every new enterprise improves the external economies of other concerns. The more factories there are, the cheaper can be the supply of gas, electricity, oil fuel, repair facilities, and the greater the expansion of the industrial labour force. Concentration as opposed to dispersion of industry particularly permits further mutual advantages in the use of raw materials, by-products, transport and other services so that a cumulative reduction of cost may be envisaged as development proceeds. Certainly dispersion of industry might moderate the growth of metropolitan centres and reduce the heavy social costs attendant upon large urban areas, and it might also reduce the impact of the growing dualism in the economy, but it is rarely favoured on economic grounds.

The system of protection deserves criticism if it is given in an unplanned economy to haphazard industrial promotions that never become competitive, for the higher prices are a burden on the consumer and contract rather than expand the market. Experience also shows that high profits obtained in certain protected manufacturing industries lead to the establishment of competing firms. The domestic market is usually too small to sustain several firms which leads to under-used capacity and high-cost production and this implies wasteful use of capital. The further effect of protection is that the rural population is financing industrialization, for protection raises the price of manufactures relative to agricultural products. To some degree this may be necessary and must be accepted, but the danger is that inequality between rural and urban incomes grows and a severe drift from the land into urban unemployment takes place.

The range of government help and methods that can be enjoyed is very great. Frequently tariffs are levied on selected categories of imported goods, roughly in the form: nil on machinery, low on raw materials, moderate on semi-finished goods and heavy on finished manufactures. Internal freight rates to and from ports and factories may also be adjusted on similar lines, with especially favourable rates of moving indigenous raw materials. Other forms of help may be as loans at low interest rates; subsidies especially to goods seeking export markets; exemptions from certain taxes for a stated period and, in some countries, preferential treatment by government order departments.

All this indicates that many of the young industries depend for their profits largely upon government intervention. An unfortunate but natural response is to lobby and bring pressure to bear on the government for further support, rather than to seek greater efficiency of operation and the cutting of costs.

Preparing the plan

The drafting of a plan for economic development follows the basic decisions on social and economic aims. These would be expressed in terms of permitted annual percentage increase in consumption, the degree of unemployment to be tolerated, and the amount of foreign exchange deficit to be allowed. A United Nations publication has described the procedure as follows:

The basic principles having been formulated are expressed mathematically by a system of equations, the next step – the operational part of planning – would consist in aggregating the relevant economic and technical information in a programming matrix; the system would then be 'solved' for those variables which it is sought to evaluate. In fact the whole process begins by drawing up as large a list as possible of economic projects both existing and proposed, the inclusion of an activity involving no commitment whatever as to its retention in the final plan or its numerical importance. The list should contain not only such conspicuous and much talked about labour-saving and capital-intensive projects as modern steel production, aluminium production, heavy fertilizer production, etc., but also a number of labour-intensive activities … such as road building, slum clearing, minor irrigation, handloom weaving, etc. Only by including a sufficiently large spectrum of such activities will it be possible at a later stage to find optimum solutions that can really satisfy the desired conditions of employment in the transition period. Each listed activity will be described by economists and engineers, who will tabulate current operations and capital requirements for both existing and proposed enterprises. Information concerning current operations, that is, activities resulting in a more or less continuous flow of goods and services, will relate to input – wages, salaries, ownership income, taxes, purchases from other enterprises, imports and such items – and output of given products or groups of similar products ('product-mix') for any given period; the input and output data will also cover the physical quantities involved. Information concerning capital investment will relate to size, required construction period, type of ownership, etc. The information, together with data relating to the supply of domestic and foreign capital, will then be aggregated in a programming matrix; the mathematical solution of the system, obtained by a method based on linear programming, will provide the answer to such questions as the optimum combination of industries, the respective levels of investment in, and rate of growth of, producer and consumer goods industries, the maximum rate of expansion, etc., corresponding to the stated goals.[8]

9 The progress of industrialization
1: Ghana and Nigeria; Chile;
Argentina; Hong Kong

Every nation runs an individual course in the cross-country
development race; each faces and must overcome a series of
obstacles and difficulties, some of them being individual to its own
course. It seems appropriate, therefore, to scrutinize certain aspects
of industrial development in a few selected countries in order to
demonstrate from actual examples the character of the problems
to be faced and the varying progress being made. Full treatment is
impossible here; instead a variety of facets have been selected to
exemplify aspects of the body of theory previously advanced, with
finally an examination in some detail of one country's progress in
industrialization.

Ghana and Nigeria

West Africa provides us with a region where environmental
difficulties pose severe problems to economic development but
where a number of African states are attempting to co-ordinate
their resources and plan for their future. Ghana and Nigeria are
examples of such countries. Both countries exhibit social and
economic conditions widely different from a number of other
developing lands. Both have had early development plans disrupted
by revolution and, in the case of Nigeria, by civil war. Both exhibit
a high rate of population increase but each has land still available
for agricultural expansion. Low *per capita* incomes here result
from chronic under-utilization of resources rather than substantial
utilization with too many people sharing the returns. Early plans
for developing industrial sectors were modest, then Ghana raised
the pace in the early 1960s before the fall of President Nkrumah,
and now Nigeria is speeding industrial projects with the oil boom
of the 1970s.

   The rate of increase of Ghana's population (totalling 11 million
in 1979) at 3.6 per cent is among the world's highest. If this rate

continues the population will double before the end of the century. The increasing weight of population is to be found in the prosperous southern part of the republic, which includes fast growing towns such as Accra (the capital, population *c.* 1 million), the Sekondi–Takoradi port area (population, 200,000) and Kumasi (population, 500,000). The south possesses all the railways and most of the road network; the north remains relatively inaccessible and undeveloped.

Ghana's wealth is derived mostly from the large African-owned and -operated cocoa-farming business. It was the cocoa-tax revenues that provided much of the development capital during the 1950s. The Cocoa Marketing Board between 1939 and 1958 is estimated to have accumulated £107 million net surplus. This sum gives some indication of the important part cocoa plays in the economy; in recent years cocoa exports have accounted for between 50 and 60 per cent of export revenue. The vulnerability of Ghana to fluctuation in world demand and the seriousness of falling prices need little emphasis, and led to plans for diversification by promoting the expansion of the timber industry and of the industrial sector in her economy. In addition, growing food consumption has outstripped local food supply and an increasing volume of food is now imported. Either local agriculture and industry must become more productive in order to reduce imports, or exports must be increased to pay for the growing food imports. The growth of import-saving local industries is therefore one of the goals of development.

In 1951 a first Development Plan was prepared involving a public investment of £102 million. The then Gold Coast government put most emphasis upon the building up of the less spectacular but essential public services – communications, education, water supplies, health – realizing that the existing infrastructure was quite inadequate to sustain substantial development. The following years saw £34 million devoted to communications and harbours, including a considerable programme of road construction, railway modernization, construction of power stations and harbour developments at Takoradi and the commencement of the building of another major port at Tema. The second Development Plan (1959–64), suspended in 1962 in favour of a Seven Year Plan (1964–71), was far more ambitious; it required £243 million investment, more than double that of the first plan and was to be completed in five years. The spending of a further £100 million on a major hydroelectric scheme on the river Volta was also proposed.

The allocation to commerce and industry in both plans was

small since it was hoped that with the development of a firm infrastructure, private capital would be attracted to exploit industrial opportunities. The range of manufactures developing during the period of the first plan followed the customary pattern and included brick and tile manufacture, beverage industries, food-processing, biscuit and soap manufacture, pottery, nails and foundry products and the assembly of bicycles and refrigerators. The more ambitious second plan led to a steel mill, a ship-repair yard, the introduction of textile industries, boot and shoe manufacture, cement, milling, the manufacture of fertilizers and insecticides, rubber and plastic products, radio and motor-car assembly. Only one tenth of the investment of this plan was allocated to agriculture – a proportion far too small in a country where great opportunities both for the expansion of agriculture and, locally, its intensification are present and where food imports increase. Professor W. A. Lewis in his report on the prospects for industrial development in the Gold Coast (1953) has stated categorically:

The most certain way to promote industrialization in the Gold Coast is to lay the foundation it requires by taking vigorous measures to raise food production per person engaged in agriculture. This is the surest way of producing that large and ever-increasing demand for manufacture without which there can be little industrialization.[1]

Cocoa revenues, based on fluctuating prices and declining production, are no longer commensurate with the widening scope and rising costs of development, and the difficulty of raising the necessary capital (internally and externally) caused the second plan to be described as an act of hope. Saving and investing are still foreign to the African's nature. Small personal incomes are not conducive to capital accumulation and if money is available better returns are obtained from trading and money-lending. Ghana would have been able to supply less than half the planned development expenditure of her moribund second plan and the heavy loans and grants she solicited from international sources for the separate great venture – the Volta river aluminium and hydroelectric power schemes – made it more difficult to obtain further international funds (from virtually the same bodies) for the plan. Attempts at self-help through community development projects for secondary roads, wells, irrigation channels, etc. made some easement of demand on capital but the main problem remained.

Indeed the difficulty of raising sufficient capital and the temptation besetting the young newly independent state have been well exemplified in Ghana. The desire to maintain prestige as the first ex-colony in Africa to gain independence and to assure pan-African leadership led to the dissipation of money needed for development. Loans were made to Guinea and Mali and financial support given to various African nationalist movements. Ostentatious displays, prestige building projects, the inevitable quota of mismanagement that every young nation must expect, underlined the wasteful unreality of many projects begun under President Nkrumah. The over-ambitious Seven Year Plan, scrapped by the new government after the ousting of Nkrumah, had scarcely begun to be implemented. This plan aimed at an annual rate of economic growth of 5.5 per cent; the rate attained in 1964 was 4.5 per cent, and in 1965 fell to 3.3 per cent. The balance of payments deficit reached a record of £79 million in 1965 and loan and interest repayments on £205 million advanced in the late 1950s, mainly from overseas, were falling due in 1965–6. The new government inherited a state on the verge of bankruptcy and, owing to a growing dependence on imported foodstuffs, short of many essential foods.

There is no doubt that the economic chaos into which the country had drifted by 1966 resulted from the autocratic and often high-handed methods of the former president. The disdaining of economic advice, grandiose planning with inadequate means of implementation, a proliferation of inefficient state-owned corporations ('of 37, representing an investment of £82 million, hardly one was making a profit in 1965 and few showed any promise of ever making any', *The Economist*, 5 March 1966), preoccupation with pan-African power politics, all reduced the country's credit worthiness in international eyes. After a promising start, economic advance in Ghana had faltered.

Ghanaian governments immediately after 1966 adopted stringent non-inflationary policies which involved severe cutbacks on development projects and a low rate of growth. They inherited international debts of well over £200 million and the economy remained in a precarious position well into the 1970s. Since 1966 the many state-owned industries have been reorganized in the Ghana Industrial Holdings Corporation, and in some cases private investment capital has been invited to assist ailing enterprises. A general problem has been the operation of many of the industries (for instance, the meat factory, jute bag manufacture, ship repairing) at well below design capacity because of import restrictions on essential raw materials and machine parts.

What must be appreciated is that in recent Development Plans (as in those of Nigeria) a very high proportion of expenditure has been necessary for the development of transport, communications and harbour facilities. This is partly a reflection of the antagonistic West African environment. The variation in intensity and the seasonal character of the rainfall necessitate irrigation and water conservation projects in the north, but cause serious drainage, bridging and maintenance problems in the well-watered, forested south. The heavy rainfall here is conducive to soil erosion, to the rapid deterioration of roads and helps to create conditions sympathetic to the spread of debilitating diseases. Railway and road construction in West Africa has been accomplished in the face of almost inconceivable environmental difficulties. Often the surveying of a line was the initial survey for that part of the country, valleys subject to flooding and tsetse fly had to be avoided in the rain-forest areas where the construction of innumerable bridges over streams, rivers and swamps, all with imported equipment, has required prodigious drive and very high expenditure. Ballast materials especially needed by both roads and railways in the wet south are particularly scarce there. Road builders have mainly had to use the materials they found along the line of the road, varying from sand to lateritic gravels, with a wide range of response to weather conditions. In Ghana, out of 14,000 miles of motorable roads in 1970, only some 2200 miles were bitumen-surfaced. All these difficulties become translated into monetary terms when transport, communications and harbour facilities are created, and subsequently enlarge the heavy and unavoidable repair and maintenance charges.

A serious problem for Ghanaian development is that her coast provides no natural site for a deep-water port. From the Ivory Coast to east of the Niger delta most of the coastline suffered submergence during the Tertiary era and has since been smoothed by the creation of sand bars from the action of south-west winds and waves and a powerful longshore drift. Tidal range is small and this coast now exhibits the double obstacles of surf and sand several hundred miles long, through which muddy rivers struggle desperately and add their own great volume of silt. In the Ivory Coast a canal was cut through the sand bar in 1907. It was badly sited and became silted up in a few months.

In 1937 because of high water in the lagoon a metre wide ditch was cut through the old choked canal to release the flood. In three days the metre ditch had a 100 metre wide mouth which in another five days had become 300 metres wide. Yet after a week the flow of water had ceased and six months later the outlet was blocked by the action of the sea.[2]

It is natural forces such as these that delay harbour development. As far back as 1928 an artificial harbour was created at Takoradi near the former unsatisfactory railhead port of Sekondi. Long breakwaters obstruct the west to east drift and keep the narrow entrance to the rectangular deep-water basin clear. The growing Gold Coast economy, with its export of cocoa, timber, palm oil, manganese and bauxite, by the end of the war strained the resources of this chief port and a several million pound enlargement programme was put in hand. This, completed in 1953, doubled berth capacity, mechanized the loading equipment and necessitated the removal of an eighty-foot hill covering twenty-four acres to provide level land for the siting of new railway yards and spoil for other reclamation. Except for sand, timber and aggregate from a quarry eight miles away, practically every item from cement, steel and construction plant to all-important DDT had to be sent out from Britain.

The continuing growth of Ghana's economy has led to the construction of a second deep-water port at the former fishing village of Tema, 18 miles east of Accra and due south of the Volta hydroelectric power station at Akosombo. Road, rail and water supply connections with Accra were completed in 1952 at a cost of over £3 million. The development of the port, providing deep-water berths, a dockyard, warehouses, railway sidings and marshalling yards, has been completed at a cost of £35 million. An entirely new town (population, 150,000), including an industrial area with an oil refinery, a steel mill and a large aluminium smelter, has grown beside this new port as the Volta river hydroelectric and aluminium scheme has developed.[3] The Volta River Project, which secured approval and funds from the United States in December 1961, was a major step forward in Ghanaian planned development. It comprises a £46 million aluminium smelter, presently operating on imported alumina, but ultimately to utilize huge local bauxite deposits, supplied with power by a £70 million hydroelectric station. The project was completed (*c.* 1968) and aluminium production for export has risen to 220,000 tonnes annually. The continuing dependence of the Volta Aluminium

Company on imported alumina and the low price they pay for their electricity has been used as an example of the problems of the participation of multinational companies in industrialization, in this case the American Kaiser Corporation. Yet without the electricity, which is also available to other users, the cost of imported energy would have seriously hindered industries in recent years. An additional hydroelectric power scheme has now been completed at Kpong on the Volta just downstream from the original dam at Akosombo and this will add 120 megawatt capacity.

From 1972 to 1979 the military took over the country's government and generally these were years of mismanagement. There were budget deficits, acute inflation and export earnings unwisely used. Low local prices paid to cocoa farmers led to reduced production and, from being the world's leading producer satisfying over one third of the world market, by 1979 production was down by a half and less than one fifth of the world market was supplied. Ageing and low yielding trees have not been replaced and labour has drifted to the towns. Attempts in recent years to return to self-sufficiency in food have been unsuccessful. The lack of price incentives, the high cost of fertilizer, a succession of three drought years, labour problems and poor weather led to disappointing progress and the continuing need for substantial food imports.

Foreign exchange difficulties led to a shortage of imported raw materials and spare parts and over a considerable period Ghanaian industry has operated at only 20–30 per cent of capacity. This situation offers no incentive to the establishment of new industry, and generally throughout the 1970s the growth of the economy was scarcely greater than the rate of population increase. On average some 62 per cent of the country's industrial raw material is imported – 94 per cent of the inputs of the metallurgical industries, 90 per cent of the chemical industries and 76 per cent of the textile industries. This latter industry now accounts for 17 per cent of the manufacturing output of Ghana and the 25 textile and 28 clothing concerns employ over 18,500 workers, about one quarter of all the employment in the manufacturing sector. A large cotton growing scheme in northern Ghana will halve imports of raw material but leaves a considerable shortfall. The import-substitution industries themselves generate considerable imports and are vulnerable when government policy is reducing imports by strict licensing. In 1979 Ghana's glass factory at Aboso had been virtually at a standstill for over two years because of import licensing problems, with 300 workers redundant but being paid and the country continuing to import glass that could have been manufactured locally.

Food- and agriculture-based industries import 48 and 47 per cent respectively of their raw material input and the erratic supply of local raw materials must be improved as a first priority. Recent government policy suggests that this is recognized but many existing industries need rehabilitation before there can be further growth. Such measures may restore foreign confidence but the economic malaise will not be solved without better economic management and leadership.

Nigeria, independent since 1960, is a vast and populous nation. It is four times the size of the United Kingdom or Ghana and has a population of over 80 million. Thanks to oil resources it is now one of the rich states of Africa, a situation that only developed during the decade of the 1970s and materially changed the pace and direction of development. With a larger area and unevenly distributed population, transport problems and costs are relatively greater than those of Ghana. The main concentrations of population lie in the south and north, separated by the thinly populated 'middle belt'. An extensive network of transport and communications is needed and their cost of provision, operation and maintenance is high, irrespective of the high costs arising from varied environmental disabilities. Early development plans differed in emphasis from those of Ghana. Much stress was laid upon education, public health, agriculture, urban and rural water supplies and road development. Industry was not ignored, but the need for a firm infrastructure was appreciated; industrial development was initially steady but cautious.

Nigerian manufacturing industry effectively began during the Second World War. Afterwards, in 1953, an International Bank Mission suggested various lines of industrial development, including vegetable-oil industries (such as soap and margarine manufacture), cocoa products, food canning, sack manufacture and associated fibre products, textiles, leather, wood products, cement and glass manufacture. Since then many of these industries have been established and the country is now the most industrialized country of West Africa. It possesses cotton ginneries, plywood factories, palm-oil processing plant, breweries and factories making cement, textiles, soap, margarine, leather and plastic goods, paper and chemical products. Nevertheless, in 1980 industry accounted for only 7 per cent of Nigeria's GDP; there were 1000 industrial establishments employing 170,000 workers.

The reluctance of Nigerians to forsake trade for industry where returns are less assured helps to explain the moderate pace of early development. To assist in the problems of finance the government enacted the Aid to Pioneer Industries Ordinance in 1952. Under this, any undertaking satisfying the condition that it was favourable to the Nigerian economy was granted a Pioneer Industry Certificate and obtained various tax reliefs. A Federal Loans Board also exists to give moderate financial aid to industrial projects. These measures, supported by aid revenues, have helped to bring about a marked expansion in consumer goods industries in the last five years, especially at Lagos and Port Harcourt. There are now over forty factories on the Ikeja Industrial Estate near Lagos, manufacturing such things as tyres and inner tubes, asbestos cement products, paints, beer and soft drinks.

The fuel and power situaton was radically changed during the 1960s by the successful exploitation of oil and natural gas, mainly in the Niger delta. Previously fuel and power for industrial development in Nigeria had been limited almost entirely to the coal from Enugu. This was one reason why a major hydroelectric project, the Niger Dam at Kainji in northern Nigeria (completed in 1969), was included in the Six Year Plan, 1962–8. Now with the completion of the third oil refinery (inland at Kaduna) and the beginning of an internal pipeline system there is occurring a shift from reliance on Enugu coal for industrial energy and electricity generation. Crude oil production in 1979 was over 110 million tonnes, and most of this was exported. The economy will benefit for many years to come, for mineral oil and natural gas are expected to be Nigeria's principal exports, and earned as much as £8000 million in 1979 – forty times the value of all Nigeria's exports in 1964.

The civil war, which broke out in 1967 with the abortive declaration of independence of the south-east under the name of Biafra, underlines Nigeria's greatest problem: that of tribalism. With more than 200 tribes and as many as 100 languages it has proved impossible yet to create one nation in Nigeria. The greatest division and distrust is between the three main regional population groups, the Hausas of the north, the Yoruba of the south-west and the Ibos of the south-east. The numerical superiority of the north has been seen as a threat by the rest of the country and one result is that the old British division with three administrative regions has been changed now to nineteen regions. Development progress is much hampered by mistrust and jealousy which again became overt when the military dictatorship, which had held the country together with an impartial hand, in 1979 handed over power to democratic civilian rule.

The Six Year Plan foundered in the civil war. The two National Development Plans of the 1970s changed the pace and character of Nigerian development, reflecting the increase of crude oil production up to 1975 and the great increase of oil prices between 1973 and 1980. Nigeria, a member of OPEC saw her oil export revenues increase from £1800 million in 1973 to over £8000 million in 1979. The sudden affluence saw a surge forward in consumer goods manufacture, in 'Nigerianization' of enterprises (some reserved for absolute ownership by Nigerians and others where no more than 40 per cent foreign participation was permitted) and in attaining a high increase of self-sufficiency by emphasis on import-substitute industries and the establishment of steel manufacturing plants and of petro-chemical industries.

Unfortunately the infrastructure was inadequate for such plans. Ports, railways and roads were congested or broke down under the enlarged volume of traffic and agriculture, replaced by oil as the main source of revenue, as in so many developing countries, became the poor relation – unromantic, unattractive and neglected for urban ways and promises of new life-styles. Thus the government allocated more resources to agriculture in the Fourth National Development Plan for 1981–5, to attempt to bring about a 'green revolution', to increase domestic food and cash crop production and to restore the traditional exports of palm oil, cocoa and groundnuts which declined dramatically with the oil boom of the 1970s. The oil revenues are also being utilized to establish an iron and steel industry.

The Enugu coal and iron ore deposits near Lokoja were regarded as a possible basis for an iron and steel industry as far back as 1958. The first post-independence National Development Plan (1962–8) put the creation of a steel industry into a prominent place, but by the end of the plan period no more than discussion with overseas interests and investigation of the resources had taken place. The United Nigerian Iron and Steel Company (UNISCO) was established but a setback followed, for the iron ores had a high phosphorous content and the Enugu coals were unsuitable for coking. However, the discovery of the oil-gas deposits in the south-east offered another possibility, that of a direct steel reduction plant fuelled by gas from the oilfields. West Germany, Austria and Japan were to become technical partners, but the civil war rendered the project abortive. A search for new ore and coal deposits was undertaken under the second Development Plan and Nigeria turned to the USSR for assistance. Meanwhile demand for steel products was increasing: over £70 million was spent on steel imports in 1971 and consumption during the 1970s grew at 12 per cent per annum. By 1973 suitable iron ore deposits were located near Itakpe and coal suitable for blast furnace operation was found at Lafia. In 1974 the site of Nigeria's first iron and steel plant was decided upon: Ajaokuta in Kwara state. There followed disagreement between the French technical advisers and the Russians regarding both the size of the plant and the form of the steel production (flat or long or mixed). Little progress followed until 1979 when a contract was signed with the Russians for the construction of the plant, initially with an output of 1.3 million tonnes of steel – at which rate the iron ore reserves would last 60 years. Until the Lafia coalfield is developed the plant will be fuelled by imported coking coal blended with Enugu coal. The building of the plant and the necessary infrastructure of roads and railways and power lines has been slow. Some steel is promised for 1983 although the plant would be unfinished. The cost of the plant will be over £2000 millions and 7000 Soviet technicians and their families are required to build and operate it.

Meanwhile a gas-operated direct reduction steel plant first mooted in 1977 had been constructed near Aladja in Bendel state not far from the Niger delta on the Warri river, which has been deepened to accept iron ore imports. The project was begun by a German–Austrian consortium in 1979, and compared with the Ajaokuta project showed impressive progress. Iron ore is imported from Brazil and Liberia and steel production commenced in 1982. The plant produces wire rods, bars, medium and light sections and billets for steel mills at Katsina, Jos and Osbogdo.

The outline of the chequered history of Nigeria's attempts to establish an indigenous steel industry has been given in order to underline a number of features that such a developing country has to face. First, these large advanced-technology projects are outside the experience of local contractors and businessmen. Planners and technologists from advanced countries become involved, opinions are sought of international bodies, the technocrats from one country disagree with those of another and years may pass without material progress. Nigeria, blessed with iron ore and coal deposits, and for the last decade rich with petro-dollars, has seen almost twenty years pass in talk on the size, form and location of its proposed steel industry, while its demands for steel increased annually. Second, an iron and steel plant has complex demands upon infrastructure and on a range of fuel and raw materials; it is quite unlike establishing a factory. Mineral exploration to locate suitable ores and coal in adequate quantity may take years. Their situations influence the location of the plant; when that is decided, expensive infrastructure of railway links, road links, power supplies, river dredging, etc. must be put in hand, and on the site costly workers' housing, services and amenities must be provided for the four or five years of plant construction. Third, for a number of years the plant needs to be operated by foreign technologists while indigenous labour is being trained. This and the infrastructure costs make for high-cost production for a considerable time, although an inland situation gives a measure of protection to inland markets because of freight rates on imported steel. Fourth, the Aladja steel-works near the coast have been more quickly and more cheaply established; a gas pipeline and river dredging being the most costly infrastructure provision. Imports of high quality ore are readily available – mineral exploration and mining are unnecessary. In terms of time and initial costs the coastal situation has advantages, although in the longer term the Ajoakuta plant with its linkages with coal and iron production will offer more to the Nigerian economy. Steel consumption in Nigeria is now 3 million tonnes a year and by 1985 is expected to be 5 million tonnes. Both plants, then hopefully in full production, will supply only half this amount. If self-sufficiency is still pursued a further plant and enlargement of the first two may be required.

Among other industries especially basic to development are those concerned with the creation of constructional materials. Of these the cement industry takes a paramount place yet it is rarely one of the earliest industries in a developing country. Reasons for this may be discerned from Nigeria, which now has the largest cement industry of West Africa. The industry dates from 1957; a prime reason for its seeming leisurely promotion is that a cement works needs to be large to be economic and must be kept in full production if disproportionate rises in costs are to be avoided. A further requirement, often difficult to meet in developing countries, is for good transport facilities to assemble raw materials not *in situ* and to distribute the bulky low-value product. The rise in demand for cement has made it feasible to establish three major plants in Nigeria. Cement consumption has increased from well below 100,000 tonnes to almost 1 million tonnes annually and continues to expand.

Proximity to the low-value raw materials of limestone and clay, and to the market, are important in such an industry where the product is both bulky and heavy in relation to its value and loses little weight in manufacture. Proximity to fuel deposits is less essential although an added advantage, since a modern works requires 25 tonnes of coal to make 100 tonnes of cement. The first Nigerian cement works (and the first in West Africa) was established at Nkalagu in the former Eastern Region in 1957. The plant is sited near limestone and shale deposits some thirty miles from the Enugu collieries and also obtains electricity from the Oji river power station. The site was completely undeveloped and required an eight-mile branch line and road connection to be made. The cement finds a market in the centre and north of the country.

Other cement works subsequently were established in the south-west and south-east, in Ogun province between Lagos and Abeokuta and at Calabar on the Cross river. That three regional cement factories can compete for the home market against one another and against imports reflects the growing pace of demand through the country's development and the careful location of the plants which enjoy the protection afforded to heavy, bulky low-value goods by transport cost which increase generally in direct proportion to the distance from factory to market. This results in each factory having a substantial 'protected' market area before meeting competition from its rivals or from imports.

Industrialization in Nigeria made distinct strides during the third Development Plan (1975–80) and for the most part followed an expected pattern of low-technology, light industries such as food, beverages, soaps, detergents, tyres, furniture and textiles. The next phase should be a move to intermediate and then capital goods manufacture, but this usually requires time to allow entrepreneurial and technological expertise to develop. Nigeria hopes to speed up the process, for her oil wealth may start to decline within twenty years and it behoves her to make use of it in laying the foundation for a modern diversified economy. Although a car assembly plant operates successfully, engineering industries are virtually non-existent. The decade of the 1980s will see efforts to expand the young industrial sector to take in the more intensive technologies of engineering in the manufacture of agricultural and industrial machinery and equipment, household electrical goods and transport equipment. Incentives to make greater use of indigenous raw materials, to develop more small-scale industries and to revive agriculture will, in the fourth National Development Plan, show some attempt to spread development more widely. The development of export-orientated industries is also an objective in order to reduce dependence on oil and primary product exports. Success in export markets requires economic, technological and social advances of some magnitude and products of quality and competitive price. These developments cannot occur overnight and may be much delayed by the rivalry between the states and the Federal government, demonstrated in the disputing of revenue allocation and of the location of enterprises, the delays in spending allocations, and tribal feuding and squabbling; all of which weaken democratic government and threaten the forward movement and emergence of Nigeria as a powerful modern African state.

Chile

An examination of the early history of the Huachipato iron and steel plant introduces us to Chile as a representative of the developing countries of South America and to the considerations and problems brought by the introduction of heavy industry in such a country. Population 'explosions' are occurring in many of Latin America's republics and the continent's population of about 350 million is likely to double within the next thirty years. The feudal structure of society over most of the continent explains vast differences in income per head between the two classes of society. The low average level of income, owing to the under-utilization of resources, reflects this feudal frame enclosing primary activities in relatively stagnating economies. Serious disabilities, both institutional and environmental, circumscribe and retard the development of both agriculture and industry.

In most of the Latin American republics, as a result of shortages during the Second World War and periodic foreign exchange crises, there is already a high degree of self-sufficiency in the manufacture of such consumer goods as textiles and clothing, shoes, cigarettes, pottery and pharmaceutical and toilet preparations. A proportion of these industries has developed largely on private investment by foreign firms establishing local plants. These industries are generally small and exhibit high costs; their markets are relatively minute for between a half and two-thirds of the population scarcely rank as consumers. The inelasticity of demand at near subsistence level means that products of, and growth of, manufacturing industries are of little direct interest to the mass of the population. Anachronistic and inefficient systems of land tenure hold back agricultural development, but it is easier and safer for governments to plan industrial innovations than to risk political and social upheaval by instituting agrarian reforms. Consequently it is possible to find in many of the smaller countries of Latin America numerous examples of industrial growth, yet the relative neglect of agriculture – a growing state of imbalance that may well add to, rather than decrease, the disparity of incomes. Short of revolution, which might shake the agricultural sector out of its lethargy and distribute wealth more widely, the market for consumer goods at present has few prospects of expansion. Faced with this stagnation, current thought and plans for industrial expansion in the larger republics place considerable stress upon heavy industry and power production. The great hydroelectric installations and dams, the development of oil resources and establishments of refineries and petro-chemical industries, the erecting of blast furnaces and steel mills may be ambitious acts of faith but they depend on foreign loans and grants, and subsequently demand formidable, large markets. Unless the nettle is grasped and there are real agrarian and social reforms and a substantial strengthening of infrastructure, a quaking, top-heavy industrial sector may well be the outcome in many Latin American republics.

Chile fits into this general pattern. Between 1940 and 1957 she received for capital development no less than $280 million in loans from the Export–Import Bank (Eximbank) and the International Bank of Reconstruction and Development (the 'World Bank'). This money helped to further the establishment of a range of industries and services, particularly electric power, oil, coal mining, steel, cement manufacture, food processing and transport modernization. In common with many other Latin American states chronic inflation since the war has led to a series of financial crises. This has distorted prices, hampered economic development, widened income gaps, encouraged investment in land and all too often toppled governments. The resulting stagnation of the economy was marked by an actual decline in national income after 1954 and a steady lowering of income per head as population increased. The level of investment was well below the country's needs and did not show improvement until after 1957, when a serious anti-inflation programme was adopted. The success of these measures restored the confidence of the World Bank and Eximbank, to whom the government applied for loans to develop hydroelectric power and modernize the coal industry and the railways. The lack of interest of private capital stems from the extremely limited size of the home market, for barely two-thirds of the 11 million population rank as consumers. Private capital concerns itself far more with mining, especially copper – the principal product upon which the economy depends. Copper, nitrates and iron ore provide the major exports, and workers in these export industries, now nationalized, do well; for example, the Chilean copper miner earns five times the average national industrial wage.

The Huachipato iron and steel plant near Concepcion, opened in 1950, represented a serious attempt at diversification of the economy. Further aims of the project were to reduce the imports of foreign steel, to eliminate steel shortage, and the stimulation of new steel-using local industries. It was felt that new industrial growth and better economic stability would help to raise the general standard of living. Iron and steel lie at the base of modern industrial structure, and possession of an iron and steel plant only too often may have a status symbol element. This applies less in the case of Chile, which has indigenous raw materials than, say, the San Nicolás plant in Argentina based upon imported raw materials.

In the established consumer goods industries in Latin America the scale of production is small, but generally so is the capital invested. The introduction of basic heavy industry such as iron and steel manufacture has been delayed in Latin America because even a plant of minimum economic size requires a very large investment, more than foreign investors are prepared to risk in view of the limited market potential. Chile is one of the few South American countries possessing both coal and good-quality iron ore. These are certainly 500 miles apart but both are situated near the coast and bulk transport by water is cheap. The precise location of such an industrial plant in a developing country is of outstanding importance in view of the high capital investment, for faulty location is permanent and the establishment may well remain unique in the country. Raw materials, markets, transport facilities, access to power and water, are some of the major considerations in determining the location of an iron and steel plant. The best combination of these should give lowest cost production.

Chile's integrated iron and steel works have been located on St Vincent's Bay, between the port of Talcahuano and the growing town of Concepcion (Figure 11). Sheltered deep water is adjacent

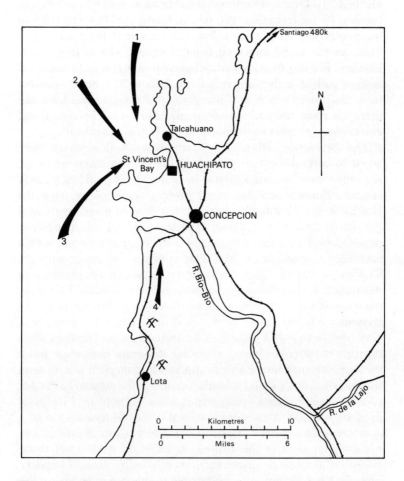

Figure 11 *The location of Huachipato: 1 iron ore (60% Fe) and manganese (45% Mn) from Coquimbo (500 miles); 2 coking coal (35% requirements) from USA; 3 limestone from Madre de Dios Island (950 miles); 4 local coking coal (65% requirements) (25 miles)*

to flat land where the plant has been built and a jetty permits the unloading of ore vessels from the El Romerel mine just north of Coquimbo, of limestone from the south and of cargoes of coking coal from the United States of America. Most of the coal used (65 per cent) is from mines at Lota and Schwager, twenty-five miles to the south, and is moved by rail. This coal is of high volatility and of poor coking quality and has to be mixed with imported medium volatile coal. Local coal-mining conditions are difficult and costs are high. Dolomitic limestone suitable as a blast-furnace flux is brought by sea from Guarello Island, Madre de Dios, 950 miles to the south. Dolomite with a low silica content for open-hearth furnaces has to be imported from Uruguay. The nearby rivers, Laja and Bio-Bio, provide hydroelectric power and fresh water (30 million gallons a day are required). Labour has been available from the nearby towns of Concepcion, Talcahuano and Lota and there are road, rail and sea communications with the capital and chief town 300 miles to the north in the fertile central valley.[4]

The 'protection' afforded by tranport costs of imported steel, allied to careful location permitting cheap bulk assembly of the low-value raw materials, have been the keys to Huachipato's success. Finance for the initial project came partly from the United States (Eximbank), from private foreign investors (mainly the USA) and from Chilean sources. One of the conditions imposed by Eximbank was that of a managerial contract with a reputable United States firm. This contract was made with the Koppers Company and still operates although the number of Americans at the plant has been progressively reduced. The initial plant consisted of fifty-seven coke ovens, one blast furnace, one Bessemer converter, two open-hearth furnaces, a blooming mill, plate sheets and a tin-plate mill. In 1954 this was expanded when thirteen more coke ovens, a second Bessemer converter and a third open-hearth furnace were added. More modern rolling plant was installed in 1956 and a fourth open-hearth furnace was added and the steel-processing plant expanded in 1959. In 1971 the plant produced 500,000 tonnes of pig iron and 515,000 tonnes of steel – as much as the domestic market could absorb. Costs of production, while higher than in the United States, still enable steel to be marketed in Chile at prices substantially below that of imports. The plant has benefited by being able to operate at capacity, but planned expansion of the plant designed to double output during the 1970s led to overproduction, with a failure to find foreign buyers. Steel-using industries in Chile have expanded notably since 1950, many plants being established around Concepcion and the steel works. New products include cars, buckets, pots and pans, pipes, wire, stoves, refrigerators, agricultural equipment.

This plant, despite its modest size, the third largest in South America, is undoubtedly a successful undertaking and ranks as a most important element in Chile's industrialization. It represents a successful utilization of indigenous resources, it has provided new industrial employment both in itself and in the new metal-using industries: it has reduced costs of steel to domestic consumers and saved foreign exchange by replacing the bulk of steel imports. It may be questioned, however, how far this enterprise has helped in the great national problem of poverty due to under-development. Was this the kind of enterprise required to revive the economy and pump fresh life into all its members?

In a sense the steel plant has operated in a closed economy within the stagnating national economy. It makes profits, but most go to service the capital loaned and to overseas participants. The moderate lowering of steel costs has made but a very limited widening of the domestic market which remains small since the purchasing power of the mass of the population has been little affected. We are led to the conclusion that the creation of Huachipato was badly timed: its full benefits will come with an expanding purposeful economy; in itself it cannot create those conditions but the money invested in it might well have done so.

An efficient iron and steel plant attached to a small high-cost industrial sector emphasizes uneven and unbalanced development. Despite great income from mining, Chile remains an agricultural country, yet her agriculture has been allowed to stagnate. For many years it has failed to keep pace with rising population so that production per head has declined, and whereas twenty years ago Chile exported more agricultural produce than she imported, now she can no longer feed herself but imports up to one quarter of her food for her growing urban population. The system of land ownership inherited from the Spaniards, whereby, for example, 3 per cent of the landowners hold 37 per cent of the land, indicates a great gap between the rich landowner and the labourer or peasant. Many landowners prefer to live in Santiago than at their haciendas, and although much of the interior may be barren mountainside, there does remain cultivable land left as rough grazing. Government price policies and inflation, whereby land was bought as a defence against monetary devaluation rather than for cultivation, have aided this situation.

Since 1940 Chile's population has grown annually by about 2 per cent, whereas *per capita* production of food has increased annually by only 0.6 per cent. The root of Chile's poverty and under-development lies in her agricultural sector where change was resisted by the landowning aristocracy. Agrarian reforms to bring about the removal of anachronistic tenure systems, to reduce the under-productive large estates and to share the land (and thus much of the national income) more equally, associated with investment in irrigation, communications and services, pumps and agricultural equipment, would seem the logical first stages to any planned development. As much as 2 million more acres could become productive. Early measures of agrarian reform were timid until the left-wing government of Dr Allende came to power in 1970 and pushed the matter ruthlessly and at times unconstitutionally. This government, with Marxist sympathies, set out to change radically the economic and social structure of the country by wide-spread nationalization of the major (including foreign) firms, state control of banks and insurance, means of communication, etc. Inflation increased rapidly and production fell. Over-rapid and badly organized agrarian reform accompanied by widespread squatting on large estates led to a fall in agricultural production of 15 per cent and necessitated record imports of foodstuffs. Lawless-ness increased and the economy was at the point of collapse when Dr Allende and his administration were ousted by a right-wing military coup in 1973.

The new government reversed the policies of its predecessor. It tackled inflation by sharp cuts in official spending, including subsidies to public enterprises and holding down wages and it quickly began the return of nationalized businesses to the private sector. It reorganized and slowed down the agrarian reform and measures were passed to welcome foreign investment and drastic reductions in protective tariffs forced greater efficiency from Chilean manufacturing industry which now had to face foreign competition. Measures were passed to control and reduce the power of trade unions and this led to a polarization of the situation into direct confrontation between left-wing led workers and the powerful right-wing government intent on getting the country back on its feet despite world obloquy as the trampler upon Chilean democracy.[5]

Argentina

Argentina is one of the most industrialized countries in Latin America and by many indices now deserves classification as a semi-developed country. Its manufacturing industry accounts for nearly 40 per cent of GNP and employs almost 30 per cent of the labour force; much of this development has occurred since 1940. Nevertheless there are wide regional differences in the levels of development: the centre–periphery theory is well exemplified and many parts of the country are under-developed. A study of Argentina's progress to development reveals social and political, as well as economic, turmoil attendant upon policies of furthering import-substitute industries at the expense of agriculture and upon her positive attempts to use fiscal and financial measures to advance these aims.

Argentina's greatest resource, developed over the last century, is the vast area of virtually stoneless level plain, the Pampa, that has been completely transformed from rough pasture of bunch grass tufts to one of the most fertile agricultural areas of Latin America, specializing in food grain, feed grain and beef production. The opening up of the Pampa for overseas agricultural markets occurred after foreign capital had created a web of railway lines over the plain, focusing on the historic deep-water port of Buenos Aires. Once given this infrastructure, the great area of temperate grassland become one of the world's major food producing areas, finding assured export markets in Europe. The country's economy became based upon this efficient agricultural sector and Buenos Aires having become the transport node of the country developed banking and insurance services and changed from an administrative to a commercial centre. It became the point of contact and inter-change between Argentina and the rest of the world. The concentration of economic activity in the metropolitan region of greater Buenos Aires is now overwhelming. This region accounts for over 50 per cent of national value added and the surrounding province of Buenos Aires for another 25 per cent.

In this century the occurrence of two wars and, between them, the great depression, led to sharp attempts to diversify the economy, to formal economic planning and to the emergence of social, political and economic problems with which the country still grapples. The great depression of the 1930s seriously affected the economy which was so heavily dependent on export of primary products. Prices paid for these products fell as demand slackened; the export of primary products by value fell by almost two-thirds between 1929 and 1932. Imports had to be severely curtailed and, with the slow recovery during the 1930s, Argentina began to seek ways of reducing its dependence on trade in primary products. This policy became reinforced during the Second World War when again imports from overseas were severely reduced. This time, however, demand for Argentina's meat and grain was strong and foreign exchange earnings accumulated since imports of manufactured goods from the warring developed world were not available. Under these conditions the domestic production of manufactures received a great fillip, and during the war years the output of manufactures increased by nearly 25 per cent. The post-war period has been characterized by strong nationalistic policies arising from a desire to be free of overseas capital, to become self-sufficient and economically independent. It was felt that too much of the national wealth lay in the hands of non-resident foreigners whose capital had established much of the infrastructure of railways, port facilities, power supplies, banking and insurance. A great part of the foreign exchange accumulated during the war became used to purchase these basic utilities for the nation, thus reducing dependence on, and cost of, foreign capital. It was the strong nationalistic spirit of the times that encouraged these moves but, with hindsight, it might have been better if the money had been used for capital goods imports and the establishment of a firm industrial base. Instead, in a spirit of autarky and to foster import-substitute industries, tariffs became levied on most imported goods.

The automatic protection of home-produced goods by wartime shortage of imports was thus perpetuated in the post-war period by tariffs. The light industries, mainly of consumer goods, that had arisen during the war needed no high level of technology nor of finance and were assured of a captive market. Most of the new industries were small, many of no more than workshop size. Much of the capital and expertise brought in by immigrants from Europe after the war became invested in such businesses, which became located mainly within greater Buenos Aires because of inadequate infrastructure and utilities elsewhere. The opportunity to establish and nurture an infrastructure of capital goods industries and to repair and revitalize utilities neglected during the war was not then grasped. The decade following the war saw marked advances in industrial techniques in the developed countries and the technological gap between them and the small-scale, poorly capitalized Argentine industries became very wide. Often there were too many enterprises in the same field and, with the small national market, there was much under-utilization of plant, but the resulting high-cost production was sustained by the protective tariffs and forced upon the captive home market. At great expense (US$300 million) a small integrated iron and steel plant was built at San Nicolás, upstream of the capital. Opened in 1962, it relies heavily on imported raw materials – coking coal to mix with Argentina's coal, iron ore (later some coming from Patagonia), pig iron and scrap. The familiar problem of an inadequate home market sufficient to sustain a plant of viable size led in the early years to particularly high production costs. Heavy industrial development was held back by the limited energy resources available and their peripheral location far from Buenos Aires. The major oilfields and working coalfield lie far south in Patagonia or in the west at Mendoza. Oil and gas pipelines were slow in being constructed, and although Argentina now produces 90 per cent of its oil requirements, its reserves are small.

Much of the post-war period was characterized by the growing power of trade unions, conceded by the government for political reasons. Wages became pushed ahead of productivity, internal consumption of agricultural products increased at the expense of exports, inflation grew to astronomical proportions, and foreign capital became scared away. It is well known that under inflationary conditions governments attempt to restrain price rises in the public sector where they have some control, and this was done in Argentina. Utilities suffered, particularly electricity supply and the railways. Maintenance was reduced, old equipment was not replaced and trading deficits grew to swell the deficits in the national budget. Again and again the peso was devalued (ten times between 1964 and 1967) but without lasting benefit: it discouraged domestic savings and frightened away much foreign capital. These frequent adjustments to the exchange rate also deterred exports, for their profitability became unpredictable and the devaluations also raised prices of imported goods including machinery and parts required for the protected import-substitute industries.

Policies of fostering import-substitute industries by tariff protection result in a bias against agriculture: the farmer must pay more for the manufactures he needs while he receives relatively less for his farm produce. During the 1960s this redistribution of income in favour of the industrial (that is, urban) sector was equivalent to a 5–6 per cent tax on the farmer,[6] and this was in addition to taxes on all sales of grain and cattle for slaughtering, a 1.5 per cent wealth tax (which is particularly severe on the farmer who has a low ratio of sales and profits to capital), plus ever-rising land taxes. Low farm prices (politically favoured to bring cheap food to the urban masses) caused a serious decline in farm morale, increased regional inequalities of income and reduced incentives to expand agricultural production. Investment was channelled away from agriculture and cropped acreage became reduced; inflated wages and low prices sharply increased domestic consumption of farm products thus reducing amounts for export. Exports, unattractive with frequent devaluations, fell seriously and led to trade deficits during the 1970s and reduced the availability of foreign exchange. At the same time growing protective policies of the EEC countries reduced customary markets for Argentina's wheat, wool and meat.

For a time after 1967 there was a change of policy. Restrictions on foreign investment were lifted, and by the end of the decade overdue investment was taking place in infrastructure and utilities: railways, power, water supplies and gas. A national investment fund raised money domestically and in Europe; other finance came as loans from the World Bank and the Inter-America bank. The Hydrocarbons Law was revised, granting concessions to foreign oil companies and projects in chemicals, agricultural machinery and motor-car assembly (mainly sponsored by United States firms) were welcomed. After twenty years ultra-nationalistic policies were reversed and a leading role in expanding the industrial sector was envisaged for private investment, particularly from overseas. A more formal approach to the country's development problems came with details of a five year Investment Plan (1970–4), giving priority to the development of energy and heavy industry. Projects, some already begun, included the construction of a nuclear power plant, hydroelectric schemes, a natural gas pipeline from Neugen to Bahia Blanca, an aluminium project on the Patagonian coast, an enlarging to 4 million tons of the steel-making capacity at San Nicolás, the expansion of car assembly and road and port improvement. The export of manufactures was encouraged by 12–15 per cent offered in tax rebates and the establishment of an export promotion agency. All branches of industry expanded during this period but still at the expense of the agricultural sector.

However this resurgence of industrial development stimulated by the welcoming of foreign capital and the import of high-level technology was short lived. Credit relaxations and numerous heavy wage and pension increases, granted for political and social reasons, spurred on both inflation and domestic demand. Reserves declined, trade fell into deficit and heavy foreign indebtedness increased, all being heightened by changing governments and political uncertainty. Reversion to more autarkic policies occurred in 1973 when restrictions on foreign investment were again imposed and existing corporations controlled by foreign capital were directed to increase the domestic capitalization to between 51 and 80 per cent or face heavier taxation. Foreign investment virtually ceased and industrial production declined. The second Investment Plan of 1974–7 revealed growing government control in banking, heavy industry (such as iron and steel and petro-chemicals), electricity generation, transport and communications. A military Junta under General Videla took over in 1976 amid economic recession and began the difficult task of stabilizing the economy. A policy of austerity was imposed, real wages actually declined, the power of the trade unions was checked, public finances were reorganized and economic revival was sought through expanding agriculture and the export sectors. Good weather, credit assistance and realistic exchange rates led to expansion of acreage and record grain crops. New markets for meat replacing those lost by the EEC restrictions were found in Eastern bloc states. Industry, which included many inefficient high-cost producers, began over five years to lose the tariff protection which had been a cornerstone of the import-substitute policies since the Second World War. Inflation remained the chief problem as the decade of the 1980s was reached. This had begun to fall with the firm government measures of budgetry control and a restrictive wage policy, but the powerful banking lobby pressed that the major weapon to fight inflation should be the exchange rate and a system of crawling devaluation was introduced after 1978. This led to over-valued currency which, with high interest rates, struck hard at the farming community who had hoped for better days. Their incomes from exports became sharply reduced and in turn their reduced purchasing power pushed the industrial sector into deeper depression.

Argentina differs from most countries of the Third World in that the adult population is highly articulate, 94 per cent of it being literate. Nearly four-fifths of the population are urban, and trade unions are well developed and have exerted powerful pressures on a succession of governments, forcing up wages and pensions and furthering measures of support for the urban-industrial sector. Left-wing violence became countered by right-wing extremists, and from the mid 1960s the country was in a state of political anarchy with assassinations, kidnappings and bombings that only became curtailed after Videla's military junta took over in 1976. It gradually restored law and order, but at considerable social cost, including loss of individual and trade union freedom. Argentina therefore displays quite distinctive features on its path to development.

It will be seen that economic development in Argentina since the Second World War has been of a sporadic nature and has been sectorally and spacially uneven. Much of this devolves from the country's espousal of autarkic policies emphasized in fostering consumer goods (and latterly in heavy capital goods) industries under tariff protection. Many of these have been of dubious efficiency and are high-cost producers, and nearly all have located in, or adjacent to, the multi-million city of Buenos Aires. Despite lip service to the notion, especially in the two published plans, there has been no real dispersal of industry. Food-processing industries for the domestic market have been expanded at Mendoza and Tucuman and engineering and car assembly at Cordoba but the bulk of the import-substitute industries became established in the traditional belt of activity from Rosario down the River Plate through Buenos Aires to la Plata, the Interior areas having little more than poorly capitalized workshop industries. Greater Buenos Aires now has a population approaching 10 million within a total national population of 26 million. The overwhelming primacy of the capital city is sustained by its being the country's major port for the ingress of raw materials, machinery and parts, by offering the largest and most concentrated market with the highest purchasing power, and by utilities being deficient away from the capital. The post-war period has seen this core area developed markedly but at the expense of the periphery. To redress the balance growth-poles were designated in the two Investment Plans (see Figure 12). Many of these relate to areas with local fuel or mineral resources: Neuquen has oil and gas, hydroelectric power, and is the centre of an area of irrigation agriculture; Jujuy and Salta have oil and gas; Puerto Madryn and Sierra Grande mine and ship ore and will produce aluminium. However, widespread industrial development

Figure 12 *Economic development in Argentina*

at these sites is dubious; external economies are lacking and local markets are small, for the centres listed do not coincide with the population concentrations in the Interior and will siphon off investment from them. It has been suggested that the emphasis on Patagonia rather than the more populous north is for stategic rather than economic reasons.[7]

Oil-fired thermal plants supply most of the electricity used by Argentina's industry and the sharp rise in world oil prices throughout the 1970s and Argentina's limited oil reserves turned attention to other sources of electric power, notably the development of nuclear and hydroelectric power. There are nuclear plants near Cordoba and at Atucha, 100 kilometres north-west of Buenos Aires (a second plant will be completed there by 1987). Hydroelectric schemes have been planned over past decades but governments have rarely survived long enough to see them established. However, swift-flowing Andean rivers are now harnessed near Neuqen and another large plant is shared with Uruguay at Salto Grande. Other schemes are under construction or planned on the Parana river. By 1985 nearly half the country's electricity requirements should come from hydro power and a firm base for industrial expansion should then be available.

Although progress has been made in supplying the home market with textiles, clothing, footwear, paper, rubber, cement and home-assembled cars and tractors, the development of industry in Argentina over the last forty years has been muddled and disappointing. Progress has been by fits and starts reflecting political, social and strategic decisions rather than economic ones. Successive governments have been obsessed with national autarky and have embarked upon policies of protection to nurture import-substitute industries, many of doubtful viability bearing in mind the limited market offered by 20 million or so in an area the size of Western Europe. These developments were at the expense of agriculture and farming has been in the doldrums. This has led to a marked movement of labour from the Pampa to the capital. Agriculture in the Interior has expanded but mainly because labour inputs there are cheaper than capital inputs and productivity is low. The substantial growth of Buenos Aires as the country's one overwhelming urban area brought political repercussions in the expansion, and the growing militancy, of trade unions. The dangers of excessive urban unemployment often led weak governments to grant fruits of development that had not been earned and to let a nation in a hurry attempt to run before it could walk.

The case studies of Argentina and Chile both representative of Latin American patterns introduce new features that should be noted. Unlike much of the developing world the populations in these countries are literate and articulate. Both countries have been independent since the early years of the nineteenth century, and their evolutionary struggles have been with a landed aristocracy and a neo-colonialism of foreign investment and control of much of their early industry and transport. It is perhaps this feature – exemplified by the British-owned railways of Argentina and American-owned copper mines in Chile – that led to xenophobia and measures of autarky, which strengthened evolving trade unions and stimulated political and ideological differences to the point where the economy and its planning collapsed with a breakdown of law and order. Under these conditions the army emerges as a power to control the country and to reverse policies, generally towards the right and sometimes harshly enforced. Democracy may well become a retarding factor in economic development if ideologies rouse passions and split a nation.

Hong Kong

Hong Kong is one of the few Third World communities that does show rapid progress in economic development; a progress that is based almost entirely upon the development of manufacturing industry. In 1951 the annual *per capita* income for its 2 million people stood at £85; in 1977 for an enlarged population of 4.5 millions it was £1250. This achievement deserves the widest publicity among other developing countries. The colony comprises 236 islands and islets and a small part of the mainland east of the Pearl river estuary. The total area is 404 square miles, made up of Hong Kong island (29 square miles), the tip of the Kowloon peninsular on the mainland (4 square miles) – these being ceded to Britain in 1842 and 1860 respectively – and the New Territories which are leased from China until 1997. Most of the area is mountainous and many of the islands are virtually waterless. Only 13 per cent of the total area is under crops, livestock and fish farming, and the bulk of the food for the population has to be imported.

In 1946 following the Japanese wartime occupation the population was reduced to 600,000, the port facilities were in a sorry state and the entrepôt trade destroyed. Many Chinese began returning to the colony and their numbers were soon augmented by hundreds of thousands of refugees fleeing from the Communist takeover of China. By 1950 the population was over 2 million – far more than entrepôt trade could support. Before the war Hong Kong existed on entrepôt trade; it served all Far Eastern countries but the greater part of its business was with China for whom it took on the attributes of a huge shop. Following the war the trade with China was much reduced and new markets were sought in such countries as Malaya, Indonesia, Japan and Korea. Such trade was inadequate for so large a population and the colony became transformed from a trading into a manufacturing economy.

The decision to further manufacturing industry was the only one possible. The rapidly growing population, considerably swollen by Chinese refugees, could not be fed from local production and there were few resources and services with which to pay for food imports amounting to seven-eighths of total consumption. The colony was in the unenviable position of having virtually no raw materials, fuel or power with which to develop industry and could only capitalize her two major resources of position in relation to world seaways and trade, and an abundant supply of cheap labour. To these, refugee capital, expertise and entrepreneurship were employed in full measure. No other country in the world has fought and overcome such handicaps, for even Japan was not utterly destitute of raw materials and fuel. Hong Kong's success is in contrast with many other Asian countries facing similar problems who have made little progress. Much of the success is due to the character and quality of the people, but credit must also be given to the form of government and its percipient policies.

Nearly all the workers and most of the entrepreneurs are Chinese, who have a world-wide reputation for diligence, perseverance and thrift. They are dextrous, skilful, quick to learn, and shrewd in perceiving opportunities. Some private saving goes abroad, often to families left in China; the rest becomes invested in the colony, in tools and machinery or as public saving, of which the government has made wise use in building up utilities. Inevitably there has been a certain amount of unemployment and this has tempered wage demands to reasonable limits.

In the immediate post-war years, when a mass of refugees swarmed into the colony, cheap and plentiful labour was a mainstay of Hong Kong's economic growth. Enterprises were mainly small-scale, often family-operated workshops. Wages today still seem low by European standards, but they are not by Asian standards, for they are the best in Asia excluding Japan. Wages paid in the textile industry are nearly double those paid in India, Pakistan and Taiwan. Hong Kong rates also represent low labour costs, because the productivity of labour is high. Daily working hours are limited to a maximum of eight for women and young persons (aged 14–17) and a total of forty-eight hours per week. There are no restrictions on working hours for men and generally men employed in manufacturing industry work between eight and nine hours a day. The notion that Hong Kong thrives on sweated and half-starved labour has long been dissipated. Cost of living for the masses in Hong Kong, particularly for food, housing and transport, is much less than in Western Europe and levels of living far surpass those of neighbouring China and other south-east Asian countries. The constant flow of illegal immigrants into the colony from China reflects the attraction of better conditions and of opportunities for personal betterment.

Foremost among these circumstances helpful to the colony's development is its geographical position and its possession of one of the best harbours in the world. These led to the growth of a great port with associated repair and servicing facilities, able to offer certain external economies to new industries. Such a port has banking, finance and insurance facilities and commercial connections with suppliers and potential customers all over the world. The very concentration of industry into so limited an area adds to the scale of external economies that accrued and to the scope and efficiency of the public utilities. The stable government, law and order, and absence of corruption attracted both the entrepreneur and the investor, many originally being Chinese refugees who did not come into the colony destitute and who were prepared to risk their capital in new manufactures and new methods, ever seeking new markets. They were favoured by low rates of taxation, a measure of Commonwealth preference, but not tariff protection, special concessions or subsidies from the government.

Over the last twenty years there has been an amazing growth both of industry and in the degree of sophistication of its products. In 1953 there were 800 establishments each employing more than twenty workers, in 1978 the number had grown to 5000. In that year there were a further 16,000 establishments each with less than

Figure 13   *Hong Kong's expansion into the New Territories*

twenty workers, indicating the retained importance of the small (and often family) enterprise. The range of manufactured goods has expanded markedly and they now account for 80 per cent of the colony's exports. Heavy industry is restricted to ship-building, repairing and ship-breaking (Hong Kong is the world's largest ship-breaking centre). Over half the scrap from broken-up ships is exported to Japan, but the colony's growing steel-rolling mills are supplied; they produce reinforcing rods and bars, some for export. Textiles form the largest manufacturing industry (with 1 million spindles, 25,000 looms and employing 45 per cent of the total labour force). The industry includes spinning and weaving, finishing, dyeing and garment-manufacturing and accounts for 50 per cent of the colony's exports by value. All types of textile goods and garments are produced and it is the garment sector that has shown the most rapid growth in recent years and is now the largest sector of Hong Kong industry as a whole. In contrast to the rest of the textile industry, firms engaged in garment production are usually very small, many employing less than ten workers. The success of the garment industry is based upon sophistication and quality. Hong Kong can now be undercut by lower wage-rate Taiwan and Korea and the era of cheap singlets is now passed. Instead quality and design have priority and Hong Kong has developed as a fashion centre for ready-to-wear clothes, supplying many famous multiple-stores in the developed world. Other manufactures include enamel ware (mainly for African and south-east Asian markets), vacuum flasks, electric torches, batteries, transistor products, metal goods such as hurricane lanterns, stove lamps, nails, metal windows, zip fasteners; footwear, rubber and leather goods, plastic ware, especially toys and artificial flowers; wig-making, printing and publishing and cement manufacture (only the clay being local raw material). In recent years the tourist industry has been particularly fostered and about 2 million tourists (a quarter from Japan) now visit the colony annually bringing in a revenue of over £400 million – the second greatest after textiles.

The colony is now moving away from the stage where it relies upon low-wage industries to give it competitiveness; it has broadened its range of products and introduced new and advanced technologies. Units of production have become larger, more research and innovation is now taking place. Newer industries include the manufacture of machine tools and steel tableware, while the electronics industry has expanded to include the manufacture of memory cores for computers and complete television sets. Education from 6 to 15 years is free and compulsory, and there is substantial provision for higher and further education. A new polytechnic, established in 1972, now has nearly 25,000 full- and part-time students. Education, the development of skills, the understanding of new technologies and of business management are regarded as keys to success in this busy, pulsating community.

The far-flung trade connections of the colony have been of benefit, but she has been assiduous in seeking out and fostering overseas markets, attending trade fairs all over the world, sending out trade missions, pushing her wares persistently and so successfully that old-established industrial centres such as Lancashire have recently cried out for discrimination against imports. In the case of Lancashire this has resulted in an agreed voluntary reduction of exports of grey cloth from Hong Kong to Britain. The United States has also sought a voluntary reduction of exports of grey cloth, while Kenya and Uganda have imposed import duties on enamelware in order to protect local industry, a form of discrimination that must be expected throughout Africa and south-east Asia as young manufacturing industries develop. France as a member of the European Common Market has also abrogated her liberal trade policies regarding Hong Kong textiles. In short, a new phase is occurring: as one critic has put it 'because her competition was too effective'.

These developments, the negation of the 'trade not aid' theme which Hong Kong has vigorously espoused, must not blind us to the colony's astounding industrial progress. Such a virile community does not let the pace of development flag. The scarcity of water and suitable land for industrial purposes are current difficulties being surmounted by water conservation schemes and the levelling of hills and use of the spoil to reclaim land from the sea. These developments are on a particularly large scale in the New Territories, in order to provide sites for three new towns each with a population of 500,000, which will be completed by the mid 1980s.[8] Earlier a scheme at Kwun Tong in Kowloon Bay had reclaimed fifty-eight acres (for twenty-two new factories) and a further large area has been reclaimed for the international airport at Kwai Tak. At Tsuen Wan, itself a new town of the 1960s, some 6000 acres of offshore and bay reclamation is now being undertaken, 711 acres being destined for industrial development.[9] Land, however, becomes more expensive – a serious matter since cost of land has always been a greater proportion of final cost of an industrial unit than is normal elsewhere. Labour, too is likely to become more expensive and Hong Kong's competitive advantage may become less pronounced during the present decade.

Hong Kong's colonial status is important. It is not a democracy for the governor, although served by advisory bodies, is all-powerful. Thus policies can be continuous and are unswayed by promises of politicians seeking votes. Unusually no series of formal development plans has ever been promulgated, instead the government has relied upon *laissez-faire* policies embodied in free enterprise, free trade and minimal taxation. The government's role has been to help industry to function efficiently by providing a stable framework of law, order and adequate infrastructure. The Chinese entrepreneur has free rein, and self-capitalization, by the constant reinvestment of profits, is the principal form of finance for Hong Kong's growing industries.

In many respects the unique character of Hong Kong's material and human situation has forced development along limited channels. She has succeeded in avoiding starvation for her growing millions by successful industrialization, whereby she realized her two great advantages of low wage rates and high productivity of labour. The limitations of her situation and resources have brought the classic response of fabricating raw materials that are light relative to their value and that require little fuel in the manufacture. We now have the abnormal situation of a developing country successfully living by the export of manufactures. The lesson to be appreciated by other developing countries, especially of Asia, is that the activities creating the links in this chain of development were not automatic and of mystical origin, but have become a reality thanks to a firm government committed to the minimum of interference with the development of the economy and to the efforts, exertion and driving force of a dedicated, disciplined and perceptive people.

10 The progress of industrialization
2: India; Egypt

India

India is now one of the most anomalous states in the world: she has developed a most impressive industrial sector with considerable capacity in iron and steel, engineering, aircraft manufacture, machine tools, electrical and electronic goods, chemicals and fertilizers. She now has acknowledged expertise in nuclear engineering. In all this she is virtually unique within the Third World; nevertheless she still has an overwhelming agrarian economy and after thirty years of immense investment and planning effort the lot of the mass of her population remains virtually unchanged. The problems India attempts to overcome are multitudinous and massive. Since 1951 she has launched six Five-Year Plans involving thousands of millions of pounds and putting to the test on a massive scale modern wisdom and theory upon the stimulation of economic growth. Much has been achieved, but to many the final goals seem as far away now as they were thirty years ago.

For much of the colonial period India's economy appears to have stagnated. The occupational structure of the population scarcely altered during the first half of the century, for in 1911 it was estimated that 71 per cent of the working population was engaged in agriculture while in 1948 the proportion was 68 per cent. The population grew by 52 per cent in this half-century (1901 census, 235.5 million; 1951 census, 365.9 million) but the expansion of the economy lagged; the sown area per person declined and yields did not increase. Sir John Russell suggests that the deterioration of the dietary had begun before the 1930s, although strictly comparable data are lacking to confirm this.[1] Under-employment in rural areas reached chronic proportions: poverty, disease and famine have come to be regarded as the traditional lot of the Indian peasantry. A policy of protection commencing in

1922 favoured the growth of a small industrial sector and the shortages during the Second World War gave India's young industries a further fillip. Textiles, iron and steel, cement and sugar manufacture were among the major industries at the time of independence and partition (1947) and a large amount of workshop or cottage industry existed. Modern type industry, however, only gave employment to 2.4 million workers. Precise data regarding *per capita* income are lacking, but estimates for 1948–9 put it at about £20 per head.

India's poverty and remedial problems are best demonstrated by certain statistics. The degree of literacy despite determined efforts at improvement is only 36 per cent (women alone, 25 per cent); there are nearly 4000 persons per doctor (750 in the UK) and 1300 persons per hospital bed (109 in the UK). Some 80 per cent of the population is rural and 125,000 of India's 500,000 villages are still primitive in that they lack pure water supply, sewerage, drainage and electricity. The grinding poverty of the masses, with their lives of leisurely toil, their unvarying and insufficient diet, often still at the mercy of the landlord or village usurer, all enveloped in a decaying caste system, serves to multiply the difficulties for the government to whom the Indian people traditionally look for succour and guidance. An Indian finance minister has said, 'We cannot afford to make a slip for our capacity to pay for our follies is very limited.' This may well apply also to the Indian peasant who lives at near-starvation level; with so little margin he dare not run risks by varying his traditional husbandry. To sap this solid wall of rural conservatism is a task demanding time, and that the planners are being denied.

A particular feature about India's planned development, taken as axiomatic by the planning commission, has been a pronounced emphasis within the industrial sector on heavy, basic capital-intensive industries such as steel, coal, oil, power and chemicals, developed as government monopolies. The rigorous implementation of these views has divided Western economists. Many believe, and events seem to support them, that much more investment should be made in agriculture, transport and education before heavy expenditure on steel mills, but others support the views of the Indian planners, pointing out that in many respects India stands apart from the majority of developing countries.[2] India has large reserves of some of the richest iron ores in the world (over 60 per cent Fe), manganese coal, bauxite and mica. There is a large potential of hydroelectric power and oil prospecting is now meeting with some small success. India's plans, influenced by these endowments and the knowledge that industrialization has the major role in securing rapid economic advance, have favoured capital-intensive projects because of the narrow base of the existing industrial sector, with little development of the basic and heavy industry that provides the foundations on which manufacturing industries depend. It was felt that India's potential to produce steel, aluminium, chemicals and other basic materials relatively cheaply should be realized as rapidly as possible, although the amount of investment required in such plants is tremendous and the initial return and numbers employed are relatively small. As has been pointed out earlier, the application of such policies requires a degree of discipline and fortitude in the population: a belief that by having no jam today, at least some will become available tomorrow.

A great deal of cottage and small-scale industry exists in rural India and considerable support for them is being given in the sixth Development Plan (1978–83). The claimed advantages are that they use more labour and less capital per unit of output than large industry and that small industries are a useful means of dispersal of industry. Futher, they decentralize economic power, distribute income more evenly and reduce the centre–periphery manifestations. Cottage establishments are largely centred on the village and use labour-intensive techniques to make traditional goods. These are now joined by small factory enterprises using power and modern production techniques and making products new to India such as umbrellas, torches, aluminium utensils and sewing machines in a considerable effort at import-substitution. Aided by tariffs and import restrictions, and government help by means of loans and hire-purchase finance for the buying of machinery, these are growing in numbers and have become a major supplier of consumer goods. By 1980 most consumer goods were Indian made. As the programme advances some of the earlier premises seem less valid. Recent studies have shown that the smaller enterprise does not always save capital; quite often small factories use not merely more labour but also more capital per unit of output. They usually have relatively more unused capacity than larger plants and seldom work more than one shift. Also the need for external economies prevents their widespread dispersal among villages.[3] Nevertheless, with 20 million unemployed and a greater number under-employed, small industries being more labour-intensive are deemed to have a growing part to play in the economy. Also the growth of these new small enterprises is bringing into being the all-important class of go-ahead industrialists and entrepreneurs, emerging from diverse social and economic backgrounds.

It is proposed to review Indian development plans in order to demonstrate the strategy employed and to take note of their fortunes and experiences. India's charted course to development began with her first Five Year Plan (in 1951) two others followed but the fourth plan (nominally 1966–70) had its commencement delayed three years owing to the economic crisis related to the brief war with Pakistan and the failure of the monsoons in 1965–7. The fifth plan (1974–9) was overtaken by the sixth plan (1978–83). The broad allocation of both public and private development investment is given in Tables 9 and 10, and the magnitude of India's task is mirrored in their totals: £2500 million, £5060 milion, £7800 million, £14,250 million, £49,000 million and £100,700 million. Each plan becomes more gigantic to sustain the momentum of its predecessor, and the returns expected at first sight might appear very modest. This is a reflection of the enormous investment in services necessary to establish an infrastructure of the size and scale deemed necessary to support and sustain the industrial growth of a sub-continent.

The first Five Year Plan was designed to raise investment from a traditional 5 per cent to 7 per cent of the national income and laid much emphasis on public utilities, services and on agricultural development. Power, transport, communications, education and health absorbed 55 per cent of the £1500 million of the public sector's outlay, while irrigation and agriculture took 31 per cent. Industry and mining rightly received a low priority. The plan was based upon an expected capital:output ratio of 3:1, a proportion deemed reasonable for developing countries by most economists. The plan proved far more successful than had been anticipated; the modest targets were more than achieved, good monsoons contributed bumper crops, national income rose by 18.4 per cent and the capital:output ratio proved to be a remarkably good 1.8:1. The second plan (1956–61) was less successful; the planners had become over-optimistic. It was intended that the national income should rise by 25 per cent at the end of the plan period and the rate of investment to national income go up from 7 per cent to 11 per cent. The capital:output ratio estimate was increased to 2.3:1, a rate that proved to be too optimistic. This plan reduced the

Table 9 *Outlay and investment in India's Five Year Plans, 1951–83*

(£ million)

Sector	First plan (1951–6)	Second plan (1956–61)	Third plan (1961–6)	Fourth plan (1969–74)	Fifth plan (1974–9)	Sixth plan (1978–83)
Public sector outlay	1470	3450	5625	10,875	30,250	54,600
Public sector investment	1170	2737	4725	9,000	28,250	46,700
Private sector investment	1350	2325	3075	5,250	20,750	54,000
Total investment	2520	5062	7800	14,250	49,000	100,700

Sources: Government of India, Planning Commission, *Third Five Year Plan* (New Delhi 1961); *Fourth Five Year Plan: Resources, Outlays and Programmes* (New Delhi 1965); *Sixth Five Year Plan, 1978–83* (revised) (New Delhi 1980).

Table 10 India's Five Year Plans (1951–83) by major heads of development

(£ million)

	First plan £	(%)	Second plan £	(%)	Third plan £	(%)	Fourth plan £	(%)	Fifth plan £	(%)	Sixth plan £	(%)
Agriculture and community development	218	15	398	11	801	14	1,900	18	4,240	14	10,030	19
Irrigation	233	16	315	9	488	9	695	6	3,250	11	6,940	13
Power	195	13	334	10	759	13	1,375	13	5,400	18	11,620	21
Industry and mining	88	6	806	24	1338	24	2,450	22	7,450	24	10,750	19
Transport and communications	392	27	975	28	1114	20	2,075	19	5,330	18	8,900	16
Social services and miscellaneous	344	23	622	18	1125	20	2,380	22	4,580	15	6,660	12
Total	1470	100	3450	100	5625	100	10,875	100	30,250	100	54,600	100

Note: Distribution of plan outlay by major heads of development (public sector).
Sources: Government of India, Planning Commission, *Third Five Year Plan* (New Delhi 1961); *Fourth Five Year Plan: Resources, Outlays and Programmes* (New Delhi 1965); *Sixth Five Year Plan, 1978–83* (revised) (New Delhi 1980).

public investment proportion in agriculture and irrigation and allocated a total of nearly £1800 million as public investment in industrial development, transport and communications.

The emphasis upon heavy industrial investment saw substantial developments in the Damodar Valley, Calcutta's hinterland in West Bengal and Bihar (Figure 14). Here in 1948 had been established the Damodar Valley Corporation based upon the pattern of the TVA, with a programme of electric-power production, flood control and soil conservation.[4] New coal mines now supplement pre-war workings and the great Jamshedpur iron and steel

Figure 14   *India's iron and steel industry*

plant of the private Tata group was enlarged and new plants established by the government at Durgapur, Bhilai and Rourkela, built by British, Russian and German groups. Fertilizer and chemical works also became established in this favourable setting. The electric power supplied by the Damodar authority to industry and to Calcutta Corporation quadrupled between 1956 and 1961. Immense strides were made in laying industrial foundations and creating great capital-intensive basic plants.

The plan, however, ran into great difficulties and was only saved after the almost complete exhaustion of foreign reserves by substantial foreign aid. The planners had made insufficient allowance for monsoonal variability which reduced harvests, and for the rate of increase of population which contributed to the necessity to import food. The plan was based upon an estimated rate of population growth of 1.25 per cent per annum; in fact the rate of population increase grew during the decade and by the end of the plan was as high as 2 per cent per annum. A limited scaling-down of estimates became necessary and at the end of the five years, food production totalled 75 million tonnes against a target of 80 million tonnes; only 2.6 million tonnes of finished steel was produced although installed capacity had risen to 4.5 million tonnes. Coal production was 53 million tonnes against a target of 60 million tonnes. National income rose by 20 per cent instead of 25 per cent. 8 million new jobs had been created but 10 million new workers had queued for them and a backlog of several million unemployed remained.

Nevertheless, at the end of the first decade (the 1950s) of planned development some notable advances had been made. Some £7500 million had been invested in the national economy. The national income, at constant prices, rose by 42 per cent; allowing for population growth of 82 million and fresh investment, this meant a *per capita* increase of 20 per cent in income and 16 per cent in consumption. The agricultural sector productivity increased by 40 per cent, and 20 million more acres came under irrigation. Basic and capital goods industry expanded eight-fold. Nitrogenous fertilizer production (in terms of nitrogen) increased from 9000 to 150,000 tonnes per annum and bicycle production from 100,000 to 1,050,000 per annum. Power-generating capacity increased from 2300 to 5800 megawatts. A definite momentum had been attained and in the private sector the beginning of an entrepreneurial class could be recognized.

The third plan (1961–6) aimed at sustaining and accelerating this momentum, at the same time profiting by the mistakes of the second plan. The emphasis on basic industries producing investment goods continued and considerable restraints on consumer goods industries remained. It was hoped to raise the rate of investment to national income to 14 per cent (and 16 per cent by 1970). An increase of at least 5 per cent in the national income was aimed at by 1966, the rate of population increase had been estimated at 2 per cent per annum and the planned capital:output ratio was 2.62:1. Unfortunately, from many points of view India's third plan was a failure. Its beginning was marred and impeded by the Chinese aggression and the necessity to increase expenditure on defence, and also by poor monsoons. At mid plan Mr Nehru's illness and death removed a firm influence and a leader of inter-national stature. Towards the close, war with Pakistan and another poor monsoon upset the economy and brought near-famine conditions in several provinces. Above all this, the rate of population increase grew steadily and by 1964 was 2.5 per cent per annum; once again a much higher rate than had been planned for. Of particular disappointment was the tardy return from the great basic industrial complexes: iron and steel plants, great hydroelectric plants, petro-chemical works, shipyards, etc. – great projects that had over fifteen years absorbed immense capital sums but still contributed little to the balance of payments or to the standard of living of the mass of the people. It had been hoped that by the end of third plan the new heavy engineering and machine-building capacity would enable much capital equipment previously imported to be made in India, and that new basic raw materials for the maintenance of many industries would be made in India and replace imports, for instance, of rayon, synthetic rubber, organic chemicals, intermediates for dyestuffs and the drug industries. Some progress was made, but the high hopes were not borne out.

In terms of achievement, agriculture reached barely 85 per cent of the target of self-sufficiency in food grains, and only 80 per cent of the planned expansion of irrigation was achieved. Installed electricity capacity reached 10,300 megawatts whereas the target was 12,700 megawatts. Artificial fertilizer production barely reached 500,000 tonnes instead of a planned 856,000 tonnes. Mining and mineral production did better. A Bureau of Mines was established in 1948 and the Geological Survey of India was expanded in 1951 to allow a systematic investigation into India's mineral potentialities. These investigations first began to bear fruit in the second plan, with increasing outputs of coal, bauxite and iron ore. The establishment of new coal mines or expansion of existing collieries took place particularly in Bengal–Bihar, Andhra Pradesh, Madhya Pradesh and Orissa. Iron ore production (10 million tonnes in 1960) increased two and a half times when new mines, mainly in Orissa, were completed during the third plan allowing 10 million tonnes of iron ore to be exported annually. Much of it went (and still goes) to Japan who provided technical assistance in establishing the new mines.

In all, during the plan period new employment was created for 13 million. However, 17 new millions were seeking jobs. With all these efforts, however, average income per head did not rise above about £26 per annum, that is a rise of £2. In India a sense of stagnation and frustration accompanied by much heart-searching attended the last months of the third plan. A number of the self-criticisms rendered Indian economists and planners more receptive of the views increasingly voiced by outside observers and creditor nations: that agriculture must receive marked priority; that the type of industrial development must ease away from the capital-intensive pattern; that all-out efforts must be made to reduce the fertility of the population, that the planning was too rigid and bureaucratic, and that the private sector must be given a greater part to play, especially if foreign capital was to be attracted. These views influenced the pattern of the fourth plan which, by investments of over £14,000 million, aimed at an annual growth of national income of 6.5 per cent. The proportions of investment are shown in Table 10 (page 203). A much greater sum was allotted to the improvement and expansion of agriculture, with the intention of raising the annual output by 5 per cent. Emphasis on heavy industry was reduced, although one new steel plant (built at Bokara with Russian aid) was included. Infrastructure investment on power and transport was not cut, but was aimed to support agriculture, with new rural roads, rather than industry. A large part (£3000 million) of the enormous cost of the fourth plan depended on foreign help; the tremendous investment needed being quite beyond India's own resources.

The inception of this plan was delayed by the war with Pakistan and severe droughts in 1966 and 1967. Three annual plans filled the gap. The fourth plan also suffered from the further war with Pakistan over the secession of Bangladesh and, like all the plans except the first, it failed to reach its targets. The fifth plan (1974–9) was scarcely more successful; it suffered from the impact of the quadrupling of oil prices, the world recession and acute inflation, and was redrafted with more realistic aims halfway through its course. Steel production was to increase from 5.8 million tonnes to 9.4 million tonnes and artifical fertilizer production from 2 million tonnes to 5 million tonnes. A significant growth of agricultural production was arrived at, particularly from the expansion of areas under the high yielding strains of wheat and rice which had introduced the green revolution to India. The agricultural sector, thanks to good monsoons and the rather patchy benefits of the green revolution, did well and by 1978 grain production at 126 million tonnes was on target, and at last surplus grain was available to be stored as a stockpile against future poor harvests. Many of the industrial targets were not attained (steel output was only 7.6 million tonnes in 1978).

A change of government in 1977 brought about sharp changes in planning policy: the forging on with heavy industrial development towards a distant goal of cheap mass production was modified. Emphasis was switched to laud small-scale labour-intensive units to absorb some of the enormous body of un- and under-employed and to generate and spread more money in the countryside. Other countries of Asia also have the problem of creating purchasing power among a growing number of landless rural poor. They will carefully watch this attempt at a solution. Thus the sixth plan (1978–83) made a fundamental break from its predecessors by shifting the weight of planned investment from heavy industry to agriculture (including irrigation and fertilizer production) and the small-manufacturing sector. The total resources directed to agriculture and rural development from those and other heads were as much as 40 per cent. This change in development strategy followed years of disappointing results from heavy industry, which had failed to make impression upon the country's great problems of poverty and unemployment. An expansion of irrigation is the basis for increasing agricultural output and efficiency, and considerable investment is directed to the improvement of rural conditions and the establishment of small-scale rural industries. The steel plants at Bokara and Bilhai are to be enlarged and a new one begun at Visakhapatnam. A target of 11.5 million tonnes of steel is proposed for 1982–3.

A number of features discussed in earlier chapters have become apparent in Indian development; the foremost among them is the need for, and the massive problem of, land reform. It was recognized that the inherited agrarian structure was an impediment to progress and the system of landownership and tenancies a source of exploitation of the peasantry. Measures have been included in development plans to abolish intermediary or 'rent-receiving' tenures; to regulate and reduce rents and offer security of tenure leading to the conferment of the right of ownership on tenants. A ceiling was placed on future acquisition of land by individuals and some attempts were made to consolidate fragmented holdings. The long-term aim of these measures is to convert the majority of India's cultivators into peasant-proprietors. The drawback of small-scale production and marketing will be met by the encouragement of voluntary co-operatives for credit, marketing, processing and distributing. Unfortunately the various agrarian reform laws have been honoured more in the breach than in the observance, thanks to the political power of landowners. As a consequence 31 per cent of the land is owned by 4 per cent of the owners and 50 per cent of owners share under 10 per cent of the land. The current green revolution is making the issue of growing importance. This 'revolution' is an outcome of the adoption of new high-yielding strains of wheat and rice. These require extra cultivation (more labour inputs), they mainly require irrigated land (new technology) and for success need application of fertilizers (capital inputs). These requirements, coupled with a general lack of 'know-how', prevent the mass of poor peasantry benefiting from these advances. It is the middle- and upper-class farmers, now joined by men of commerce and industry who have money to invest in farming, who have been receptive of the new developments. Private irrigation schemes, tractors and other mechanical appliances, the use of fertilizers and pesticides, the acceptance of the advice of agricultural officers, are the hallmarks of these new-style farmers. The benefits of the green revolution have been unevenly distributed and a split is occurring in India's agricultural society.[5] Nevertheless during the decade of the 1970s food grain output responded to these developments and repeatedly surpassed domestic demand so that a buffer stock was built up. This is necessary because so much of the Indian food grain production relies upon unpredictable monsoon rains. The expansion of irrigated areas were important aims in both the fifth and sixth plans. By 1978 some 50 million hectares were under irrigation and this, hopefully, was to be expanded to 85 million hectares (or half the total cropped area) by the end of the sixth plan. It will be seen that the impressive gains in productivity are restricted geographically to the areas of larger farms and irrigation provision (for example, the Punjab) and that these advances have done little for the incomes of the mass of small farmers, the rural poor, and this in turn restricts the domestic market for manufactured goods.

The mass market in India is very limited and most consumer industries are catering for a narrow middle-class demand. Economies of scale become difficult to achieve and protection against imports discourages efficiency and favours high prices. To some degree one may expect young industries to have higher than average costs during the teething period, but there are a number of features suggesting that a dangerously high-cost structure is being created. The early pace of development exceeded India's limited supply of technical, administrative and managerial talent. Building and bringing into operation three large steel plants simultaneously proved an enormous task, a major problem being lack of experienced staff, for each plant needed about 2000 trained men. The government hurriedly recruited 1436 engineers, to be trained for the steel industry in India and abroad. But it was soon realized that the only solution to the problem of manning the three steel plants lay in recruitment of technicians from abroad. Large-scale industry in the private sector is still aided by European management, but much public-sector industry relies for management upon experienced senior civil servants and railway officials who become remarkably ineffective when translated to manage steel or fertilizer plants or mines. One result is ministerial interference, even with industrial management.[6] Management is thus hampered and the effects penetrate adversely throughout the system.

In a country the size of India with its limited transport net, faulty industrial location can have crucial bearing upon industrial costs, and the temptation to ignore purely economic considerations in deciding locations is very high, for every part of the federal union clamours for the attention of central government in demanding the seeds of development. Some preference has been given to the location of public sector projects in relatively backward areas 'whenever this could be done without significant prejudice to technical and economic considerations'.[7] Political insistence in some cases may well have overridden efficiency and certainly causes delays in implementing plans.

After thirty years of economic planning and the investment of scores of thousands of millions of pounds it is now possible to pass some judgements on India's policies and their moderate attainments. First the Indian plans failed to develop agriculture to complement and sustain the expanding industrial sector. Indian agriculture is particularly susceptible to weather influences (that is, the monsoons) and this the planners miscalculated. They also seem to have moved industrial investment to first priority too soon, only to be caught out by bad harvests and an unexpectedly large population increment to feed and 'service'. The government's predilection for massive and sustained investment in capital goods industries is open to criticism. Wholehearted development of capital-intensive industries made but little contribution to solving growing un- and under-employment, and because of the limited size of the market they operated below capacity as high-cost producers. Only in the sixth plan were real efforts made to invest in agriculture and the villages, to develop small-scale consumer industries and thus both to increase and satisfy the purchasing power of the mass of India's population.

Second, the success of this notable exercise in planned development has been jeopardized by a rate of population increase far higher than had been expected. While more accurate counting is one contributive cause, others undoubtedly have been due to small dietary improvements and to the effects of infrastructure expenditure on medicine and hygiene whereby the crude death rate (especially the infant mortality rate) has fallen. From 1947 to 1972 the infant mortality rate fell from 146 to 73 per 1000 live births, while by 1978 the crude death rate had fallen from 27.4 to 15 per 1000 of the population. There are signs that the rate of natural increase to the population shows slight reduction, falling from 2.5 per cent in 1968 to 2 per cent in 1977, but nevertheless at this rate 13 million are added to the population each year.

Despite the vast scale of plans, at no time has enough new work been provided for the annual new entrants to the labour market, a situation that is now critical as the 'bulge' births now look for employment. If unsuccessful, their numbers worsen conditions in the countryside, or they move away to increase the numbers of squatters in the large towns. During the second plan opportunities were provided in new employment for around 8 million, of which some 6.5 million were outside agriculture. At the end of the plan period the backlog of unemployment was estimated at 8 million, with estimated under-employment at up to 18 million. The third plan may have created up to 14 million or 15 million new jobs (10.5 million non-agricultural) but the labour force increased by 17 million; in fact in each plan the provision of new jobs fell short of the labour-force increment. Thus the fourth plan started with a backlog of unemployed nearing 12 million and had to cater for a 25 million addition to the labour force during 1969–74. The increase in the labour force comprised 25 million in the fourth plan and 33 million in the fifth plan, while the sixth plan expects an addition of 53 million to the labour force by 1983. It is impossible to be precise regarding numbers of unemployed in India, but it was of the order of 19 million when the sixth plan was begun in 1978 with far larger numbers under-employed, four-fifths being in the rural areas. The growth of the industrial sector under the sixth plan is likely to engender only 7.5 million new jobs, leaving some 46 million to be absorbed mainly by agriculture. This is a further reason for the plan's main thrust being aimed at agriculture and rural improvement – expanding the area under irrigation, spreading multiple cropping and extending the new techniques of the green revolution with the need for greater application of labour. Thus rural strategy is reinforced by plans to expand small-scale and household industries for the production of consumer goods in the rural areas – in fact a turn away from Western capital-intensive technologies to the intermediate or 'appropriate' technologies advanced by E. F. Schumacher and his supporters. These figures show the immensity of India's problems and a measure of her achievement. Faith has had to be put in the cumulative character of chosen strategy, for capital-intensive basic industries offer great promise of expansion of manufacturing industry in years to come, but for a long time have little effect upon the mass of the population in an agrarian country.

India entered the decade of the 1980s with high hopes of attaining the 'take-off'. She is now the tenth industrial country in the world and has an impressive capacity in basic industries. In most products she is now self-sufficient although this rather reflects the limited size of the effective domestic market. There is no doubt that excessive population increase is the very crux of Indian problems and an early substantial fall in the birth rate is necessary. That population growth can vitiate the most strenuous efforts at development was recognized in the third plan, where no less than £18.75 million was allocated to family planning and birth control, but with the high level of illiteracy and little public interest behind the family planning programme results were slow. More organized measures were taken in the 1970s by raising the minimum age for marriage (to 18 for women and 21 for men), spreading the knowledge and means of birth control, including a vasectomy campaign. The current decline in the rate of natural increase to the population owes much to these measures.

The third noteworthy feature is the enormous scale of investment necessary when dealing with a country of sub-continental size and population. This suggests that the huge foreign aid should be by means of grants or loans at low rate of interest, otherwise payment of debt liabilities creates an intolerable strain upon the emergent economy. It is noteworthy that the foreign aid required for the fourth plan was estimated at £3000 million, but no less than £1015 million of this was earmarked for the repayment or servicing of earlier loans. The weight of debt presses heavily upon most Third World countries but in India now more and more of planned investment is being derived from domestic resources, it is repayment of earlier debts and loan interest requiring foreign currency that is an impediment. India's extensive public debt stood at US$8000 million in 1970 and at US$15,300 million in 1978, but the debt percentage of GNP dropped from nearly 15 to 13 per cent.

The mass of India's population is still little aware of the enormous efforts being made on its behalf. Often it resists the innovations demanded by the planners; general support and understanding are not great. Even the measures of land reform have had less impact than had been expected; collusion and evasion at lower levels have been widespread and a proper understanding of the integral part of land reform in development plans is rarely realized. To some degree this may be that the fruits of thirty years of planning have scarcely reached the peasant, for whereas national income has doubled, the population has grown by 300 million and income per head for the first twenty years moved modestly from £21 to about £30. A greater rate of increase occurred during the fifth and sixth plans demonstrating delayed return from the great capital intensive projects and increased revenues from the agricultural 'green revolution'. By 1980 a *per capita* income figure of £60 had been achieved but this must be set against a worsening imbalance of income distribution. The agricultural developments associated with the green revolution mainly benefited the upper and middle classes, the lot of the mass of the peasantry within a caste-ridden society has advanced very little over 30 years. The wealthiest 20 per cent of India's population share nearly 50 per cent of the national income while the lowest 20 per cent share less than 7 per cent.

Despite three decades of tremendous effort and unprecedented investment the Indian economy is only just on the move. To prise it from rest, to overcome massive inertia, has required a heavy mobilization and application of human and material resources, for development on such a scale requires a whole range of problems and difficulties to be overcome. In the industrial field gains have been made, although there has as yet been no radical change in the structure of the economy nor in the condition of the mass of the population. An inadequate use of capacity raises costs in much of India's public sector industries. These are mainly sophisticated plants demanding more skilled labour and needing a higher degree of managerial strength and expertise than is available at present. Because of the low use of capacity the capital:output ratio in the heavy industries of the public sector is as high as six to one. Valuable experience has been won; particularly it has been found that the gestation period of an industrial project, especially in heavy engineering, is longer than generally expected. Many plants (iron and steel, fertilizers and chemicals) are being completed a year to two years after the target date and teething troubles reduce early output so much that many projects expected to make a valuable contribution in one plan only start to make a substantial contribution in the next. The slowly broadening base of India's industrial structure during the past thirty years, and a growing efficiency in production, may well lessen the balance of payments problems and facilitate the growth of exports. It is certainly true that the economy today is much stronger and more resilient and that progress is more discernible. However, so long as population growth continues at the current high rates the low standard of living of the mass of the population is unlikely to show much change. Transformation in India is slowly gathering speed and it will not be simply of the Indian economy but also of Indian society and the Indian landscape, and much will ultimately depend upon urgency and dedicated endeavour permeating through the whole population.

Egypt

Egypt, over the last fifty years, provides an outstanding example of an over-populated, under-developed agrarian state passing through a disappointing period of haphazard industrial growth to an awareness of the necessity for full economic planning, but then allowing political and ideological dogma to cloud the economic design. It offers an excellent model for the display of the full suite of social, political and economic ills discussed in earlier chapters, and as an example is more manageable in scale, numbers and complexity than India. The fact that the habitable and cultivable land of Egypt, a desert state, is rigidly limited by the amount of Nile water available for irrigation from the Aswan High Dam each year, renders Egypt's problems more severe than India's. Almost 97 per cent of Egypt is desert, only 13,500 square miles are habitable and the cultivable area is only 8500 square miles; the population is 41 million and now is increasing annually at a rate of 2.1 per cent. With the amount of farmland so limited and the demand for it so great, prices and rents soared as the years passed (until the revolutionary government established some controls) delineating the typical two-class society of under-developed countries: the small group of exceedingly rich and usually absentee landowners and the great mass of poverty-stricken peasantry. The maldistribution of landownership was such that in 1950 a mere 6 per cent of landowners possessed two-thirds of Egypt's farmland; the remaining third was shared between two and a half million peasants, the majority of their holdings being of less than half an acre. Thus in addition to a growing mass of landless peasantry many of the smallest landowners also needed to seek work on the larger holdings and the over-abundance of agricultural labour kept wages at a level barely sufficient for the most primitive necessities of life.

The unequal division of wealth and the enormous number who shared the lesser portion resulted in pathetically low standards of living and negligible standards of health and education among the bulk of the population. Throughout the 1930s the Egyptian economy stagnated; the corrupt and inefficient administration closed its eyes to the worsening conditions of the mass of the people as population increase outpaced the slow development of the economy and diminishing returns steadily eroded the living standards of the rural masses. Indeed, it was the ruling class who profited most by the forcing up of land rents and the cheapening of labour.

Economic and demographic conditions in Egypt up to 1952 have been discussed in some detail elsewhere;[8] as a background it is sufficient here to underline the attraction and absorption of investment in land rather than in industry and utilities which offered lower and less-assured returns, and the dependence of the entire economy upon the cotton crop. Cotton until very recently was Egypt's sole major export and accounted for over four-fifths of total value of exports between the wars and for 60–70 per cent in the first decade after the last war. In the early 1970s cotton, raw and as fabrics, made up 50–60 per cent by value of all exports, indicative of a slow export diversification.

The limited industrial development in Egypt between the wars received a considerable stimulus in 1930 when graduated tariffs were imposed on imports of raw materials, semi-finished and fully manufactured goods. This stimulated some fresh industrial promotion, but the lack of capital, the poor quality of the labour and the very limited home market were heavy restraints. The period of the Second World War saw the virtual cessation of imported manufactures and local industry found itself in command of the home market. A boom period followed, but many of the less efficient establishments went out of business in the early post-war years with the return of competition from better quality and cheaper imported goods. Investment once more swung to land and agriculture. By 1952 industry contributed barely 10 per cent of the national income. The principal industries up to that time were those customary in under-developed agrarian countries and were based almost entirely upon indigenous raw materials, mainly of agricultural origin. The textile industry (using cotton, wool and rayon) took first place and had grown to satisfy almost the entire home demand; among the food industries were sugar refining, oilseed crushing, milling, brewing, fruit and vegetable preserving and canning; certain chemicals were manufactured; and also boots, shoes and leather goods, glass, cement, tobacco and cigarettes. The narrowness of the home market (being insufficient to sustain competition between several large firms) was overcome in some industries by the development of monopoly and cartel features. Sugar, cement and glass are examples of the former; textiles, cigarettes and brewing the latter.[9]

The structure of Egyptian industry in the period immediately after the Second World War revealed a multitude of small concerns of workshop rather than factory character; 92 per cent of industrial establishments in 1948 each employed less than five workers and 80 per cent of firms had a capital investment of less than £E100 (then £E = £1 0s. 6d. sterling). At the other end of the scale, and with little in between, were a few really large firms of substantial financial and productive power (particularly in the textile, sugar and cement industries). These few large fully mechanized establishments were responsible for the bulk of the country's industrial output. Such a pattern is not unusual in developing countries (India shows a similar pattern); small firms are likely to proliferate where capital is scarce and labour abundant, for they make small demands upon investment and reduce the handicaps stemming from a lack of managerial ability and limited knowledge of accounting, costing and statistical techniques. The growth of a few large firms was dependent upon monopoly or cartel features and on the fact that capital was more readily available to large firms than to small. Tariff protection, by reducing competition, furthered monopolistic development and helped to perpetuate inefficient high cost production; this in turn limited still further the small home market.

In 1944 the first Census of Industrial Production in Egypt permitted an analysis of manufacturing costs and revealed that salaries and wages made up only 12.6 per cent of industrial expenses, but raw materials accounted for 79.8 per cent, a situation very different in developed countries.[10] Most of the raw materials were home produced and their high cost reflected low labour productivity, manual rather than mechanical methods of extraction or production, high transport costs, wasteful and uneconomic use in the factories. Costs of production were also inflated by weakness in management, revealed by lack of foresight, exaggerated scales of expenditure and poor factory organization. Management claimed disproportionately high salary scales, and widespread nepotism and favouritism permeating the whole of Egyptian industry resulted in uneconomic staffing with a high proportion of administrative and clerical grades. The textile industry classed 19.9 per cent of its employees as administrative, technical or clerical staff; in Britain the proportion was 6.3 per cent. For the leather industry the comparative proportions were 20 per cent and 10 per cent.

This industrial development – haphazard, unco-ordinated, expensive – made but a minor contribution to the national income and to the depressing population situation. After twenty years of protection it offered employment to barely one tenth of the working population and had little effect upon the lives of the rural masses. The government did little to stimulate industry during the post-war years. It was responsible for the enforcement of an 'Egyptianization' policy after 1947, whereby 75 per cent of employees and 90 per cent of workmen in joint-stock companies had to be Egyptians, while 51 per cent of the capital of all new joint-stock companies had to be owned by Egyptians. These measures were contrary to Egypt's real industrial interests; they aggravated the lack of technical, skilled and foremen staff by the withdrawal of foreigners and discouraged potential foreign investors. Nationalist feeling also led to changes in mining law, making operations and prospecting prohibitive for a number of foreign oil firms who withdrew or reduced their capital outlays.[11]

The subjection of the Egyptian economy to the vagaries of international cotton markets was amply demonstrated with the Korean war boom and the subsequent slump in 1950–2. Prices and exports rose during the boom but little of the heavy profit was reinvested, much went on luxury imports and there were substantial trade deficits. Manipulation on the Alexandria market priced Egyptian cotton out of the contracting world market in 1952 and there followed a severe economic crisis with the country on the verge of bankruptcy. The almost bloodless revolution of July 1952 was the act of a group of young army officers sickened by the corruption, bribery, favouritism and general ineptitude of the ruling class and the unappetizing spectacle of Egypt's decadent political and social life. They were almost unprepared for the sweeping success of their coup; they had virtually no political nor economic plans and found themselves coping with government on an *ad hoc* basis. To this, and the sheer size and state of the Augean stables they sought to cleanse, we must attribute the slow progress of the economy during the next few years.

It was suggested that little short of revolution might seem likely to bring about the social, political and economic upheaval necessary to free feudal-type agrarian economies from the domination of the landowning ruling class. The Egyptian revolution served such a purpose but was less drastic than if it had been a rising of the peasantry and working classes rather than of the middle class. A Land Reform Act was one of the first measures of the new government, its object being to strike at the 'feudal mentality' enslaving the peasantry and to curb the power of the large landowners. The maximum-sized individual holding was restricted to 200 feddans plus 50 feddans for each of two children (1 feddan = 1.038 acres); excess land was expropriated and redistributed in plots of up to *c*. 5 feddans among the peasantry. This was indeed a moderate measure, for property of 300 feddans was then worth between £8000 and £9000 a year to its owner. In all, some 2000 landowners were first affected. Subsequently, amendments have reduced family holdings to a maximum of 100 feddans, and rather more than 15 per cent of Egypt's farmland has been redistributed, but thousands of peasant families are still landless. This merely underlines the lack of cultivable land in Egypt, for even if all farmland were divided into small peasant plots, there would still be landless peasantry. The transference of the land, spread over a number of years, was facilitated by the prevailing habit of the large landowners to rent out most of their land rather than farm it themselves; in fact, their large estates were farmed in small plots using a plenitude of labour and the change of title deeds did little to upset the pattern of agricultural production. Co-operative societies were successfully established to replace the landlord, as a provider of finance, seeds, fertilizer and marketing A further major feature of the Act, affecting two-thirds of Egypt's farmland, was the fixing of annual land rentals at seven times the value of the low Land Tax assessments of the 1940s (a case of the biter bit, for the low rates of tax emanated from self-interest of the rulers). This reduced rents by at least a half and was a further measure to redistribute income in favour of the peasantry. Another revolutionary measure was that holdings could not be divided on the death of the owner. Descendants must decide as to the inheritance of the land; thus it was hoped to stem the fragmentation of holdings, a system prevalent under the Moslem law of equal inheritance.

In 1951 over a fifth of rural income went to the large landowners, in 1956 only one tenth; the total increase in the income of the small landowners was about £E30 million, representing only a small amount per family but vital to their well-being. Practically the whole of the increase was spent on food; the position when Egyptian-made manufactures can be bought by the mass of the people is still some way off. Unfortunately much less was done for landless labourers, comprising nearly two-fifths of Egypt's rural population. Their lot was not improved and with rising prices may well have worsened. Land reform eased the demand for labour on large estates and economic conditions undermined attempts at establishing a minimum daily wage. Agricultural output rose, thanks to incentives to better farming provided by the spread of co-operatives, the new ownership policy and the widespread adoption of a triennial rotation system.

Measures in the industrial field after the revolution were less prompt and less sure. The pressing population problem requires greater production from agriculture, more land to be reclaimed from the desert and delta and the provision of water for its irrigation, and greater output from industry. Land reform was aimed at improving agriculture and shifting the attraction for investment from land to industry; the highly expensive and grandiose High Dam Scheme came to be the cornerstone of the government's plan to increase the cultivated area, but co-ordination of industrial development was delayed. Efforts were made to ease restrictions on foreign capital, particularly in the oil and mining industries, and certain measures such as the exemption of new industries from taxes on profits for seven years, were passed. These measures were insufficent to make industry particularly attractive to investment, for the market for home manufactures remained stagnant. By 1954 the prestige of the revolutionary government was becoming linked with economic development, but neither an overall plan nor investment priorities had yet been formulated. The principal difficulty was finance: estimates by the National Bank of Egypt for 1954 suggested net capital formation at £E54 million per annum or about 6 per cent of the national income and in 1955 at £E68 million, or 9 per cent of the national income.[12] With the high rate of population increase this latter rate was sufficient to maintain existing standards of living, but gave little margin for financing large-scale development. Nevertheless a number of major and somewhat ostentatious projects were begun; an agreement to establish an iron and steel industry was signed with a West German firm, the government oil refinery at Suez was enlarged, plans for a big fertilizer plant at Aswan were prepared. Public loans and funds confiscated from the royal estate financed the earlier measures, than came a period of assistance from the United States, followed, after the Suez crisis, by aid from the Eastern bloc.

Gradually the revolutionary government, stifling all opposition, extended its power and after the Suez crisis, when it emerged triumphant, secured a firm grip on the whole economy by its sequestration of foreign business, banks and insurance in addition to securing the revenue of the canal itself. A new and vociferous wave of nationalism had surged over the country supporting these 'Egyptianization' measures, which effectively ousted foreign commercial influence and made the government, through its

Economic Development Organization, a major owner and controller of capital. Even at this stage no national economic plan had been prepared to point the way to the 'New Industrial Egypt' listed as one of the aims of the revolution.

A hasty industrial plan, little more than a list of projects, appeared the next year, 1957. In many respects it was quite unrealistic and demonstrates miscalculations even more glaring than those of India's second Five Year Plan. The plan aimed at raising the industrial sector of the national income from £E100 million to £E184 million in five years, assuming that the rest of the economy would expand at the rate of 2 per cent per annum and that the *per capita* income should double in twenty years. Manufacturing industries were to need £E181 million, while the mining and oil industries and training schemes took a further £E70 million. Thus about £E50 million in new investment would be required each year – an amount about equal to the total annual saving of the nation and from which provision also had to be made for agriculture, communications, social service investment, and so on. The means of obtaining the necessary capital, especially the estimated £E123 million of foreign currency, were not made clear. Even more optimism is to be found in the assumption that up to 500,000 new jobs would be created in secondary and tertiary occupations – when most existing Egyptian industry was on single-shift working and hard pressed to find markets. Where the extensive markets for the spate of new manufactures were to be found was not specified, but it was not likely to be self-engendered, for even if all the new jobs were created, practically the whole income of the workers would need to go on food, housing and transport; their capacity to buy industrial products would be small. For want of a better plan this was first accepted by the government and a four-year credit of about £E60 million was obtained from the USSR. The need for a comprehensive development plan for the whole economy was becoming apparent and this was put in hand in 1958 with the industrial 'plan' undergoing modification to fit within it. The first Five Year Plan was eventually announced in July 1960.

Egyptian industrial production had shown substantial, if uneven, growth during the 1950s, a good deal of the expansion occurring near the end of the period when infrastructure investment, especially in power and transport, was beginning to mature. A substantial renewal and renovation of the railway system, a considerable road construction and improvement programme, and improvement of inland river navigation representing some £E60 million investment had gradually been completed.

The general advance in Egyptian industrial and mineral production is shown in Table 11. Much of the increased production to 1960 came from established plants and not new creations. By 1970 the textile industry (Egypt's largest single industry) was processing 40 per cent of the domestic cotton crop and exporting 30 per cent of its yarn production and 20 per cent of its textile manufactures. A valuable post-war industry has been the manufacture of fertilizers, urgently needed by Egyptian agriculture. Calcium nitrate and superphosphate are produced by a plant at Suez and a new factory at El Khattara, just north of Aswan, which relies on hydroelectric power from the Aswan High Dam.

A small iron and steel industry had earlier been established at Helwan, just south of Cairo. There were serious locational problems in establishing this plant, for Egypt possesses no coking coal and the iron ore (about 50 per cent Fe) is obtained from the Eastern Desert, near Aswan. No matter where such a plant were located in Egypt, high transport costs on raw materials would be incurred. The plant at Helwan is 500 miles from the ore fields and over 100 miles from the ports where the coke is imported. Initially the plant was very small, being well below economic size. Original estimates put the cost of the plant at £E17 million. Production was 220,000 tonnes of rolled steel from 265,000 tonnes of pig iron. By 1960 when the plant was working at about half capacity, the construction cost had reached £E28 million. The result of these features was steel produced at costs above world prices. The plant began as little more than a costly prestige project and has never been profitable. Under the second Ten Year Plan the plant was to be expanded to a more economic size, to produce 1.2 million tonnes of steel from 1.5 million tonnes of pig iron by 1976 – a target not attained. Other industries that have expanded and now have a firm place include food processing and the manufacture of a wide range of consumer goods, extending from the assembly of lorries and cars to the manufacture of razor blades. The growing chemical industry produces pharmaceuticals, cosmetics, medical supplies and fertilizers, and other manufactures include sanitary ware, glassware, rubber tyres, leather goods, soaps, paints and varnishes.

The geographical distribution of Egyptian industry shows a high concentration on Cairo and Alexandria. These two centres include

Table 11 *Egypt: industrial and mineral production*

(thousand metric tons)

	1939	1956	1960	1964	1966	1968	1970	1972	1974	1976	1978
Extractive industries											
Crude oil	749	1828	3319	6979	6884	9890	18,945	10,720	5832	19,020	24,299
Phosphate	578	615	566	613	661	1441	716	563	507	489	539
Manganese	120	201	286	328	186	4	4	2	5	4	–
Iron ore	–	–	239	447	440	447	451	427	1302	1,087	1,399
Manufactures											
Cotton yarn	24*	75	102	131	142	157	164	179	179	193	212
Cotton fabric	20*	52	64	88	97	102	110	116	120	563†	604†
Refined sugar	233	287	338	382	357	380	547	604	577	497	590
Alcohol (thousand litres)	5	15	17	20	21	27	32	32	29	30	29
Superphosphate	20	170	188	209	277	306	411	566	504	463	502
Nitrate of lime	–	208	257	255	261	168	285	293	327	1,085	1,396
Cement	368	1351	1903	1733	1764	2309	3,684	3,822	3263	3,362	3,028
Paper and cardboard	–	32	49	103	110	116	125	152	131	n.a.	159
Tyres and tubes (thousands)	–	220	485	614	1136	1832	1,566	1,829	1679	1,725	1,763

*Large factories only.
†Million metres.
Source: Federation of Egyptian Industries.

about two-fifths of the total number of industrial establishments, giving employment to half the industrial labour force. The spread of industry into suburban and adjacent areas of the contiguous provinces of Giza, Qalyubia and Beheira increases the industrial concentration in and around the two cities and now gives employment to 70 per cent of the country's industrial labour force. A change in the coverage of industrial censuses and tabulation after 1950 makes it impossible to make direct comparisons between the most recent and earlier censuses. However, the increasing attractiveness of the two major cities is clear and their rate of population growth (now holding 6 million and 2.2 million, or one fifth of the entire population) has been about 5 per cent per annum during the last decade – double the national rate. The agglomeration of industry in and around these cities provides a clear example of the disproportionate pull of the few locations in a developing land where efficient public utilities such as gas, electricity, pure water, telephones, are available with other amenities of civilization and where there is a provision of labour and an effective market. This selective urban growth, while up to a point economically advantageous, is regarded as less desirable on social and political grounds, and attempts are being made to curtail future growth and to spread new industrial growth into the revivified Canal Zone, and to a number of newly founded satellite towns in the Delta.

The structure of modern Egyptian industry by size of establishment demonstrates a pattern similar to that of India and one that may be regarded as typical of an industrially young country. The change in census methods, already mentioned, precludes direct comparison with earlier returns but in 1954 some 80 per cent of industrial establishments employed less than ten workers each. The graph in Figure 15 suggests that large-scale industry forms only a tiny proportion of the total number of establishments, but in fact it employs a majority of the labour force and accounts for the bulk of value added. Value added per worker gives a rough measure of economies of scale available to factory rather than workshop concerns, but is also likely to reflect a more efficient use of labour and better management and administration. The attractions and advantages of small-scale establishments where skilled labour, management and capital are relatively scarce are emphasized by their proliferation. Between 1952 and 1954 the vast majority of the new industrial establishments were of small size. The 341 new businesses represented an increase of 10 per cent in total number of establishments, but barely 1.5 per cent more workers were employed. During this period the index of industrial production rose by an estimated 5 per cent. This suggests that if a very large expansion in industrial production materialized it would be insufficient, from the point of view of employment, to make any real impression upon the growing annual population increase and the population problem as a whole. The industrial census of 1964 recorded 93 per cent of industrial establishments as employing less than ten workers. This suggests a not unexpected proliferation of small concerns, but if 'one worker only' establishments are removed, one discovers that between 1960 and 1964 the proportion of employees in the group of establishments employing two to nine workers fell from 39 per cent to 35 per cent, while those in the group employing 'over twenty persons' rose from 41 per cent to 55 per cent of all workers.

A review of Egypt's succession of development plans underlines both familiar and new problems that beset the path to modernization. The first Five Year Plan, 1960–5 (the first half of a ten-year

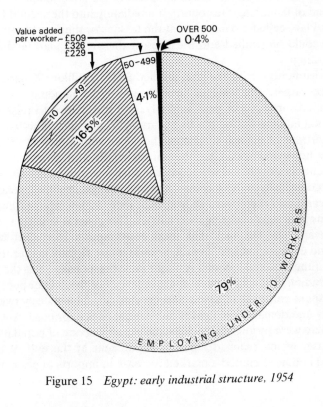

Figure 15   *Egypt: early industrial structure, 1954*

scheme) aimed at increasing the national income by 40 per cent. It provided for a total investment of £E1577 million, of which 25 per cent was allotted to agriculture and 37 per cent to industry and power. This reflected the special importance which the government attached to industry and also was a reflection on the gross under-employment in Egyptian agriculture, where there was little prospect of creating more jobs until the farmland area could be expanded when water from the Aswan High Dam became available after 1968. Some £E650 million of foreign currency was required, mainly for the industrial sector. The growing population, making heavier demands on existing acres for food, prevented an increase of agricultural exports, the mainstay of the economy.

The plan was very ambitious. It was based on a capital:outut ratio of 3:1 and aimed at a compound rate of growth of the national income of just over 7 per cent. Many economists felt that this was too optimistic. In fact, at its conclusion in June 1965 a considerable measure of success had been achieved. However, a greater air of realism was then apparent in the government which, instead of launching the country immediately into the second Five Year Plan, called a pause so that the lessons of the first Five Year Plan could be studied and the lines of the second plan modified accordingly.

Investments during the plan totalled £E1513 million, 96 per cent of the target. The rate of investment to the national income averaged some 20 per cent annually, and this helped to raise the national income during the five years by 37 per cent. This was an annual rate of growth of almost the 7 per cent aimed at. There were, however, also a number of shortfalls and shortcomings. Bottlenecks developed where inter-industry requirements had not been co-ordinated; deficiencies in organizational structure became apparent, and there were shortages in technical manpower and a serious shortage of foreign exchange. The general situation was aggravated by the fact that total consumption increased well beyond expectation and, in fact, grew at a rate slightly higher than that of the national income. A major factor responsible was the re-distribution of the national income in favour of the poorer people, who spent rather than saved and created an imbalance between supply and demand and caused substantial rises in prices.[13] Above all, there were serious effects from the expanding rate of population increase, which reached almost 2.8 per cent at the end of the period and necessitated a marked increase in imports of grain and other foodstuffs. Excessive imports resulted in a growing deficit in the balance of payments.

At the end of 1965 and in preparation for the second plan the government faced this situation by raising retail prices on a wide range of goods and slightly raised taxes, in order to withdraw excess purchasing power. Further, investment priority was directed to raising output of existing factories to their maximum capacity rather than to starting new ones, and to give high priority to projects not relying on imported inputs. Finally a definite policy regarding the population problem was formulated, for with population increase surpassing 2.8 per cent per annum, even a high expansion of the national income was not likely to leave much margin for investment and improvement of living standards. An estimate of the *per capita* income in 1952 was £E30, in 1960 £E38 and in 1969 about £E78. However, official statistics are not entirely reliable and sometimes differ from one ministry to another.

The duration of the second Five Year Plan was extended to seven years and subsequently abandoned: a reflection mainly of external disturbance arising from military assistance to Yemen and the June 1967 war with Israel, the subsequent Israeli occupation of Sinai and the closure of the Suez Canal. Thus, as might be expected, the first Five Year Plan came closer to targets than the second and by 1970, although the planned decline in the relative importance of agriculture was occurring, the shift was less in favour of industry than in the distribution and service sectors.

The decade of the 1960s saw a marked swing of government policy towards autarky and the widespread nationalization of industries and businesses. A series of decrees in 1961 gave the government sweeping financial and economic powers. Banks, insurances and fifty companies engaged in basic and heavy industries were nationalized. Another eighty-three companies were partially nationalized through the state acquiring at least half of each company's capital; this group was mainly engaged in light industries. A third group of 145 companies was also partially nationalized through the government's acquisition of all personal shareholdings in excess of £E10,000. These companies mostly comprised textile factories and other light industries mainly owned by a limited number of private individuals or families. A quarter of profits of all companies had to be retained for the workers' benefits; the boards had to conform to a prescribed pattern and directors' fees were limited. Income tax was increased on incomes above £E1000, and maximum landholding for individuals was halved from 200 feddans to 100 feddans, the excess holdings were distributed among the poor and landless peasantry. In 1963 all cotton exporting and ginning firms and pharmaceutical factories were completely nationalized, as were most of the companies in which the state held a half-share of the capital.

These measures had a number of purposes: to enlarge the public sector of the economy to allow greater control of development and ensure the reinvestment of profits, to foster a spirit of self-sufficiency by broadening the range of Egyptian industry and to continue the redistribution of the national income, cutting down even further the number and power of the wealthy, both landowners and industrialists. In a sense these measures signify the failure of the government to enlist the support of an important stratum of Egyptian society in its development planning. That political pressures overcame economic realism is suggested by these decrees being followed, under the guise of overcoming the 'dictatorship of capital', by the confiscation of the property and assets of several hundred persons, mainly from Egypt's commercial middle class, an admixture of Syrians, Greeks, Italians, Lebanese, Jews and Copts. This was particularly serious, in that this class includes the entrepreneurs, businessmen and managers; a class of person in which Egypt is notably deficient, yet a class essential for the industrial expansion to which the regime was committed.

Inflationary pressures became particularly manifest after the 1967 war and a number of annual development programmes followed until, belatedly in 1973, under President Sadat, the second Ten Year Plan was announced. Three elements that constitute bottlenecks on the road to development for most developing countries had been identified: inadequacy of real domestic savings, the weak growth of exports and an underestimation of external obligations. It became realized by the end of the first Ten Year Plan that industrialization through import-substitution soon expends itself by increasing the burden on balance of payments instead of reducing it. Policies of autarky were no longer favoured in the second Ten Year Plan. It was intended to increase industrial production by 10 per cent annually and agricultural production by 5 per cent annually. Included in the plan was the expansion of the Helwan iron and steel plant, the construction with Russian help of an aluminium plant costing £E60 million and of a phosphorous plant costing £E66 million. The decade of the 1970s soon showed the impress of President Sadat who introduced more liberal policies, swung Egypt from the Eastern bloc once more to the Western, restored democratic elections and linked the faltering nationalized economy once more with capitalism. More realistic industrial appraisals replaced President Nasser's autarkic views, foreign companies and capital were welcomed and encouraged with tax holidays of 5–15 years, guaranteed repatriation of profits and capital, exemption or deferment of custom duties, etc.

The economy, stumbling with the weight of successive wars with Israel, with the high rate of population increase, with stagnation of agriculture and increasing food imports, with sluggish industrial performance, was surprisingly sustained by four new or renewed sources of income: remittances from the 1 million to 2 million Egyptians who moved out of Egypt to work in other (and richer) Arab states – as much as US$2000 million a year; growing oil revenues which overtook remittances in 1980; transit dues from the Suez Canal, reactivated since 1975; and a return of tourists in large numbers as peace with Israel became a reality. It was these sources of income that helped sustain Egypt through a period of war with Israel and in the difficult time of reconstruction and reorientation after peace was agreed (and when, in retaliation, Arab aid was withdrawn). Thus surprisingly Egypt emerged from the 1970s showing a modicum of real economic growth and, after years of deficit, a surplus balance of payments. It was with a new spirit of optimism that the 1980–4 Five Year Plan was announced.

In 1979 manufacturing industry employed about 1.4 million people (11–12 per cent of the working population) and its products were valued at US$5700 million; of this only US$1800 million came from private industry. The bulk of manufacturing industry, including the largest firms, had been nationalized under President Nasser and inefficient production in this public sector with over-manning and massive bureaucracy was to be tackled by rationalization and foreign participation in updating plant and technologies and by competition from the expanding private sector. The Five Year Plan gave priority to agricultural projects and agro-industries, for years given insufficient attention by the planners. The yields of practically all food crops except wheat had fallen throughout the 1970s and in the closing years of the decade an average of £E500 million-worth of food was imported annually. Cotton yields had also fallen and amounts exported had declined. The construction and tourist industries also had priority in the plan, reflecting urban renewal and economic development in the Canal Zone and the building of new towns in the Delta to relieve the urban pressure on Cairo. A sense of realism began to sweep through Egyptian industry in its peacetime rehabilitation. Managers have greater freedom in decision-taking, market forces and growing competition are now a spur to efficiency and to some extent the economy is moving out of the hands of the politicians and into those of the technocrats.

After almost thirty years of revolutionary government the foundations of a socialist state have been laid, but in terms of economic achievement progress has been slow. The purchasing power of the masses, the real market for manufactures, remains low and industrial development continues at high-cost levels, a situation of mutual exclusion that will persist so long as the rate of population increase remains high. Nevertheless the pace of industrial development has been quickening and now equals the share of agriculture (28 per cent) in the gross national product. After the Republic of South Africa, Egypt is the most industrialized state in Africa, now having a wide range of food and consumer goods industries.

President Nasser's legacy, whereby the state controlled almost the entire economy and created, nourished and protected industry, only slowly underwent change during the 1970s. Now the more liberal policies of President Sadat continue to be pressed boldly and, with foreign participation and advice, the decade of the 1980s may well see Egypt enter the take-off stage. Textile plants are being modernized and the expansion of food-processing and other agro-industries has begun. The engineering and metallurgy sector is expanding its already wide range of goods and the Fiat car assembly plant may be joined by other major international automobile and lorry-making firms. Steel and aluminium production is planned to increase and valuable experience and technological transfer may occur if the United States agrees to the production of military equipment under licence. The decade of the 1980s should see a real surge forward with the burdens of war and misjudged policies of autarky left behind.

A new spirit is becoming apparent within Egypt and a new image is being presented to the world. The previous coffee-sipping, place-hunting, government-job seeking attitude of the student population is passing. To work in a factory or on an oilfield is no longer a disgrace or embarrassment. The new sense of purpose and more effective use of human resources offers real hope for the future. However, geographical limitations to Egypt's habitable area are decisive factors affecting her development, rendering the margin for the expansion of agriculture and its productivity relatively small and leaving to industrial development a task seemingly beyond its capacity and potentiality. The new and renewed sources of revenue (oil, remittances, Suez Canal dues, tourists) if wisely used will provide the means for the spurt forward in the economy; but with growing emphasis on efficiency, expanding industry will supply only a limited number of new jobs. For Egypt to make substantial forward progress the rate of population increase must quickly be reduced.

11 Conclusion

With thirty years of development experience completed, it is now possible to attempt some tentative conclusions. The developing world entered the 1980s with mounting debts, disappointing economic growth, populations increasing over-fast, food scarcities, and rising energy costs. This is a sombre list, but a number of lessons have been learned and, if they are acted upon, there is a chance of real progress being attained during the decade. Much development planning has had mediocre results because the concept of the wholeness of a country's economy had been disregarded. Industrialization alone can provide no panacea for economic backwardness and poverty, for it is but one form of development and its advance is closely related to that of the other sectors of the economy. Infatuation solely with industrialization can bring dire results as the recent history of Argentina shows and, nearer home, the case of Yugoslavia whose agricultural exports withered away with programmes of over-industrialization that ignored the agrarian sector. In 1950 when Yugoslavia suffered famine it was discovered that only 70 per cent of the arable land was being cultivated through lack of incentive because of low-price ceilings relative to industrial products and heavy taxation. There is no hope of success for any country if economic advance is one-sided, yet this is precisely what has been occurring in many developing countries during the 1970s. Only at the end of the decade was it coming to be realized that even moderate industrialization contains a multiplier element that works adversely against the agrarian sector. As we have seen, policies furthering import-substitute industries penalize the rural sector but boost the urban-industrial cities. Further, these cities hold the rulers, planners and administrators. These town-dwellers often have little understanding of rural ways and rural requirements and are all too conscious that the town exhibits progress and modernization, the much lauded side of the dual economy. Urban ways and urban occupations become favoured.

Almost everywhere Third World agriculture has suffered neglect and has seen its most active and virile members move to the cities. Production has fallen and country after country now spends scarce resources on the import of food for its urban masses.

The second major conclusion concerns the dynamic but often obstructionist character of demographic factors. Again and again in South-East Asia material gains are cancelled out by unexpectedly high rates of population increase. It seems that Asia can abolish poverty or she can increase her numbers, but it is becoming clear that she cannot do both simultaneously. At the moment too many of the fruits of development are wasted in supporting more people in poverty instead of being used to abolish poverty. The whole problem of development, and particularly the furthering of industrialization, becomes more and more intractable with soaring population totals. These problems beset parts of South-East Asia today but tomorrow will grip Latin America and then Africa. There is no hope of success under these conditions – rates of population must moderate. A population policy to that end should be actively furthered within development plans.

These examples also support the further conclusion that present-day conditions necessitate planned development. The developing countries need to do in a relatively brief period what took several generations in the richer countries that had an early start. The need for planning, to mobilize resources and deploy them effectively and economically to the achievement of a definite aim, is not an ideological manoeuvre but a common-sense and logical approach to the highly complex parts of the central problem. The plan should be a business prospectus laying down aims, directions, priorities and phasing. But planning that becomes too rigidly nationalistic and bureaucratic loses the support of the people and checks the flow of aid from most external sources. Psychology also plays a part. The poor of the world now have rising expectations for, thanks to the media, they are aware of their plight and see and know of other life-styles. Thus politicians and leaders no longer have time on their side, for discontent may topple governments and democratic processes may fall beneath the extreme right or extreme left, as a number of Latin American states show. All this makes a vast task much more difficult and the economic history of the advanced states becomes less relevant. In the developed world capital formation and industrialization were well advanced before the rate of population growth increased. The West never had to face the intractable difficulties now besetting the Third World; they had no need to formulate plans for development.

The fourth conclusion is that there can be no hope of successful industrialization without the establishment of a firm foundation both in social services and public utilities, for the infrastructure concerns human as well as material resources. Here the more adverse influence of environmental factors in extra-temperate climates upon efficiency of labour and costs of basic works must be recognized. The infrastructure requires substantial investment but offers delayed returns.

The example of Hong Kong suggests that something more than doles of capital will be required for successful industrialization. Increasingly 'trade as well as aid' must become a world slogan. Poor countries over-populated in relation to their primary resources must turn to industry for succour; industrialization here cannot be effective if overseas markets are closed to their products. Hong Kong, indeed, may be but a harbinger of things to come. Jeremiahs will not be slow to ask what will happen to world trade if developing countries flood the market with manufactures. The answer is that trade is a two-way process and that both primary and secondary products in the world as a whole must increase together. Growing incomes create greater demand; world trade may well grow faster than ever, for food and raw materials will be urgently needed by the overpopulated newly industrializing countries as well as capital goods and more 'difficult' manufactures. Degrees of comparative advantage may play a notable part in determining patterns of specialism, but it is clear that the simpler manufactures will be made increasingly by developing countries.

Fifth, the struggle for betterment by the developing countries has now gone on long enough for paths to be evaluated and lessons to be learned. What is becoming disturbingly clear is that while economic growth has been taking place (according to indicators such as GNP, *per capita* income, etc.), the mass of the population in so many countries seems to have received little benefit. Economic growth alone is not development; social improvement in terms of education, health and welfare is an integral part of the 'modernization' process. 'National levels of development need to be measured against human, social and cultural values rather than solely economic values.'[1] Income maldistribution has worsened; the urban elite and the growing commercial and industrial middle class cream off much of the newly engendered wealth, and in recent years the rise of trade unions has seen the rewards of urban workers raised well beyond the income of the mass of the people living in the countryside. There is a growing gap between the incomes of the rich and the poor within developing countries, and it is accepted that successful development requires this to end.

Another conclusion is that there can be little prospect of successful economic development without goodwill and harmony between all countries. Further it is clear that substantial help from the more fortunate advanced countries has become a *sine qua non*. The call for aid from the developed world, already of massive proportions, will continue to increase at an accelerating rate, as the case of India has shown. Here a new and formidable problem has become apparent: the growing indebtedness of Third World countries. According to World Bank estimates the international debts of about 100 developing countries amounted to US$33,000 million in 1964, to US$80,000 million in 1971, and US$370,000 million in 1980. Many developing countries are now using more than one half of their foreign exchange earnings merely to service their debts (with little prospect of paying them off) and this figure is rising sharply. This is a major issue that must be tackled quickly by the world community, particularly since it is coming to be realized that the speed of development is far slower than optimistic forecasts of one and two decades ago. The idea of 'development in a decade' is giving way to 'development in a half-century'. Figures show that during the first Development Decade the gap between rich and poor nations' incomes widened. The rich countries maintained rates of growth 5–6 per cent a year; the developing countries rates of about 4 per cent. This meant, for example, that each year the United States added to its national income the equivalent of the entire national income of the African continent – some US$30,000 million.[2]

Thirty years ago a group of experts reported to the United Nations that to increase real income per head in under-developed lands by about 2 per cent per annum would need annual capital investment of the order of US$10,000 million – a figure that would be substantially higher today.[3] The estimate was particularly high because industrialization was deemed the most urgent problem of many of the countries and the figures were based upon an estimated annual transfer out of agriculture of 1 per cent of the total working population. The capital required for each person absorbed into non-agricultural work was put at US$2500. Many disagree with or qualify these figures, but they provide a rough guidepost. Aid to the Third World in 1977 totalled US$47,000 million, of which nearly one third came from the United States. Owing to inflation this figure has scarcely changed in real money terms over the last few years although the developed countries have become richer. The United Nations, when the idea of the Development Decade was formulated, hoped for progress towards an annual transfer of 1 per cent of the national incomes of the wealthier countries to the developing world which, as more development plans gather way, can absorb three to four times the present amount of aid. The developing countries have become dissatisfied with numerous aspects of the aid system during the 1970s. These poor countries are beginning to recognize that united they have power, in that they control large proportions of natural resources, foodstuffs and raw materials, upon which the economies of the industrialized countries depend. While there are unlikely to be dramatic effects such as those created by the alliance of the oil-producing states, nevertheless a changing relationship between the Third World and its customers evolved during the 1970s. Changing economic relations between rich and poor are inevitable, with the era of cheap food and cheap commodities passing from the advanced countries, and with a diminution of the 'poor relation' status that so far has been part of these relationships.

The rising cost of oil and its derivatives has hit the poorest nations very hard (for example, oil bills consume 60 per cent of export earnings of Sudan and Tanzania) and the loose term 'Fourth World' is sometimes applied to this group. What can now be discerned is a number of successful newly industrializing countries (NICs); a group of poorer countries whose economic development has progressed to the stage when successful export of manufactured goods is attained. It includes Hong Kong, Taiwan, South Korea, Brazil and Singapore. These countries are still far from the ranks of the first or second worlds; their industry yet lacks innovative and multiplier effects, their occupational structures are still heavily inclined to primary production, the maldistribution of income remains severe. Nevertheless they offer a small measure of progress amid generally disappointing results.

Notes and references

Chapter 1   Development and under-development

1 L. Wolf-Phillips *et al.*, 'Why Third World?', *Third World Foundation Monography*, no. 7 (1980).
2 N. B. Guyal, 'Energy consumption and economic development', in N. Ginsburg (ed.), *Geography and Economic Development* (Chicago 1960), p. 68.
3 A. Bonné, *Studies in Economic Development* (London 1957), p. 7.

Chapter 2   The demographic factor: the global setting

1 United Nations, *Demographic Yearbook 1978* (New York 1980).
2 J. Huxley, 'Population and human fulfilment', in *New Bottles for New Wine* (London 1957), p. 174.
3 J. Huxley, 'Population and human destiny', *World Review* (1950), pp. 7–8.

Chapter 3   The demographic factor in the under-developed lands

1 P. T. Bauer and B. S. Yamey, *The Economics of Under-developed Countries* (Cambridge 1959), p. 31, and W. A. Lewis, *The Theory of Economic Growth* (London 1955), pp. 201–13.
2 A. B. Mountjoy, 'Million cities: urbanisation and the developing countries', *Geography* (1968), pp. 365–74.
3 A. B. Mountjoy, 'Urbanisation, the squatter and development in the Third World', *Tijdschrift voor Economische en Sociale Geografie* (1976), pp. 130–7.
4 T. Lynn Smith, *Population Analysis* (New York 1948), p. 132.
5 P. Gourou, *The Tropical World* (London 1961), p. 7.
6 T. E. Hilton, 'Land planning and resettlement in northern Ghana', *Geography* (1959), p. 230.

Chapter 4   Industrialization: the panacea?

1 W. W. Rostow, *The Stages of Economic Growth* (Cambridge 1960), pp. 4–16.

2   C. Clark, *The Conditions of Economic Progress* (London 1951), p. 401.
3   A. M. Carr-Saunders, *World Population* (Oxford 1936), p. 113.
4   Elaborated in A. B. Mountjoy, 'Vegetable oils and oilseed', *Geography* (1957), pp. 37–49.

Chapter 5   Industrialization: theoretical considerations

1   D. E. Keeble in R. J. Chorley and P. Haggett, *Socio-economic Models in Geography* (London 1969), p. 247.
2   W. W. Rostow, *The Stages of Economic Growth: A Non-Communist Manifesto* (Cambridge 1960).
3   G. Myrdal, *Economic Theory and Under-developed Regions* (London 1957).
4   A. O. Hirschman, *The Strategy of Economic Development* (New Haven, Conn. 1957).
5   J. R. P. Friedmann, 'A general theory of polarized development', in N. Hansen (ed.), *Growth Centres in Regional Economic Development* (New York 1972), pp. 82–107.
6   B. J. L. Berry, 'Essays on commodity flows and the spatial structure of the Indian economy', Research Paper 3, University of Chicago (1966), p. 239.
7   F. Perroux, 'Note sur la notion de "pole de croissance"', *Economie Appliquée* (1955), p. 307–20.
8   A. B. Mountjoy, 'Planning and industrial development in Apulia', *Geography* (1966), pp. 376–80.
9   H. Singer, 'Dualism revisited', Institute of Development Studies, University of Sussex (1969).
10 K. Sutton, 'Industrialisation and regional development in a centrally planned economy: the case of Algeria', *Tijdschrift voor Economische en Sociale Geografie* (1976), pp. 83–94.

Chapter 6   Problems of industrialization

1   M. Ionides, Letter to *The Economist* (20 February 1960).
2   United Nations Economic Committee for Asia and the Far East, *Economic Bulletin for Asia and the Far East*, (1959), pp. 33–45.
3   R. Nurkse, *Some Aspects of Capital Accumulation in Under-developed Countries* (Cairo 1952), p. 1.
4   Quoted in United Nations, *Processes and Problems of Industrialization in Under-developed Countries* (New York 1955), p. 5.
5   A. G. Chandavarka, 'The nature and effects of gold hoarding in under-developed economies', *Oxford Economic Papers* (1961), p. 138.

6   N. Islam, 'Economic inter-dependence between rich and poor nations',
    Third World Quarterly (1981), p. 239.
7   G. Myrdal, *Economic Theory and Under-developed Regions* (London
    1957), p. 12.
8   P. T. Bauer and B. S. Yamey, *The Economics of Under-developed
    Countries*, (Cambridge 1959), p. 247.
9   H. Myint, *The Economics of the Developing Countries* (London
    1980), ch. 7.
10 A. O. Hirschman, *The Strategy of Economic Development* (New
    Haven, Conn. 1960), pp. 50–119.

Chapter 7   Environmental and human problems

1   E. Huntington, *Climate and Civilisation* (New Haven, Conn. 1924).
2   S. F. Markham, *Climate and the Energy of Nations* (Oxford
    1942), p. 32.
3   D. H. Lee, *Climate and Economic Development in the Tropics* (New
    York 1957), p. 100.
4   N. C. Chaudhuri, *A Passage to England* (London 1959), pp. 26–7.
5   F. B. Wells, 'Transport in the Rhodesian Copper Belt', *Geography*
    (1957), pp. 93–5.
6   A. M. O'Connor, 'New railway construction and the pattern of
    economic development in East Africa, *Transactions of The Institute
    of British Geographers* (1965), pp. 21–30.
7   B. Harris, 'Urbanisation policy in India', *Proceedings of The Regional
    Science Association* (1959), p. 187.
8   J. E. Orchard, 'Industrialisation in Japan, China Mainland and India',
    Annals of The Association of American Geographers (1960), p. 211.
9   D. H. Meadows, *et al.*, *Limits to Growth* (London, 1972).
10 D. R. Pendse, 'The energy crisis and Third World options', *Third
    World Quarterly* (1979), pp. 69–88.
11 C. Sofer, 'Working groups in a plural society', *Industrial and Labour
    Relations Review* (1954), p. 73; quoted by P. T. Bauer and B. S.
    Yamey, *The Economics of Under-developed Countries*, p. 69.
12 W. A. Lewis, *Aspects of Industrialization* (Cairo 1953), p. 31.

Chapter 8   The form of industrialization

1   *The Times* (14 March 1960).
2   I. Little, T. Scitovsky, M. Scott, *Industry and Trade in Some Developing
    Countries* (London 1970), p. 61.
3   A. B. Mountjoy, 'Worlds without end', *Third World Quarterly* (1980),
    pp. 753–7.

4 United Nations, *Industrialization and Productivity*, Bulletin 1 (New York 1958), p. 13.
5 ibid., p. 14.
6 K. Mukerjee, 'Employment and substitution of capital for labour', *Indian Economic Journal* (1956), p. 105.
7 E. F. Schumacher, 'Rural industries', in M. W. Clark (ed.), *India at Mid-passage*, (London 1964), pp. 30–9.
8 United Nations, *Industrialization and Productivity*, p. 12.

Chapter 9   The progress of industrialization 1

1 W. A. Lewis, *Report on Industrialization and the Gold Coast* (Accra 1953), p. 2.
2 R. J. Harrison Church, 'The sea in West African development', *West Africa* (1951), p. 74.
3 D. Hilling 'Port development and economic growth: the case of Ghana', in B. S. Hoyle and D. Hilling (eds.), *Seaports and Development in Tropical Africa* (London 1970), pp. 127–145.
4 C. L. White and R. H. Chilcote, 'Chile's new iron and steel industry', *Economic Geography* (1961), pp. 258–66.
5 'Chile's counter-revolution: a survey', *The Economist* (1980).
6 I. Little, T. Scitovsky, M. Scott, *Industry and Trade in Some Developing Countries* (London 1970), p. 177.
7 A. Morris, 'The regional problem in Argentine economic development', *Geography* (1972), p. 301.
8 A. B. Mountjoy, 'Housing and New Towns in Hong Kong', *Geography* (1980), pp. 53–7.
9 D. C. Y. Lai and D. J. Dwyer, 'Tsuen Wan: a new industrial town in Hong Kong', *Geographical Review* (1964), pp. 151–69.

Chapter 10   The progress of industrialization 2

1 Sir E. J. Russell, 'India's people and their food', *Geography* (1952), p. 136.
2 Sir F. Benham, *Economic Aid to Under-developed Countries* (London 1961), p. 100.
3 C. H. Rao, *Cottage and Small-scale Industries and Planned Economy*. (New Delhi 1967).
4 W. Kirk, 'The Damodar Valley', *Geographical Review* (1950), pp. 415–43.
5 A. Chakravarti, 'Green revolution in India', *Annals of the Association of American Geographers* (1973).
6 'India revisited', *The Economist* (1961), p. 343.
7 Government of India, Planning Commission, *Third Five Year Plan* (New Delhi 1961), p. 455.

8   A. B. Mountjoy, 'Egypt, population and resources' in J. I. Clarke and W. B. Fisher (eds.), *Populations of the Middle East and North Africa* (London 1972).

9   A. B. Mountjoy, 'The development of industry in Egypt', *Economic Geography* (1952), p. 215.

10 Government of Egypt, *Census of Industrial Production, 1944* (Cairo 1947).

11 A. B. Mountjoy, 'Problems of industrialization: an Egyptian example', *Indian Geographic Journal*, souvenir vol. (1951), p. 22.

12 National Bank of Egypt, *Economic Bulletin* (1956), p. 312.

13 ibid. (1965), pp. 243–8.

Chapter 11   Conclusion

1   D. J. Dwyer, 'Economic development: development for whom?', *Geography* (1977), p. 333.

2   B. Ward, *The Decade of Development: A Study in Frustration* (London 1965) p. 5.

3   United Nations, *Measures for the Economic Development of Underdeveloped Countries* (New York 1951), p. 79.

Bibliography

Chapter 1 Development and under-development

Annel, L. and Nygren, B., *The Developing Countries and the World Economic Order* (London 1980)

Clifford, J. and Osmond, G., *World Development Handbook* (London 1971)

Furtado, C., *Development and Underdevelopment* (Berkeley and Los Angeles 1964)

Ginsburg, N., *Atlas of Economic Development* (Chicago 1961)

Lewis, W. A., *Theory of Economic Growth* (London 1959)

Mountjoy, A. B. (ed.), *Developing the Underdeveloped Countries* (London 1973)

Mountjoy, A. B. (ed.), *The Third World: Problems and Perspectives* (London 1980)

Myrdal, G., *Economic Theory and Under-developed Regions* (London 1963)

Todaro, M., *Economic Development in the Third World* (London 1981)

Chapter 2 The demographic factor: the global setting

Cipolla, C., *The Economic History of World Population* (London 1974)

Clark, C., *Population Growth and Land Use* (London 1967)

Clarke, J. I., 'World population and food resources; a critique', Institute of British Geographers, *Special Publication*, no. 1 (1969), pp. 53–70

Linton, D. L., 'Population and food in the tropical world', *Advancement of Science* (1961), pp. 391–401

Sauvy, A., *General Theory of Population* (London 1974)

Chapter 3 The demographic factor in the under-developed lands

Abu-Lughod, J. and Hay, R., *Third World Urbanization* (London 1979)

Beaujeau-Garnier, J., *Geography of Population* (London 1966)

Clarke, J. I., *Population Geography and the Developing Countries* (Oxford 1971)

Grigg, D., *Population Growth and Agrarian Change* (London 1981)

Osborn, F. (ed.), *Our Crowded Planet* (London 1963)

Trewartha, G. T., *The Less-developed Realm: A Geography of its Population* (London 1972)

United Nations, *Demographic Yearbooks* (New York annually)

Chapter 4   Industrialization: the panacea?

Cohen R., *The Economics of Agriculture* (Cambridge 1959)

Dumont, R. and Rosier, B., *The Hungry Future* (London 1969)

Griffin, K., *Land Concentration and Rural Poverty* (London 1976)

Grigg, D., *The Harsh Lands* (London 1970)

Warriner, D., *Land Reform and Development in the Middle East* (London 1962)

Warriner, D., *Land Reform in Principle and Practice* (London 1969)

Chapter 5   Industrialization: theoretical considerations

Brookfield, H., *Interdependent Development* (London 1975)

Friedmann, J. and Wulff, R., *The Urban Transition* (London 1976)

Myint, H., *The Economics of the Developing Countries* (London 1980)

Patman, C. R., 'Economic planning: paths to development', in A. B. Mountjoy (ed.), *The Third World: Problems and Perspectives*, pp. 45–54

Chapter 6   Problems of industrialization

Lall, S., 'Transnational and the Third World: the R and D factor', *Third World Quarterly* (1979), pp. 112–18

Little, I. K. D. and Clifford, J. M., *International Aid* (London 1965)

Morton, K. and Tulloch, P., *Trade and Developing Countries* (London 1977)

Pearson, L. B., *Partners in Development* (London 1969)

Chapter 7   Environmental and human problems

Chorley, R. (ed.), *Water, Earth and Man* (London 1969)

Dorner, P. and El-Shafe, M., *Resources and Development* (London 1980)

Ginsburg, N., 'Natural resources and economic development', *Annals of the Association of American Geographers* (1957), pp. 197–212.

Hodder, B. W., *Economic Development in the Tropics* (London 1980)

Hoyle, B. S. (ed.), *Transport and Development* (London 1973)

Robinson. E. A. G. (ed.), *Economic Consequences of the Size of Nations* (New York 1960)

Tosi, J. and Voertman, R., 'Some environmental factors in development in the tropics', *Economic Geography* (1964), pp. 189–205

Trom, G. (ed.), *Transport Investment and Economic Development* (London 1966)

Chapter 8   The form of industrialization

Estall, R. C. and Buchanan, R. O., *Industrial Activity and Economic Geography* (London 1980), especially ch. 2

Hay, D., 'The location of industry in developing countries', *Oxford Economic Papers* (1979), pp. 89–103

Hoover, E. M., *The Location of Economic Activity* (New York 1948)

Katzman, M. T., 'Regional development policy in Brazil', *Economic Development and Cultural Change* (1975), pp. 75–109

Schumacher, E. F., *Small is Beautiful* (London 1975)

Stewart, F., *Technology and Underdevelopment* (London 1977)

Tinbergen, J., *Development Planning* (London 1967)

Chapter 9   The progress of industrialization 1

Ghana and Nigeria

Benveniste, G. and Moran, W., *Handbook of African Development* (New York 1962)

Darkoh, M., 'The distribution of manufacturing in Ghana', *Scottish Geographical Magazine* (1971), p. 38–57

Hay, A., 'Imports versus local production: a case study from the Nigerian cement industry', *Economic Geography* (1971), pp. 384–8

Chile and Argentina

Benham, F. and Holley, H., *The Economy of Latin America* (New York 1946)

Furtado, C., *The Economic Development of Latin America* (New York 1976)

Gilbert, A., *Latin American Development* (London 1974)

Hong Kong

Benham, F., 'The growth of manufacturing in Hong Kong', *International Affairs* (1956), pp. 456–63

Yung, C. T., *The Economy of Hong Kong* (Hong Kong 1978)

Chapter 10   The progress of industrialization 2

India

Bhagwati, J. N. and Desai, P., *India, Planning for Industrialization* (London 1970)

Clark, W. *et al.*, *India at Midpassage* (London 1965)

Desai, P. B., *Planning in India, 1951–78* (London 1980)

Government of India, Planning Commission, *First Five Year Plan* (New Delhi 1951)

Government of India, Planning Commission, *Second Five Year Plan* (New Delhi 1956)

Government of India, Planning Commission, *Fourth Five Year Plan: Resources, Outlays and Programmes* (New Delhi 1965)

Government of India, Planning Commission, *Fifth Five Year Plan* (New Delhi 1974)

Government of India, Planning Commission, *Sixth Five Year Plan*, revised (New Delhi 1980)

Kuriyan, G., 'Industrial development in India since independence', *Indian Geographical Journal* (1958), pp. 71–8

Orchard, J., 'Industrialization in Japan, China mainland, and India', *Annals of the Association of American Geographers* (1960), pp. 193–215

Egypt

Hansen, B. and Marzouk, G. A., *Development and Economic Policy in UAR (Egypt)* (Amsterdam 1965)

Issawi, C., *Egypt in Revolution* (London 1963)

National Bank of Egypt, 'A decade of planned development in Egypt', *Economic Bulletin* (1972), pp. 154–75

Saab, G., *Egyptian Agrarian Reform, 1952–62* (London 1966)

Chapter 11   Conclusion

Bairoch, P., *Economic Development of the Third World since 1900* (London 1975)

Benham, F., *Economic Aid to Under-developed Countries* (London 1961)

Brandt Report, *North–South, a Programme for Survival* (London 1980)

Mende, T., *From Aid to Re-colonization* (London 1973)

Index

abortion, 55
Afghanistan, 20, 145
Africa: agriculture, 22, 79, 110; agriculture and land tenure, 72–3, 215, 219; agriculture and surplus population, 74–5; climate, 167; commercial crops, 120, 164–5, 169–70, 216; diet, 59; energy, 129, 131, 133, 164, 169–71, 220, 222, 226; exports, 152; foreign aid, 165–6, 169, 173–4, 220–1, 229–30; incomes, 19–20, 75, 108, 165, 219, 233; industrial forms, 143–4, 147, 155, 158, 162; industrial problems, 105, 111; industrial progress, 163–76, 214–31; industry, 76, 89, 134, 138–9; juvenility, 51–3, 56; literacy, 61, 137; over-population, 22, 71, 97, 163–4, 170; planning, 164–7, 225–30; population growth, 37–41, 215, 226, 233; population theory, 30; population vital statistics, 78; resources, 23, 120, 172–5, 223; transport, 119–21, 164, 167–8, 170, 172, 221–2; under-population, 22; urbanization, 124, 164, 222, 224; wars, 171–2, 229; *see also individual countries*
age: at marriage, 47, 213; and sex pyramids, 48–53; -specific birth rate, 45–51, 55; structures, 45–7; *see also* population
agrarian reforms, 100, 182, 209, 218–19
agriculture, 22–3; balanced development of, 79–80; and climate, 67, 211; commercial crops, 120, 164–5, 169–70, 183–4, 216–18, 229; decline of, 198, 229; disabilities of, 66–70; efficient, 64–6, 68, 79; growth of, 92, 110–11, 205–9, 212–13, 219; incomes, 64; investment in, 83, 110; and land tenure, 67, 72–4, 83, 181–2, 209, 213, 215, 218–19; neglected for industrialization, 62–3, 92, 151, 158, 177, 181–2, 186, 211, 229, 232; and over-population, 32, 38, 42, 70–5; plans, 172, 182, 206–19; and population distribution, 35, 37
Albania, 20
Algeria: energy, 133; incomes, 20; industrialization, 92–3, 147; occupations, 65; population, 40, 78; resources, 23
Allende, S., 182
aluminium, 168–9
Angola, 20
appropriate technology, 157, 212
Argentina: agriculture, 183, 186, 232; bibliography, 245; energy, 186, 188–90; foreign aid, 186–7; incomes, 19, 185–6; industrialization, 62, 120, 139, 183–91; literacy, 187; population, 188; resources, 183, 185, 188–90; transport, 120, 183, 188; urbanization, 124, 183, 187–90
Asia: agriculture, 22, 74, 79, 95–6, 110, 198; agriculture and land tenure, 72–3, 83; agriculture and planning, 206–19; climate, 119; demographic transition,

Asia – *continued*
41–5; diet, 59; education, 61,
145, 195–6; energy, 129, 131–3,
135, 145, 171–5, 198, 204;
exports, 196; foreign aid, 104–5,
205, 207, 210, 213; health, 60;
incomes, 19–20, 191, 199–206
passim, 214; industrial forms,
143–4, 147, 152, 155–8;
industrial problems, 96, 110–11;
industrial progress, 191–214;
industry, 76, 82, 94, 138–9;
juvenility, 51–2, 56; literacy, 61,
136–7, 199; over-population, 22,
71–3, 97; planning, 23, 82, 96,
104, 110, 122, 145, 170–6,
200–13 *passim*; population
growth, 22, 33–41, 191–3, 198,
206, 211–12, 233; population
theory, 31–3; population vital
statistics, 78; resources, 23–4,
38, 97, 199; transport, 121–2,
145–6, 191–3, 196, 210;
urbanization, 123–4, 196; wars,
207; *see also individual
countries*
Australia: agriculture, 64–6, 102;
climate, 118; incomes, 16, 19;
occupations, 65; population, 78
Austria, 19

balanced growth, 79–80, 107–11
Bangladesh, 19–20, 60, 65, 78
Basutoland, 72
Bauer, P. T., 237, 239
Belgium, 19, 95
Benham, F., 240, 246
Benin, 20
Berry, B. J. L., 88, 238
birth control, 47, 50, 55, 60, 77–9,
212–13
birth rates, 42–5; age-specific,
45–51, 55; and industrialization,
75–9; urban, 58, 77; *see also*
population
Bolivia, 20, 65, 78

Bonné, A., 237
Botswana, 20, 40
Brazil: agriculture, 22; energy,
131, 135; incomes, 19; industrialization, 151–3, 236; population, 22; resources, 16, 24, 120,
124, 153; transport, 120; urbanization, 124
Bulgaria, 19, 40, 74
Burma, 19–20, 131

Cameroon, 20
Canada: energy, 131; incomes, 16,
19; industry, 83; occupations,
65; population, 78; resources,
16, 102
capital, 97–9; attraction of, 102–5;
coefficient, 53–4, 82; formation
of, 99–102; -intensive industrialization, 154–6; lack of, 143,
153–4, 159; and multinationals,
106–7; problems, 97–105;
productivity of (-output), 53–4,
81–3, 96, 108–9, 121, 201, 214
Carr-Saunders, A. M., 76, 238
cement, 174–5
Central African Republic, 20
Central America: agriculture, 74;
energy, 129, 131; income, 20;
industry, 147; literacy, 137;
population, 40, 71, 78; urbanization, 124
centre–periphery theories of
industrialization, 87–9, 114, 157,
183, 188
centripetal tendency, 122
Chad, 20
Chakravarti, A., 240
Chandavarka, A. G., 238
character of industrial development, 153–8; capital-intensive,
154–6; labour-intensive, 153–4;
technologies, choice of, 156–8
Chaudhuri, N. C., 119, 239
Chilcote, R. H., 240
Chile: agriculture, 177, 181–2;

TAQUARA, TAQUARI *Panicum sanguinale.* A plant of the grass family; any bamboo, usually of the smaller species, used for making arrow shafts and also flutes. [44, 58, 66, 84, 114]

TASSIT A water root shaped something like an onion. After cooking, it has a yam-like taste. [27]

TATARUIÁP TATU + ARUIÁP—a spirit armadillo of monstrous proportions. [216]

TATORÍ The Kamaiurá. term for a creel or wickerwork basket trap for fish. [148]

TATU-AÇU *Priodontes giganteus.* The giant armadillo, also called the *tatu-canastra,* which is now rare. Some of the Alto-Xingu tribes make head ornaments, associated with the JAKUÍ flute spirit, from its claws, but never eat its meat. [124]

TATUPEBA *Euphractus sexcinctus.* The hairy, banded armadillo. [76]

TATU-PEQUENO A small armadillo. [85]

TAUARAUANÃ Both a Kamaiurá festival song and a dance performed by the Trumái are known by this name. The dance, frequently seen in the Xingu, involves a number of men dressed in BURITI-fiber skirts, feather headdresses, and leafy branches which are tied to arms and shoulders. The leaves (see ENEMEÓP) are from a highly aromatic bush that is of great importance in the curing rituals of the tribal shamans. The center of the village plaza is the usual area for tribal dancing, and the music is provided by two men who sing while keeping the rhythm with a rattle and a percussive instrument made from a hollow bamboo tube beaten on the ground. [24, 151]

TAVARÍ The mask of a water spirit; the spirit itself, which is associated with the JAKUÍ flute. [160]

TAVARIRÍ The spirit which dwells within the tree; the name of the tree itself: its characteristics are that it is weak, burns easily, and topples with no difficulty. [207]

TEPARATÊ The coarse MANIOC dough which has been grated and squeezed in the first part of the process required to remove its high content of poisonous cyanogenetic glucosides. [195]

TERRETÉ The fruit of the JATOBÁ tree. [27]

TIMBÓ *Leguminosas.* The common name of a great number of plants and lianas with toxic properties that, when crushed and released in a small stream or pond, stun the fish, causing them to float upon the surface of the water, from which they may easily be collected in great numbers. [9, 41, 123, 149]

TIPITÍ   An elongated cylindrical basket made of palm-tree fiber in which MANIOC pulp is placed and squeezed to remove its poisonous juice. [40]

TIRIVA   *Pyrrhura.* The medium-sized, primarily green parrots which are noted for the scale-like design on their upper breasts. [9]

TRACAJÁ   *Podocnemis cayennensis.* A semi-aquatic, fresh-water turtle, one of six species in the Amazon region, whose eggs are dug out of the sandbars and beaches of the rivers, and boiled and eaten by the tribesmen. [9, 160]

TRAIRÃO   *Hoplias malabaricus.* A scaly fish, similar to the *tríara,* which is found in fast-moving rivers and is known for the excellent taste of its meat. [6]

TSITSICÁ   A type of black bird. [58]

TUAVÍ   The Kamaiurá term for the bast or palm-fiber mats which are used by the Alto-Xingu tribeswomen to squeeze and press out the poisonous juices from grated MANIOC pulp. The mats also act as sieves through which the juices run into large clay pots. The finest MANIOC flour is found in the residue at the bottom of the pots which held the poisonous juice. [128]

TUCANO REAL   *Rhamphastos.* The largest species of toucan, it has a large beak, black plumage, and a maw of white, yellow, or red. It eats mostly fruit and seems more to jump from tree to tree than to fly. The toucan sleeps with its head tucked under a wing and its tail lifted forward and up so that it appears to be sleeping on its back. [9]

TUCUMAIÁ   A drink made with PEQUI. [199]

TUCUNARÉ   *Cichla ocellaris, C. temensis.* A highly valued fish among the Xingu tribes and widely consumed during the dry season. The large black spot on the tail makes it easy to identify, and the flesh has a renowned trout-like taste and relatively few bones. [6, 67, 68, 113, 143, 161, 201, 203, 205]

TUIM   *Psittacula.* A small green parakeet or parrot with a short tail and blue markings. It flies in large flocks and when landing on a tree immediately separates into pairs. [9]

TÚIM   A white EMBIRA fiber; a term for the vaginal ornament or bibliography, 245; energy, 131, 178–80; foreign aid, 177–8, 180, 182; incomes, 20, 178; industry, 176–82; population, 40, 181–2; resources, 23, 178–80; transport, 178–80

China: education, 61; energy, 132; incomes, 20; industry, 76, 96, 139; population, 38, 97; resources, 124; urbanization, 124

Chorley, R. J., 238, 243

cities, *see* urbanization

Clark, C., 64, 238, 243

climate: and agriculture, 67, 211; and industry, 205–7; and man, 115–19; and population, 35; and transport, 119–21, 167

coal, 132–3; development of, 145; and heating, 116; and industrialization, 125, 171, 173, 175, 178–80, 204–5, 207; lack of, 125; *see also* energy

Colombia, 20, 139

commerical crops, *see* agriculture

Congo, 20

consumer demand, 159–60

consumption of resources, 127–31

contraception, *see* birth control

core–periphery, *see* centre–periphery theories of industrialization

Costa Rica, 19, 147

Cuba, 20, 22

cumulative causation and industrialization, 84–7

Czechoslovakia, 19

DDT, 43, 60

death rates: decline, 37, 41, 43, 46, 51, 60, 76, 78, 211; infant, 46, 76, 78, 211; *see also* population

demographic: effects of industrialization, 75–9; factor, global setting, 31–44; factor in underdeveloped lands, 45–62; transition, 41–4; *see also* population

Denmark, 19, 24

developing countries, differences in, 18–23; *see also* industrialization; under-development

development: Decades, 15, 235–6; path to, 26–9; and underdevelopment, 15–30

diet, 59, 198, 211

differences in developing countries, 18–23

diminishing returns, law of, 31

disabilities in agriculture, 66–70

diseases, 43, 59–60, 117–18; *see also* health

Dominican Republic, 20

dualism in industrialization, 90–3, 157, 161

Dwyer, D. J., 240–1

East Germany, 19, 65, 78

economic: factor and population, 33–4, 96–8; growth, geometric, 23–4; *see also* industrialization

Ecuador, 20, 65, 78, 133

education, 195–6

Egypt: agriculture, 75, 79, 110, 215–19, 229; bibliography, 246; diet, 59; energy, 131, 220, 222, 226; foreign aid, 105, 220–1, 229–30; illiteracy, 61; incomes, 20, 75, 219; industry, 76, 105, 111, 138–9, 155, 214–31; occupations, 65; planning, 225–30; population, 22, 40, 71, 78, 97, 215, 227, 229; resources, 222–3; transport, 221–2; urbanization, 124, 222, 224; wars, 227, 229

El Salvador, 20

emigration, 56, 229

employment, 54–5, 62, 79; *see also* industrialization; unemployment

energy: development of, 168–75, 178–80, 186, 188–90, 199, 204–6, 220, 222, 226; map of,

energy – *continued*
129; problems, 17–18, 130–5;
see also coal; hydroelectricity;
nuclear power; oil
entrepreneurs, 139–40, 192–3
environmental and human
problems, 115–42; climate,
115–21, 167; resources, 17–18,
124–41; utilities and services,
121–4
Ethiopia, 20, 131
Europe: agriculture, 64–7, 74;
climate, 116; energy, 129, 131;
incomes, 18–19, 23–4, 100;
industry, 28, 83, 89–90, 94, 123,
125–6, 138; industry, forms of,
143, 146; industry, problems of,
95–7, 99, 102, 111; literacy, 137;
overseas investment, 103;
population, 32, 35–43, 46–51,
76, 78, 97; resources, 17, 24–6,
130; transport, 120, 123; under-
development, 89; war, 74; *see
also individual countries*
European Economic Community,
89
exports, 125–6, 144, 149, 152–3,
184, 186, 196

factors influencing selection of
industries, 142–5
Fiji, 20
Finland, 19
Food and Agricultural Organization, 28
food imports, 169, 182, 226, 229
foreign aid, 102–3, 140, 235–6;
to Africa, 165–6, 169, 173–4,
220–1, 229–30; to Asia, 104–5,
205, 207, 210, 213; to Latin
America, 177–8, 180, 182, 186–7
Fourth World, 236
France, 19, 40, 95, 103
Friedmann, J., 87–90, 238, 244
future supply of raw materials,
126–30

Gabon, 19, 147
Gambia, 20
gas, natural, 132, 171, 188–9; *see
also* energy; oil
Germany: East, 19, 65, 78; West,
19, 95, 103, 125
Ghana: agriculture, 22, 72, 164–5,
169–70; bibliography, 245;
climate, 167; energy, 131, 164,
168–9; foreign aid, 165, 169;
incomes, 20, 165; industry, 143,
163–70; planning, 164–7; population, 22, 51–3, 163–4;
transport, 164, 167–8; urbanization, 164
Ginsburg, N., 237, 243–4
global setting of demographic
factors, 31–44
governments, *see* planning
Greece, 19, 116
growth, *see* economic growth;
industrialization; population
growth pole strategy, 89–90,
188–9
Guatemala, 20
Guinea, 20
Guyal, N. B., 237

Haggett, P., 238
Haiti, 20
Harris, B., 239
Harrison Church, R. J., 240
health, 37–8, 41, 116–19, 199; *see
also* diseases
Hilling, D., 240
Hirschman, A., 87, 90, 109, 238–9
history of population growth,
37–41
Honduras, 20
Hong Kong: bibliography, 245;
education, 195–6; exports, 196;
incomes, 19, 191; industry, 111,
138, 144, 191–7, 234, 236; population, 191–3, 196; transport,
191–3, 196
human: attitudes and develop-

ment, 95–6; and environmental problems, 115–42; factors in development, 25–6; resource problems, 135–41; *see also* man; population

Hungary, 19, 146

Huntington, E., 116, 239

Huxley, J., 237

hydroelectricity, 132–3, 145, 168–9, 171, 190, 204, 220, 222, 226

illiteracy, 60, 136–7, 187, 199, 213

import-substitute industrialization, 150–3, 169, 172, 185, 187, 200, 228

incomes: agricultural, 64; and consumer demand, 159–60; and industrialization, 62, 99–100, 178, 191, 199–206 *passim*, 214, 219, 234; *per capita*, 17–22; and population, 51

India: agriculture, 95–6, 110, 198, 205–13; bibliography, 245–6; climate, 119; diet, 59; energy, 131–2, 135, 146, 198, 204–6; foreign aid, 104–5, 205, 207, 213; illiteracy, 61, 199; incomes, 20, 199, 201, 205–6, 214; industry, 76, 82, 94, 96, 110, 143, 152, 155–8, 198–214; occupations, 65; planning, 23, 82, 96, 104, 110, 122, 145–6, 200–8, 211–13; population, 22, 51–2, 78, 97, 198, 206, 211–13; resources, 199, 204, 206–7; transport, 122, 146, 210; un-employment, 200, 207, 212; urbanization, 123–4; wars, 206–7

Indonesia, 20, 24, 64

industrialization, 16, 28: advantages of, 69–70; and agrarian over-population, 70–5; and agriculture, disabilities of, 66–9; in Argentina, 183–91; balanced development, 79–80, 107–11; and capital, 97–105; centre–periphery theories, 87–9, 183; character of development, 153–8; in Chile, 176–82; and climate, 205–7; cumulative causation, 84–7; dualism, 90–3; in Egypt, 214–31; factors influencing selection, 142–5; form of, 142–62; in Ghana, 163–70; growth pole strategy, 89–90, 188–90; in Hong Kong, 191–7; import-substitute, 150–3, 169, 185, 187; and incomes, 62, 99–100, 178, 191, 199–206, 214, 219, 234; in India, 198–214; infrastructure needs, 145–7, 157, 164–7, 170, 234; markets and balanced growth, 107–11; motives for, 62–3; multi-nationals, 106–7, 169; in Nigeria, 170–6; occupational structures, 63–6, 198; as panacea, 63–80; polarization, 84–7; and population, 42–3, 75–9; problems of 95–114, 130–5; progress, 163–232; social and demographic effects, 75–9; stages of growth, 63, 82–90, 94, 148–9; theoretical considerations, 81–94; *see also* planning; transport

inflation, 185, 187, 228

infrastructure needs of industrial-ization, 145–7, 157, 164–7, 170, 201, 207, 234

intermediate technology, 157, 212

investment, 82–4, 90–4, 96, 99–103, 110; *see also* capital; foreign aid; planning

Ionides, M., 238

Iran, 19, 136

Iraq, 19, 96

iron and steel industry, 125; in Algeria, 146; in Argentina, 185; in Chile, 178–81; in Egypt, 220,

iron and steel industry – *continued*
222, 228; in Hungary, 146; in
India, 204, 207–8, 210; in
Nigeria, 172–4; in Spain, 25–6
Islam, N., 239
Israel, 19
Italy: incomes, 19; industry,
89–90, 114, 123; occupations, 65;
population, 78; transport, 123
Ivory Coast, 20

Jamaica, 20, 65, 78
Japan: agriculture, 79, 83; energy,
131; incomes, 16, 19; industry,
101, 111, 125–6, 138; population, 38, 40, 56, 97
Java, 76, 97
Jordan, 20
juvenility, 51–6; *see also*
population

Kampuchea, Democratic, 20
Keeble, D. E., 238
Kenya: agriculture, 120; energy,
131; incomes, 20; industry, 89;
occupations, 65; population, 40,
78; transport, 120–1
Kirk, W., 240
Korean Democratic People's
Republic (North), 20
Korean Republic (South), 20, 124.
236
Kuwait, 16, 19
Kuznets, S., 98

labour: cheap, 149, 192–3; inten-
sivity, 73–4, 105, 153–5, 200, 208;
skilled, lack of, 142–3, 160
Lai, D. C. Y., 240
land: reclamation, 196; tenure, 67,
72–4, 83, 181–2, 209, 213, 215;
see also agriculture
land reform, *see* agrarian reform
Lao People's Democratic
Republic, 20
Latin America: agriculture, 22, 74,

96, 177, 181–3, 186, 232; demographic transition, 43; energy,
129, 131–3, 135, 178–80, 186,
188, 190; exports, 152; foreign
aid, 177–8, 180, 182, 186–7;
incomes, 19–20, 178, 185–6;
industry, 62, 102, 120, 139,
151–3, 176–91; juvenility, 51–2;
literacy, 137, 187; population
growth, 27, 37–40, 181–2, 233;
population vital statistics, 78;
resources, 16, 23–4, 120, 124,
153, 178–80, 183; transport,
120–1, 178–80, 183, 188; under-
population, 22; urbanization,
124, 183, 187–90; *see also*
individual countries
Lebanon, 19
Lee, D. H., 239
Lesotho, 20
Lewis, W. A., 138, 165, 239–40,
243
Liberia, 20
Libya, 133
life expectancy, 40, 50, 78; *see also*
population
literacy, 187; map of, 137; *see also*
illiteracy
Little, I., 239–40, 244

Madagascar, 20, 65, 78
malaria, 43, 59–60; *see also*
diseases
Malawi, 20
Malaysia, 20, 22–3, 147
Mali, 20, 65, 78
Malthus, T., 30, 33
man and climate, 115–19; *see also*
human
manufacturing industry, advantages of, 69–70; *see also*
industrialization
markets: lack of, 208, 210, 219,
221; need for, 107–11, 143–4,
150, 152, 180–1, 185; *see also*
industrialization

Markham, S. F., 116, 239
marriage: age at, 47, 213; rate, 47
Marxism, 33, 182
Mauretania, 20
Mauritius, 20
Meadows, D. L., 128, 239
Mexico, 20, 40, 74, 124, 131
Middle East: agriculture, 73, 96;
    energy, 16, 19, 129, 132–3;
    exports, 152; incomes, 16, 19;
    industry, 92–3; literacy, 136–7;
    population, 40, 78; resources,
    23; *see also individual countries*
military power, 169, 182, 191, 218
minerals, *see* resources
Mongolia, 20
Morocco, 51–2, 65, 78, 154
mortality, *see* death rates
motives for industrialization, 62–3
Mountjoy, A. B., 236, 238–41, 243
Mozambique, 20
Mukerjee, K., 156, 240
multinational firms, 106–7, 169
Myint, H., 239, 243
Myrdal, G., 84, 86–90, 108, 114,
    238–9, 243

Nasser, G. A., 230
nationalized industry, 227, 229; *see
    also* planning
Netherlands, 19
New Zealand, 16, 19, 66
Nicaragua, 20
Niger, 20
Nigeria: bibliography, 245; energy,
    133, 170–5; foreign aid, 173–4;
    incomes, 20; industry, 111, 143,
    158, 170–6; oil, 171–5; planning,
    170–6; population, 170;
    resources, 172–5; transport, 119,
    170, 172; war, 171–2
Nkrumah, K., 163, 166
Norris, A., 240
North, concept of, 18
North America: energy, 129, 131;
    incomes, 16, 18–19, 24;
industry, 83, 107, 125, 130, 138;
    literacy, 137; population, 35–40,
    78; resources, 16, 102, 127–8;
    transport, 122; *see also* Canada;
    United States
Norway, 19
nuclear power, 133–5, 190; *see
    also* energy
Nurkse, R., 238
Nygren, B., 243

Oceania: agriculture, 64–6, 102;
    climate, 118; incomes, 16,
    19–20; literacy, 137; population,
    39, 78; *see also individual
    countries*
O'Connor, A. M., 239
occupational structures and
    industrialization, 63–6, 198
oil: export, 15, 69, 131, 172;
    prices, 69, 208, 236; refineries,
    147, 171; resources, 132–3,
    171–5, 185, 189–90; *see also*
    energy
OPEC (Organization of Petroleum
    Exporting Countries), 15, 69,
    131, 172
Orchard, J. E., 239, 246
over-population, 22, 30–3, 96–8,
    163–4, 170; agrarian, 32, 38, 42,
    70–5

Pakistan: agriculture, 145; energy,
    131, 135, 145; illiteracy, 136;
    incomes, 20; occupations, 65;
    planning, 145; population, 78;
    resources, 17
panacea, industrialization as,
    63–80
Panama, 20
Papua New Guinea, 20
Paraguay, 20, 40, 96
Pendse, D. R., 239
Perroux, F., 89–90, 238
Peru, 20, 51–2
Philippines, 20

planning, economic, 27, 171–6, 186–8, 225–30, 233; agricultural, 172, 182, 206–19; and capital, 82, 90–3, 111–13; of infrastructure, 145, 164–5, 167, 170, 201, 207; over-ambitious, 166, 172, 221; preparation, 161–2; problems, 94–6; strategy, 158–62; technological, 157–8; utilities and services, 122

Poland, 19

polarization of industrialization, 84–7 ~~state of being~~

population: age and sex pyramids, 48–53; age structures, 45–7; birth control, 47, 50, 55, 60, 77–8, 212–13; birth rates, 42–51, 55, 58, 75–9; and climate, 35; death rates, 37, 41, 43, 46, 51, 60, 76, 78, 211; demographic factor, 31–62; demographic transition, 41–4; differences, 22; distribution of, 35–7, 115; and economic development, 33–4, 42–3, 75–9, 96–9; growth of, 33–41, 181–2, 192–3, 198, 206, 211–13, 215, 226, 233; life expectancy, 40, 50, 78; over-, 22, 30–3, 38, 42, 70–5, 96–8, 163–4, 170; stages of growth, 41–4, 49–51; theory, 31–3; under-, 32–3; vital statistics, 78; world numbers, 34–7

ports, 164, 167–8, 179, 183, 188, 191–3; see also transport

Portugal, 19

poverty, 19–23, 73–4, 199; circle of, 97–8

power, see energy

primary occupations, 64–6; see also agriculture

problems: environmental and human, 115–42; of industrialization, 95–114, 130–5

productivity of capital, 53–4, 81–3, 96, 108–9, 121, 201, 214

progress of industrialization, 163–232; in Argentina, 183–91; in Chile, 176–82; in Egypt, 214–31; in Ghana, 163–70; in Hong Kong, 191–7; in India, 198–214; in Nigeria, 170–6

protection, 160–1, 184–5, 187, 190, 198, 200, 216–17

quality of population, 58–61

railways, 119–22, 164, 167, 183, 221; see also transport

Rao, C. H., 240

raw materials, see resources

reproduction rate, net, 46–7; see also population

Republic of South Africa, 20

resources: consumption of, 127–31; distribution of, 24–6, 236; future supply, 126–30; lack of, 125, 146–8, 196; mineral, 25–6, 124–9, 149, 171–80, 185, 199, 204–7, 222–3; problems, 125–41; see also energy

rich countries, 15–16, 23, 28; see also Europe; North America

roads, 119–21, 164, 167, 221; see also transport

Romania, 19

Rostow, W. W., 63, 83–4, 158, 237–8

Russell, J., 198, 240

Sadat, A., 228–9

saving, 99–102

Schumacher, E. F., 157, 212, 240, 245

Scitovsky, T., 239–40

Scott, M., 239–40

secondary occupations, 64–6; see also industrialization

Senegal, 131

services and utilities, 121–4

sex and age pyramids, 48–53;

see also population
Sierra Leone, 20
Singapore, 19, 236
Singer, H., 92, 238
size of countries, 24, 114–15
Smith, A., 33, 108
Smith, T. L., 58, 237
social change, 26–7, 58, 75–9;
   see also urbanization
Sofer, C., 239
South, concept of, 18
South America, *see* Latin America
Spain, 19, 25–8, 66, 78
spatial variations in economic
   growth, 81–93, 122–3
spontaneous settlements, 77
Sri Lanka: agriculture, 22; energy,
   131; occupations, 65; popula-
   tion, 40, 43, 56, 78
stages: of industrial growth, 63,
   82–90, 94, 148–9; of population
   growth, 41–4, 49–51
standard of living, 62, 83–4
Sudan, 19–20, 59, 108, 236
Sutton, K., 238
Swaziland, 20
Sweden: energy, 131; incomes, 19;
   industry, 83, 102; occupations,
   65; population, 78
Switzerland, 19, 24–5, 125–6, 131
Syria, 20, 110

Taiwan: agriculture, 110; energy,
   135; incomes, 20; industry, 111,
   236; occupations, 65.
Tanzania, 20, 147, 236
tariffs, *see* protection
technical progress and industrialization, 68–9, 107
technologies, choice of, 128,
   156–8
tertiary occupations, 64–6
textile industry, 169, 195–6, 217,
   222–3
Thailand, 19–20
theoretical considerations of

industrialization, 81–94
Third World concept, 29
Togo, 20
tourism, 195, 229, 231
training, industrial, 135–40
transnationals, *see* multinational
   firms
transport: and climate, 119–21,
   167; costs, 147–50, 178–80;
   inadequate, 172; planning, 164,
   167–8, 170, 183, 221–2; ports,
   164, 167–8, 179, 183, 188,
   191–3; road and rail, 119–22,
   164, 167, 183, 221
tribalism, 171–2
Tunisia, 20
Turkey, 20

Uganda: agriculture, 72, 120;
   energy, 131; incomes, 20, 75;
   industry, 89, 136; transport,
   120–1
UNCTAD (United Nations
   Conference on Development),
   106
under-development: demographic
   factor in, 45–62; and development, 15–30; reasons for, 23–6
unemployment, 198, 200, 207,
   211–12; *see also* employment
Union of Soviet Socialist
   Republics: agriculture, 67, 83;
   education, 61; energy, 132;
   incomes, 19; industry, 28, 101;
   occupations, 65; population, 78
United Arab Emirates, 16, 19
United Kingdom: agriculture,
   64–5; energy, 131, 134; incomes,
   18–19, 23–4, 100; industry,
   94–7, 99, 111, 125, 138, 143;
   occupations, 65; overseas aid,
   102–3; population, 40–3, 46–51,
   78, 97; transport, 120
United Nations: Conference on
   Development, 106; Development Decades, 15, 235–6; on

United Nations – *continued*
    financial aid, 102; statistics, 28,
    30, 34, 108
United States: energy, 131;
    incomes, 16, 18–19, 24, 235;
    industry, 83, 107, 125, 130, 138;
    occupations, 65–6; overseas
    investment, 103–4; population,
    78; resources, 127–8; transport,
    122
Upper Volta, 20
urbanization, 27, 75, 157; in
    Africa, 124, 164, 222, 224; in
    Asia, 123–4, 196; and birth rate,
    58, 77; in Latin America, 124,
    183, 187–90; and population
    growth, 56–8
Uruguay, 19
usury, 199
utilities and services, 121–4

Venezuela, 19, 102, 131
Videla, Gen., 187–8
Vietnam, 20

Wales, 114
war, effect of, 50, 171–2, 206–7,
    227, 229

Ward, B., 241
water power, *see* hydro-
    electricity
waterways, 121–2, 222; *see also*
    transport
Wells, F. B., 239
West Germany, 19, 95, 103, 125
West Indies, 20, 65, 71, 78
White, C. L., 240
Willcox, W. F., 39
Wolf-Phillips, L., 237
women, employment of, 79
World Health Organization, 28
world maps: energy resources,
    129; income *per capita*, 21;
    literacy, 137; population distri-
    bution, 36
world setting of demographic
    factor, 31–44

Yamey, B. S., 237, 239
youthful population, 33, 47, 51–6
Yugoslavia, 19, 65, 74, 78, 232

Zaire, 20, 76
Zambia, 20, 23, 76, 120–1
Zimbabwe, 20

Index compiled by Ann Hall

shield traditionally worn by Alto-Xingu women in the Karib language of the Kuikúru. [74]

TUPÃ   A Tupi-language term for thunder. [218–20]

TURUÁ   The manifestation of a forest spirit that lives at the top of the JATOBÁ tree. Hemorrhaging and serious illness are sometimes diagnosed by the Shamans as being caused by this spirit. [158]

UAIACAÊP   A hardwood tree; see MANUCAIÁ. [58]

UANDARÉ   In Juruna, "sun's cudgel," the ringed boa; see also SALAMANTA. [96]

UAPANÍ   A type of eagle in the terminology of the Kamaiurá. [179]

UARAIM   Canis thous. The "wild dog" which resembles both the fox and the wolf and lives in the forest in packs which feed on small birds and mammals. [227–31]

UÉGOVI   A tree. [72]

UERAVAPIRUM   Enxenura maguari. The Kamaiurá name for the JABIRU MOLEQUE, or American stork. [149]

UETSIMÓ   A fish of a species that can jump very high out of the water. [203]

UGÚVU-CUENGO   Gypagus papa. The term for the king vulture (urubu-rei) in the Karib language of the Kuikúru. This large, bald-headed bird can be seen circling alone in the skies and is treated with respect by the smaller vultures, who move out of his way if he wishes to eat their carrion and sit waiting until he has finished before continuing themselves. [108, 109]

UIRAPAREÁT   An archer in the Kamaiurá language. [183]

UIRAPẼ   Thrasaetus harpyia. The harpy or giant crested eagle which is kept as a pet, in large tepee-like cages, by the Alto-Xingu tribes. It is rare to find more than two in a village, as the eagle's owner must accept the added responsibility of hunting frequently to feed his pet. The tail and wing feathers of the eagle are removed periodically and distributed among the tribesmen to be used on arrows and in headdresses. [177]

ULURI   A small triangular vaginal ornament of whitish bark which is attached to a palm-fiber belt and worn just above the labia by the women of the Alto-Xingu; it is less commonly called the TAMEÓP. [27]

URUÁ   An important spirit dance of the Kamaiurá and other Xingu tribes; the flute played to accompany it. [69, 115, 207, 208]

URUÁGUI   *Catharista atratus brasiliensis.* The term for the common vulture among the Karib-speaking Kuikúru. [108]

URUBU   *Catharista atratus brasiliensis.* The bald, black Brazilian vulture which circles in flocks, high up in the sky, in search of carrion. The two species of a larger vulture, both known as the *urubu-caçador,* are distinguishable from each other by the yellow or red coloring of their heads. [9, 25]

URUBUTSIN   *Gypagus papa.* The term for the king vulture (*urubu-rei*) in the Kamaiurá language; see UGUVU-CUENGO. [89–93]

URUCU   *Bixa orellana.* A dye-yielding shrub which produces pods filled with seeds covered in a pasty red coating that the tribesmen separate from the seeds and repeatedly boil to make an orangish-red substance. This hardens and is used both as a body paint and in the decoration of pottery and spirit masks. Men cover their hair, chests, and backs in intricate geometric patterns, whereas women tend to paint a red stripe across the forehead and lightly cover the rest of their bodies in a shade of URUCU which is slightly more orange than that which the men use. URUCU· is also known as *annatto* and is not italicized in the text. [26, 41, 43, 60, 93, 101, 109, 124, 205, 210, 229]

URUMACH   A large pot once made by the Trumái. [27]

VATÁ   See PAU-AMARELO. [72]

XEXEU   *Cassicus cela.* An oriole, frequently called the *japim;* it is a black bird with a brilliant yellow rump which gathers in groups in a single tree and has the ability to mimic other birds. The yellow feathers are used in Alto-Xingu headdresses and in the trading rituals usually held during the rainy season. [89, 91]